Birds Over America

WINNER OF THE JOHN BURROUGHS AWARD

Birds Over America

ILLUSTRATED WITH
105 PHOTOGRAPHS BY THE AUTHOR

NEW AND REVISED EDITION

Roger Tory Peterson

DODD, MEAD & COMPANY
NEW YORK

First published as a Dodd, Mead Quality Paperback in 1983

Published by Dodd, Mead & Company, Inc.
79 Madison Avenue, New York, N.Y. 10016
Distributed in Canada by
McClelland and Stewart Limited, Toronto
Manufactured in the United States of America

Library of Congress Cataloging in Publication Data

Peterson, Roger Tory, 1908–
Birds over America.

Originally published: 1964
Includes index.
1. Birds—United States.   I. Title.
QL682.P473   1983   598.2973   83-16364
ISBN 0-396-08269-6 (pbk.)

Foreword

As I followed birds, their elusive trails have taken me to all of the fifty states of our country. Though such deeply felt pleasures are hard to share, I wanted, as the years went by, to put on paper my impressions of some of the different facets and sidelights of the world of birds and to describe some of the ornithological spectacles I have seen; hence this book.

As worthy of our contemplation as the birds themselves are the men who follow them, and who play the game of "birding" for all it is worth. With most of them it is a diversion—a sport, if you will—and it is my belief that this aspect should be put on record. More formal works on ornithology, concerned primarily with the science of bird study, rather than the sport, cannot tell this story.

One cannot give a large share of his life to this carefree hobby without soberly reflecting on the mechanics of the well-integrated world of nature. One inevitably becomes a fervent conservationist. But merely being a protectionist is not the same thing, for to do the birds and other wildlife much good one must have some understanding of the biological basis of conservation. Such understanding comes slowly, but it does come if one inquires more deeply into the lives of birds and is not satisfied solely with being able to identify them.

A book on birds, then, cannot avoid the all-important topic of conservation. I have watched birds since the year 1920, and have witnessed sweeping changes during those sixty-five years. Some species have vastly increased, others have dangerously declined. The forces at work that influence the fortunes of birds are as fascinating as a detective story. To me there is no more dynamic side to ornithology than the study of bird populations.

Impatient with my brush and paints, I have often found my camera the best way of preserving a record of some of my bird adventures. The hundred photographs in this book are among the best of the thousands I acquired prior to 1948, when I was in my large format black and white period. Most have not been published elsewhere. For the benefit of those who photograph birds I have included in the back of the book a short *photographic postscript*. Today I use 35 mm cameras and shoot mostly in color.

Birds Over America, first published in 1948, was revised in 1963 with a minimum of changes so as not to impair the flavor of the original book. For the benefit of the newer recruits to the burgeoning army of bird-watchers who may have missed the earlier editions, this paperback reprint is offered without further change so as to present a picture of the way things were in the world of birds in mid-century. Much has happened since. The passage of years has seen the passing of most of the people mentioned in these chapters, and allusions to them must be shifted from the present to the past. Circumstances also change, and some factual statements no longer hold true in the light of new findings. The story of birding in the 1980s remains to be told.

Acknowledgments

Inasmuch as I have drawn so freely not only upon the literature of North American birds, but also upon the things I have learned from innumerable friends who share with me the pastime of bird-watching, I cannot give adequate acknowledgments. However, the following persons have contributed something tangible to the physical makeup of this book, either through scrutiny of a portion of the manuscript, by helping me to take one or more of the photographs, or in some other way: Robert P. Allen, John H. Baker, Adrey Borrell, Herbert W. Brandt, Charles L. Broley, Mrs. Herbert Busse, James Callaghan, Dr. Clifford Carl, William Carr, Garrett Eddy, John J. Elliott, Guy Emerson, Arthur Fast, Ludlow Griscom, John Hamlet, Charles A. Harwell, Harry W. Higman, Irving Kassoy, Junea W. Kelly, Ralph Lawrence, Mr. and Mrs. Charles W. Lockerbie, John B. May, Margaret McKenny, Luff Meredith, James Murdock, Michael Oboiko, Barnie Parker, Dr. and Mrs. Eric Reynolds, Chandler Robbins, Walter R. Spofford, Josselyn Van Tyne, John Aldrich, and Sigred Lee. Most of all, I am indebted to Barbara Coulter Peterson, who, doubling as counsel and secretary, has made my task a smoother one.

Fragments of chapters which since have been expanded or rewritten first appeared in *Audubon Magazine* and the New York State *Bulletin to the Schools*. To the editors of these journals, I am much indebted, and also to the staff of Dodd, Mead and Company, especially John Blair, Raymond Bond, Edward Dodd, Jr. and Phelps Platt.

All of the photographs with three exceptions were taken by myself. These three pictures, in which I appeared, were taken by Lester Walsh, Peter Stackpole and Walter Spofford. The eagle photographs were taken by me while covering an assignment for LIFE magazine and are reproduced with that magazine's kind permission.

Roger Tory Peterson

July 1, 1948.
Revised July 1, 1963

To
BARBARA

Contents

Illustrations

ILLUSTRATIONS

Birds Over America

FIRST FLIGHT. This young osprey took off from its Long Island nest and balanced on this pole when I approached. (Notice the band on its leg.)

ERRATIC. Golden evening grosbeaks spill across Canada into the northeastern states in a great wave one winter, may be rather scarce the next year. Migration students are not certain as to the cause of these irruptive movements.

YELLOW EYES. Within a twiggy fortress a brown thrasher
studies its mottled eggs. Many more thrashers skulk unnoticed
in the thickets than are seen in the course of a day's birding.

NOT A "SEA GULL," the Franklin's gull or "prairie dove" nests in the interior of the continent. It has vastly increased because of the federal waterfowl refuges, and a flight of a million southbound birds has been estimated in South Dakota.

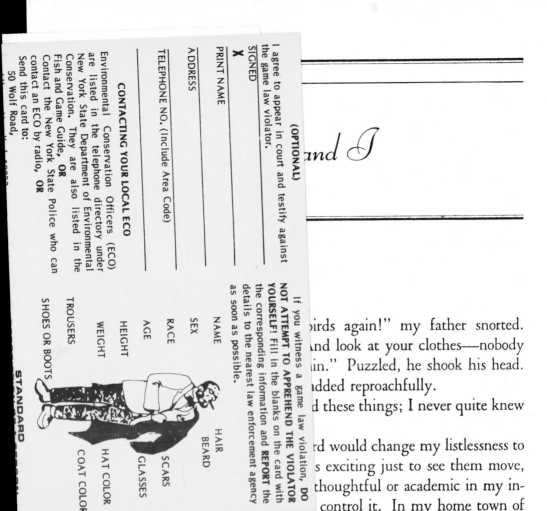

(OPTIONAL)

I agree to appear in court and testify against the game law violator.

SIGNED

X

PRINT NAME

ADDRESS

TELEPHONE NO. (Include Area Code)

CONTACTING YOUR LOCAL ECO

Environmental Conservation Officers (ECO) are listed in the telephone directory under New York State Department of Environmental Conservation. They are also listed in the Fish and Game Guide, **OR**

Contact the New York State Police who can contact an ECO by radio, **OR**

Send this card to:

50 Wolf Road,

If you witness a game law violation, **DO NOT ATTEMPT TO APPREHEND THE VIOLATOR YOURSELF!** Fill in the blanks on the card with the corresponding information and **REPORT** the details to the nearest law enforcement agency as soon as possible.

NAME — HAIR / BEARD

SEX

RACE — SCARS

AGE — GLASSES

HEIGHT

WEIGHT — HAT COLOR

TROUSERS — COAT COLOR

SHOES OR BOOTS

STANDARD

birds again!" my father snorted. ...nd look at your clothes—nobody ...in." Puzzled, he shook his head. ...dded reproachfully.

d these things; I never quite knew

rd would change my listlessness to ...s exciting just to see them move, ...thoughtful or academic in my in- ...control it. In my home town of Jamestown, New York, there are youngsters today whose eyes light up the same way at the sight of a bird. And so it always will be.

Many have tried to explain this pastime of bird watching. Joseph Hickey writes: "By some, it is regarded as a mild paralysis of the central nervous system, which can be cured only by rising at dawn and sitting in a bog. Others regard it as a harmless occupation of children, into which maiden aunts may sometimes relapse." James Fisher, the British ornithologist, comments: "The observation of birds may be a superstition, a tradition, an art, a science, a pleasure, a hobby or a bore; this depends entirely on the nature of the observer."

Doctor Frank Chapman used to say, "Everyone is born with a bird in his heart." But I wonder. Why will a dozen boys in a classroom become mildly absorbed when their teacher starts a bird club, but only one or two really take hold? Many older women are enthusiastic bird watchers, but how is it that so few teen-age girls go in for ornithology? And why the exceptions—attractive girls like the late Lorene Squire who became so engrossed in her magnificent waterfowl photography that she lost consciousness of all else whenever she saw a bird she wanted to picture. On the whole, however, birding is more of a boy's hobby.

How does it happen that so many of our best ornithologists started at the age of ten or eleven? Some of the top men—John James Audubon, Frank Chapman, Alexander Wetmore and Ludlow Griscom—began even earlier than that. Professor Arthur Allen, of Cornell, sent a questionnaire to the fellows of the American Ornithologists' Union a few years ago and found that every last one of them was launched before he was out of his teens and ninety percent by the age of ten.

A few years ago, on a Tuesday night, during a meeting of my old bird club, the Linnaean Society of New York, I sat in the back of the room where I could see everyone present. There were boys not yet seventeen, men past seventy; several housewives; a man who lived in a hall bedroom in lower Brooklyn and at least two millionaires. One man, unshaven and with gravy stains on his tie, sat beside a distinguished banker in a pinstriped Brooks Brothers suit. A lad of particularly dull intellect sat two rows in front of John Kieran, paragon of quick wit and fabulous memory. What is the common denominator? Here is a challenging opportunity for a group survey by some analyst. Instead of a behavior study of birds, why not a behavior study of bird watchers?

Would symbolism be the key? What do birds symbolize anyway? As with all symbols they probably represent different things to different people. Certainly the Linnaean Society or the American Ornithologists' Union or the Audubon Society or any large group seems to be a representative cross-section of humanity. Kings, presidents, prime ministers, generals, admirals, governors, senators, motion picture stars, and all manner of glamorous folk have been interested in birds. So have unnumbered plain people without particular distinction, right down to the maladjusted souls in mental wards and prisons. (I once received a letter from a lifer who asked for a check-list of American birds so he could give appropriate nicknames to his fellow "jail-birds.")

Every state has a state bird. These, chosen as they often are by garden clubs, school children and popular vote, usually favor such familiar birds as meadowlarks, bluebirds, goldfinches and chickadees. They are seldom the birds the ornithologist would choose as his personal favorites. If a questionnaire were sent to all the members of the American Ornithologists' Union, asking each to name his favorite three species, we might through the association of ideas gain some clues to the emotional appeal of birds. To say that people are attracted to birds because of their color, music, grace, vivacity and that sort of thing is superficial rationalization. I suspect a more fundamental reason is that birds suggest freedom and escape from restraint.

I have been astonished, on putting my friends to the test, how often the peregrine falcon, the fastest of all the birds, is indicated. Even more suggestive is the symbolic similarity of those birds that take second or third place. If a man's favorite is the peregrine, the chances are his second choice will be a hawk, too—perhaps a red-tail. Asked to name a bird that is not a hawk, to my surprise several replied "pileated woodpecker." What do the dashing peregrine and this big wild woodpecker have in common?

If a gentleman from Georgia tells me his favorite bird is the mockingbird, I know that his second choice will be the cardinal, and his third— you might guess—the Carolina wren, of course! All these stable, dependable garden birds represent the same thing; the gracious living of the old South. For a similar reason, in Ohio, the song sparrow and the cardinal are likely to share the honors.

Irving Kassoy, whose story I tell in the chapter *Ghoulies and Ghoosties*, spent more than two hundred nights in an abandoned mansion studying barn owls. He told me he sometimes heard queer sounds as of footsteps on the stairs. I ventured that he must enjoy creepy things or he would not have gotten himself into such a state of mind.

He replied, "That's not it at all; I don't like mysterious things—and that also goes for backward ideas too. That's why I study barn owls," he added. "There is so little known about them. People believe all sorts of things about owls. They did in the old days, and they still do."

"Irv," I said, "if you did not watch barn owls what would you work on?"

He thought a moment and replied, "Screech owls."

"Forget the owls," I countered, "take a marsh bird."

He furrowed his brow and suspected it would be a rail, "probably the black rail." Here was the same pattern—a clicking voice in the dark; the bird rarely glimpsed as it skulks through the salicornia, and almost unknown.

"Choose a sea bird this time," I prompted.

Without hesitation he replied "Leach's petrel." Again a bird of mystery, seldom seen as it roams the sea by day, a voice heard at night as it flutters over its dark burrow.

Granted there are special reasons why some individuals like birds, there is far more general interest in birds now than there was a half-century ago. In those days a man who scouted around the woods for "dickey birds" felt self-conscious about it, almost apologetic. Today so many people are taking to the out-of-doors that a man who does not watch birds or grow flowers, collect minerals, study the stars, or show a little interest in at least one of the natural sciences is likely to feel uneasy about it and offer his excuses.

Why this flood-tide? It has swept across the land from East to West; and even in the Northwest, the nearest thing to a frontier we have left, people are taking time out to look at birds.

Massachusetts can be called the cradle of American ornithology, although Philadelphia could make just claim by pointing out that both Wilson and Audubon once lived there. In 1871, twenty years after the death of Audubon, two young men, William Brewster and Henry Henshaw met each Monday night in the attic of Brewster's pre-revolutionary home on Brattle Street in Cambridge, Massachusetts, to read Audubon aloud and to discuss what they had read. Soon others climbed the stairs each week to pore over the pages and to take part in the talks. After two years of these informal seminars the Nuttall Club, named after the early New England ornithologist, was formed. This, the oldest bird club in America, of which I am proud to be a member, still holds its meetings in Cambridge.

The American Ornithologists' Union, the top scientific bird organization in the new world, has often been called a lusty offspring of the Nuttall Club, but actually the two are half-brothers. Brewster and some of the other early Nuttallites were among the charter members of the A.O.U. They decided it would be too much duplication if there were two journals, so the *Nuttall Bulletin* was continued as THE AUK, the new organ of the A.O.U. In 1884, a committee of the A.O.U. initiated what became the Audubon movement, which today is embodied in such organizations as the National Audubon Society, the various state Audubon Societies, and hundreds of local clubs. Thus we can trace the roots of the whole great movement to John James Audubon himself.

Bird watching became a respectable pursuit in New England long before it was countenanced elsewhere. It is a hobby that seldom thrives where men are pushing frontiers; it takes hold when life has settled down to the civilized complexities. The appeal of birds seems to be greater the more life is restrained.

As frontiers dissolved and communities weathered, the center of ornithological interest moved westward, until now we find the more progressive work (ecological studies, behavior studies and the like) being turned out in such states as Ohio, Michigan, Wisconsin and California. Massachusetts still has more bird watchers per square mile and probably produces more expert field observers than any other state, with the possible exception of New York.

In large cities like Cleveland, St. Louis and Detroit, bird clubs that numbered 100 members twenty-five years ago now have more than 1000. As an "Audubon Screen Tour" lecturer I have been astonished at the size of the audiences that filled the halls—1800 in Daytona, Florida; 1600 in Kansas City. In Detroit they do not publicize the lectures too much because the hall holds only 1000, and 3000 would turn up! Two hundred and some odd cities are now on the Audubon Screen Tour circuit and the yearly audiences are estimated at nearly a million.

The number of children in Junior Audubon Clubs is climbing, too. The idea started fifty years ago, and since that time more than eleven million children have been enrolled. The influence of these clubs is widening like the ripples on a pond.

In a way, the story about the small girl who informed her father that she had joined the "Junior Atom-bomb Society" is a commentary on the times we live in. We have gone through a bad nightmare and have awakened in what we are told is the atomic age. People are hopeful, frightened and puzzled. Everyone wants a higher standard of living; they all talk about it, while a few, aware of our diminishing natural resources and a constantly increasing population, believe that if the world gets much more crowded it will burst at the seams and the Malthusian principle may operate on a global scale.

Life is getting more and more complicated; but it seems that the more artificially complex man's affairs become the more he yearns for the fundamentals, the things of the earth. There has been a tremendous Renaissance in nature study since the beginning of World War II, not only here, but in Europe, particularly in England. Several British ornithologists with whom I have talked lately tell me that bird study has almost become a national hobby. Bird clubs are swamped with new members. This "boom in birds" seems to be an antidote for the pressures and artificialities of the modern world.

Some would say this is a form of escapism and perhaps it is, in a way—but not an escape from reality; rather a flight from the unreal things—from the "somnambulism of the hive" as Louis Halle calls it. In this gadget civilization which man has built to insulate himself against the world, he finds himself entrapped, not knowing whence he came or where he is going. Halle, in his *Spring In Washington,* observes that "it becomes necessary, occasionally, simply to throw open the hatches and ventilate one's psyche, or whatever you choose to call it. This means an excursion to some place where the sky is not simply what you see at the end of the street."

We invent systems, Socialism, Fascism, Communism and Capitalism. Each despises the other. Yet, as Professor Aldo Leopold of the University of Wisconsin pointed out, they all espouse one creed: *salvation by machinery.* Is it any wonder that when these systems prove faulty and men detect the synthetic nature of the civilization of their devising they turn to nature? In a world that seems so very puzzling is it any wonder birds have such appeal? Birds are, perhaps, the most eloquent expression of reality.

If we were to believe for one moment that Audubon was the Lost Dauphin, the son of Louis XVI and Marie Antoinette, a legend fondly clung to by the great naturalist's descendants but doubted by his biographer, Professor Herrick, it would not be hard to guess why birds became the most important interest in his life. A little prince imprisoned, before his final disappearance, in a tower—birds in a cage, his only pets—creatures with wings but imprisoned as he was. It takes little imagination to see the symbolism here. The Dauphin, psychologically at least, could have become Audubon.

A bird can fly where it wants to when it wants to. I am sure that is what appealed to me when I was in school. Regimentation and restriction rubbed me the wrong way; and the boys in my neighborhood were either younger or older, so I had to dream up my own fun. Birds seemed wonderful things. There were times when I wished that I could fly as they did, and leave everything. When Miss Hornbeck, teacher of the seventh grade, started a Junior Audubon Club, birds became the hub around which my life revolved. For the first five or six years, I could remember the dates of every field trip I had ever made and could recall just what I had seen. During the first years it was the joy of discovery. Then it became a competitive game, to see how many birds I could identify in a day, to discover rare birds, or to record a bird a day or two earlier in the spring than anyone else, or a day or two later in the fall. This was the listing stage. But as I tore about the countryside, ticking off the birds on my check-list on the run, I gradually became interested in their way of life. At home I pored over ornithological journals like *The Auk, The Wilson Bulletin,* and *The Condor.*

As I learned more about birds I found they are not quite the gloriously unrestrained things I had imagined them to be. They are bound by all sorts of natural laws. They go north and south almost by the calendar. They seem to follow certain flyways and routes between their summer and winter homes. A robin that lives in Connecticut this year will not think of going to Wisconsin next year. In fact, we are cautioned by Tinbergen, Lorenz and the other behaviorists against saying that birds *think.* We are told they are creatures of action and reaction, "releasers" and responses. A night heron, newly arrived in the rookery, goes through a step-by-step ritual of song and dance. Leave out any one of the steps, and the sequence is disrupted—the reproductive cycle does not carry through. If a female whose legs are still yellowish approaches a performing male she is rebuffed; if her legs are coral pink she is accepted. Bird psychology is a baffling thing!

I learned, too, that most birds have "territory." The males hold down a plot of ground for their own—it may be an acre or it may be five. They are property owners just as we are—and song, instead of being only a joyous outburst, is a functional expression—a proclamation of ownership, an invitation to a female, a threat to another male.

Most thought-provoking of all was to discover the balance between the bird and its environment—the balance of nature that we hear so much about (a swinging balance, it is true), the interrelation that exists between the hawk that eats the bird, the bird that eats the insect and the insect that eats the leaves, perhaps the very leaves that grow on the tree in which the hawk nests. I learned that each plot of ground has its carrying capacity and that predation only crops a surplus that otherwise would be levelled in some different way; hence putting up fences and shooting all the hawks and all the cats will not raise the number of redstarts or red-eyed vireos to any degree at all.

Birds then, are almost as earth-bound as we are. They have freedom and mobility only within prescribed limits. It was down-right disillusioning to read Mrs. Nice's technical papers on behavior, Kendeigh's studies of environmental factors and Rowan's discussions of migration. But my interest survived this phase and has grown deeper. It has followed the pattern of a thousand other ornithologists I have known. What had started as an emotional release has swung over to an intellectual pursuit.

Reluctant at first to accept the strait jacket of a world which I did not comprehend, I finally, with the help of my hobby, made some sort of peace with society. The birds, which started as an escape from the unreal, bridged the gap to reality and became a key whereby I might unlock eternal things.

The Lure of the List

WHEN Field-marshal, the Viscount Alanbrooke was chairman of the joint chiefs of staff of the allied armies during World War II, his associate, General Dwight Eisenhower, presented him with a book on birds. Lord Alanbrooke was not the only military leader who found bird watching a good relief for tension during those deeply troubled times. A few months later, a general in command of the British Zone in Germany was picked up in Berlin by the Russians as a suspicious character because he was wandering about, looking into the trees with a pair of binoculars. He was released immediately when his identity became known.

The highest ranking general to lose his life in the service of this country during World War II was Lieutenant-General Simon Bolivar Buckner who died on Okinawa. Mrs. Buckner told me that on one of her husband's brief visits to his home in San Francisco he spent an afternoon in Golden Gate Park, watching the waterfowl on one of the small lakes. In a marshy spot he glimpsed something that piqued his curiosity, and, disregarding his spotless regalia, he crouched low and crept through the reeds. Parting the cattails to see better, he came face to face with another stalker, creeping through the rank growth, a bearded gentleman. Both were momentarily startled, but the graybeard, obviously a biologist, found his tongue first.

"How do you do, sir," he said. "I'm looking for gallinules."

"What kind," inquired the general, "purple or Florida?"

And so, two men whose professions were in different spheres, found a congenial meeting ground in their mutual interest in birds.

"Bird listing," or just plain "birding," call it what you will, is becoming a popular game. Boys go in for it, of course, but so do many professional men who have only Sundays to spare. They cruise the roads, scan the lakes, investigate new places, and keep a year-to-year record of what they find. Housewives, more confined, keep lists of what they see in the backyard.

Guy Emerson, as a banker, used to engineer his business trips to distant cities so that he would be there at the best time for warblers, shorebirds, or ducks. Birds, he said, gave him a closer tie with America than any other medium. Through them he often met people in walks of life with which he would otherwise have no contact—people with long vistas before their eyes. And he set foot in places that were untrod by the multitude—from remote groves in our National parks, the most beautiful places this side of heaven, to city garbage dumps.

Even the seamy places appeal to some birds and to the men who pursue them. One day, Geoffrey Carleton of New York set out in his rattletrap of a car to see a rare gull that had been reported on one of the city dumps. He became lost, and, chugging up to the nearest policeman, called out over the asthmatic sobbing of his engine:

"How do I get to the dump?"

The policeman, visibly indignant, replied, "I'm sorry—you can't leave that old hack here. It's not a junk yard, you know."

Mr. Carleton, an inveterate bird-lister, has become callous to such brushes with his uncomprehending fellow man. Even the scientific ornithologist is not too sympathetic and often looks down his nose at such goings on. "So you broke a hundred today!" he taunts. "What does that prove?" He forgets that he went through the same stage himself and that the "lure of the list," as Guy Emerson calls it, came first, before the science. Scratch a fellow of the American Ornithologists' Union and you will find, beneath, a boy who stood open-mouthed when he first heard a thrush sing; a boy who made lists for years before he put his hobby on a more intellectual basis. Many of the leaders of American ornithology, men like Robert Cushman Murphy of the American Museum and Alexander Wetmore of the Smithsonian, are not ashamed to enjoy a good day's birding whenever they can, even if it adds not one scrap to science. Arthur A. Allen, Professor of Ornithology at Cornell, still keeps lists, and even goes out for an exhausting "Big Day," once in a while.

"What makes a good field-man? I once knew a guide at Barnegat who could identify the ducks as they rose in a smoky cloud on the horizon, so distant that we could scarcely distinguish what they were with our binoculars. "There go your cannies," Oscar would say, "and them's broadbills over on the end." He was always right. Of course, he went partly by location. He was out on the bay every day so he knew approximately where to expect things. I knew another guide on Great Salt Lake who could tell the different ducks by the murmur of their wings. Without hesitation, one night, he called pintails, redheads, teal, shovelers and mallards. I believed him, even though the sky was so black I had no way of checking.

There are many, like Oscar, the Barnegat bayman, who, on familiar ground, can call off the birds before anyone else; but I think the test of a good field observer is how quick and accurate he is away from home. I am sure you could put George Sutton, the bird artist, anywhere on the continent and he would know immediately what to look for in that particular area. Sutton has a technique all his own. He doesn't stick to the paths the way most of us do, but wanders off into the dark thickets and makes squeaks on the back of his hand. In this way he turns up a lot of things, little obscure warblers and the like, that most of us would miss.

Ludlow Griscom, of Cambridge, Massachusetts, was often called the "virtuoso of field identification." He knew many of the birds by their flight alone, and 500 or more by their songs. Very few North American birds had eluded him, and his world life list was well over 2500. After 10,000 field trips he had learned to call off birds in a split second—so quickly and surely that his scientific colleagues sometimes had strong doubts. But when they checked he was invariably right. What gave Griscom this edge? Let us look at his early background. Brought up in a family with a tradition of international diplomacy, he crossed the Atlantic fifteen times before he was twenty-eight. He spoke French and German, not as an American speaks them, but like a European. All told, he learned to speak five languages fluently, could read ten easily and translated up to eighteen with a little help. As a youngster, he played the piano so proficiently that by the time he became a young man he had to make a choice between the career of a concert pianist and that of an ornithologist. There came a time when he could further his art only by devoting eight hours a day to the keys instead of four, and this meant he would have to give up the birds. Although he continued to play for pleasure, ornithology won out. Languages and music both demand the control of great masses of detail, so organized that they can be sorted out with unconscious speed. Griscom's achievements in these fields undoubtedly conditioned his way of thinking, and, in addition to his training as a first-rate botanist and museum ornithologist, helped make him the field-man he was.

The mind of a good field observer works just like a kaleidoscope, the gadget of our childhood, wherein loose fragments of colored glass fall quickly into symmetrical patterns. We see a bird. With an instinctive movement we center it in our glass. All the thousands of fragments we know about birds, locality, season, habitat, voice, actions, field marks and likelihood of occurrence flash across the mirrors of the mind and fall into place—and we have the name of our bird.

A new bird, seen for the first time, is called a "life bird." It goes on a "life list." Herbert Brandt, one of Cleveland's leading business men, and Ludlow Griscom were about tied with life lists of around 980 species and subspecies for the North American continent. There were not too many North American birds left for either of these men to see. However, even Griscom could not separate most subspecies in the field, so he contended that they ought not be counted as sight records, even if they are found within the range outlined by the Check-List. Only full species should be counted, he believed. I agree with him.

In a single year, Dr. William Helmuth, a physician, ran up a list of 672 species and subspecies. Guy Emerson nosed him out with a score of 674. For a time, the largest one year's list, even topping Emerson's, was 681, made by Arthur Allen. Then word came out of Boston that Dr. Morton Cummings had piled up a grand total of 752. All records seemed to topple until it was noticed that his list ran very heavily (contrary to modern rules) to subspecies—eleven different horned larks, ten song sparrows, eight nighthawks. But when the lists of Allen, Emerson and Cummings were broken down to full species, Emerson came out ahead with 497. In 1953, the year of the great trip with James Fisher, I gained the title with a score of 572. Three years later, Stuart Keith retraced our path and amassed a total of 594.

All of us had traveled to the far corners of the country, but local lists of 250 species or more are made every year by birders who live close to salt water, particularly around such cities as Boston, New York, Philadelphia,

Washington, Charleston, San Francisco and Los Angeles. Inland, 150 to 200 is a good year's total.

As in any other sport, "scores" seem exciting chiefly to those who play the game. If, in this chapter, or in one or two of those that follow, I seem to be placing too much emphasis on sheer collecting, it is because I have an academic interest in these games men play with birds and believe the phenomenon should be recorded.

Griscom, in his late fifties, and with scientific prestige enough to satisfy any museum man, still played the game of his youth for all it was worth. I watched with fascination his acceleration of pace. Two decades earlier, when he was at the American Museum, he made the statement that it was physically impossible for one man to see 250 species of birds in the New York City region in one year. On the very last day of that year, Frank Watson, an entomologist in the American Museum, saw his 250th bird, a razor-billed auk. Griscom, after duplicating the feat himself, moved to Boston, where reputedly there were leaner pickings. In due time he was getting lists of 250 there, and eventually 290! Later, he developed a state-wide grapevine. His friends telephoned him immediately when they discovered anything rare. They tipped him off to all the strays: birds from Europe, the far north, the south and the far west. Thus, he did not have to travel outside the state to get his birds. The world came to his door; the mountain came to Mohammed. In 1941, he attained a list of 304, all in Massachusetts. Then he wrote: "The war and the tire shortage will make a repetition of 1941 impossible for some years to come. I trust this will be written up in some detail as a record of a way of life and a technique of bird study, so that it will have historical rather than purely passing interest . . . I shall never again even try to duplicate 1941." That is what he wrote, but, in 1945, the very year the war ended, his year's total was 307. Then post-war inflation set in. In 1946, his personal list soared to such heights that he refused to publish it! When I asked Griscom, late the following year, whether it was a secret, he said no, but he had felt, at the time, that publishing it would emphasize unduly a relatively unimportant side of ornithology. Be that as it may, Griscom's list for 1946 was 317. I said, surely that would be his top record for all time. With a wry smile, he informed me that he had just that week reached 318, with two months of 1947 still left to go. His latest bird was a painted redstart! I thought he said painted bunting, and I was not too impressed, but then it dawned on me that he meant the gorgeous butterfly-like warbler with the red belly and white wing patches that lives in the mountains of southern Arizona, the most stunning of all the warblers, bar none!

Two women, Mrs. de Windt and Mrs. Searle, newcomers to the fold, were scanning the trees on Marblehead Neck when they made their incredible discovery. The bird flitted among the branches overhead like a vision. They could not find it in their eastern Field Guides, so they called up Russell Mason at the Massachusetts Audubon Society. He could think of nothing that fitted their description but suggested it might be a towhee. The two ladies were indignant. They knew towhees. Then Mason had a hunch. He called up Griscom and the following morning they both went to Marblehead Neck. Within two minutes after their arrival they found the bird—a painted redstart—2400 miles from its home in the desert mountains. During the day this rare visitor was seen by 100 to 150 observers from all over the state, including a busload of Massachusetts Audubonites on a scheduled trip. Even Kodachrome movies were taken for the record.

That is the way they do things in Massachusetts. When a rare straggler turns up, so many people see it that there is no question as to its authenticity. One winter a sea eagle from Europe was studied by forty people on the ice of the Merrimac River. In January, 1946, an ivory gull was discovered sitting disconsolately on a rooftop by a busload of Audubonites. They thought it was a pigeon and kept right on. The second bus stopped and forty people made the acquaintance of this rare gull from the Arctic whose scientific name, *Pagophila alba*, means "white ice-lover." On the very last day of the same year, a green-tailed towhee, an olive-backed bird with a rusty cap that lives in the Rockies and should spend its winters in Mexico, switched its direction detectors and turned up at a feeding tray in Northampton, Massachusetts. For three months, the Risleys, who entertained this distinguished finch, did not have a Sunday to themselves. At least one hundred New England bird students dropped in to pay their respects.

Every state in the Union has its quota of rarities, stray birds out of their normal range. Joseph Grinnell once remarked that, given enough time, every North American species would be recorded in California.

The field-glass amateurs need not apologize to the professionals. To the beginner, advanced ornithological research seems as dull and pointless as bird listing seems to some biologists. Yet they blend, one with the other. There is no reason why the bird lister should justify his hobby on scientific grounds any more than should the sportsman. Still, he inevitably adds something to our knowledge of birds. To the rank and file of field-glass observers we owe much of what is known about the sweep and movement of migration, of invasions, distribution, extension of range and periodic increases and declines.

But the game of listing pays smaller dividends the longer it is played. Rare birds no longer seem rare when you have seen them a dozen times. After a few years, even the most fanatical bird chaser takes things easier. He no longer gets up at the crack of dawn on every field trip. I remember how the rest of my party once despaired of me when near Cobb's Island, Virginia. They got up at daybreak to see what they could find before breakfast. I stayed in bed. In the two hours they were gone they listed forty-two species. My own list when I came downstairs was forty. I had heard them all from my pillow and only once did I raise my head to look out the window—when a flock of curlew flew by.

It used to take a lifetime to learn to identify all the birds; now it can be done in several years. That does not mean that bird study stops when you can no longer add new birds to your list. Some expert field men, like John Baker, plunge into conservation work; he became president of the National Audubon Society. Others, like Allan Cruickshank, transfer their interest from seeing new birds to photographing them. Cruickshank has seen almost everything there is to see. Now he has set out to photograph all 650 North American species. He is past the 500 mark, but I am afraid if he doesn't pin down the hardest ones soon, birds like the cerulean warbler and certain others which nest high up, he won't ever get them. He will no longer be able to make the hazardous climbs.

There is a point of transferal that bridges the gap from the bird lister to the bird watcher. Joseph Hickey had gone through the usual cycle with his field glass and little white check-lists. The law of diminishing returns had set in and his zealous interest lapsed. He still went on a few field trips, but it looked as though another follower of the cult had been lost when Ernst Mayr, brilliant young ornithologist of the American Museum, took an interest in Hickey and opened his eyes to the limitless untapped possibilities of his hobby. He taught him not to identify a bird and then pass on quickly to the next one, but to slow down, watch it and inquire into its way of life.

Joseph Hickey changed from a lister to a full-fledged bird watcher and to pay off his debt wrote his classic book, *A Guide to Bird Watching*. It takes one by the hand and demonstrates that bird study can last a lifetime. Written when Hickey was still an amateur, it points out what the amateur can do to add his bit to the science of ornithology.

Some men settle on a favorite bird. They try to find out everything they can about it. It gives them pleasure to feel they know more about that species than any other man living. Irving Kassoy became fascinated by the barn owls that lived in the Bronx, while his friend, Richard Herbert, who lived a few blocks away, spent all his spare time going over to the Palisades to watch the peregrines. No falconer knew more than he about the prince of predators. One Brooklyn bird watcher, or, I should say, bird listener, specialized in thrushes' songs. When I met him in a wooded canyon near Salt Lake City he was looking for the willow veery. He wanted to compare its song with that of the veery he knew in the East. The late Prentiss Baldwin, a retired Cleveland lawyer, had an elaborate system of bird boxes on his estate. Each box was wired electrically to charts and graphs in his laboratory. A wren could not make a move on the nest without Baldwin's knowing about it. It was he who revealed the bigamous marital relations of "Jenny." Some say he knew more about a single species of songbird than any other man has ever known; others contend that this honor goes to Mrs. Margaret Morse Nice, a former Columbus, Ohio, housewife who watched song sparrows for ten years while she raised a brood of four children of her own.

In a way, the amateur is in a better position than the professional to add to our knowledge of the living bird. The museum man is condemned to a life of inhaling paradichlorobenzene fumes from trays of skins while he works out problems in taxonomy. The university professor teaches, and becomes an arm-chair strategist, while his students, working for degrees, do the creative work. Wildlife management experts get outdoors more than the others, but they are committed to game species.

If you are a thoughtful person you will probably graduate from Christ-

ANCIENT BIRDS are the white pelicans here shown floating on the sun-flecked water of Bear River in Utah. They nest on Gunnison Island far out in Great Salt Lake, but the water there is so salty that many go fifty miles or more for food.

MUSICAL ACCOMPANIMENT to spring is provided by the silvery-voiced song sparrow. Systematists have split this familiar passerine into twenty-seven subspecies, ranging from small pale desert races to large dusky Alaskan forms.

HOME IN A GOURD. The cheerful enthusiastic house wren is always glad to accept a proffered bird house in lieu of an abandoned woodpecker hole.

LIKE A MAGNET, the colony pulls its members together from a vast range. Brown pelicans, above, find security on an island in the Laguna Madre of Texas, while Caspian terns, below, gather at Hat Island in Lake Michigan.

mas counts to breeding-bird censuses, and from there on to life histories, or studies of song, territory or whatever strikes your fancy. The exact requirements of many birds—their ecology—is still not well known. Nor do we know too much about plant succession, and just what happens to the birds when the plants change. If you wish to become really profound, you might even probe into bird psychology.

So don't think that as an amateur you are not important. The vistas of ornithology stretch out to the horizon.

The Big Day

AT THREE o'clock in the morning a large open touring car parked just off the highway in the hills of northern New Jersey. After switching off the ignition and the headlights, the driver relaxed while the other occupants of the car leaned out and listened. Two state police saw the suspicious-looking automobile. The six silent, roughly dressed men within appeared to be a hard-boiled and dangerous lot.

"What do you gents think you are doing?" inquired one of the patrolmen.

"Listening for whip-poor-wills," replied the driver.

"Wise guys!" retorted the officer.

It took these men a full hour to convince the skeptical police that they really were listening for whip-poor-wills. Furthermore, they were trying to find as many birds as they could within a twenty-four hour day. They were starting with the night birds; that is why they had parked in this lonely place.

Some years ago, when the star of the field-glass ornithologist was rising and it was no longer necessary to check every observation over the sights of a shotgun, some fellow with good legs and sharp eyes found he could list over 100 species of birds in a day. In the north this would be in mid-May, at the time the spring migration was at flood tide.

This all-out May-day tournament was something I had never heard of before I came into contact with the birdmen of the big cities along the East coast. New Yorkers and Bostonians call it the "Big Day"; the New Jerseyites the "Lethal Tour"; Philadelphians the "Century Run," and Washingtonians the "Grim Grind." One museum man, with a note of scorn, has dubbed it "ornithogolfing." Lately it has become a tradition, planned for weeks in advance. Each hour is mapped out so that the most productive places are visited at the most opportune time. From dark to dark the field-glass forces invade the realm of the birds with military thoroughness. Crossing a field, they deploy their ranks on a wide front so that no bird slips by. Fast travel between strategic areas, with a tankful of gas and good brakes, is part of the tactics.

A dozen pairs of eyes are better than one pair, or two; and although there is dead wood in every Big Day party, the larger the group the better the list. In Massachusetts, half a dozen of us usually went together, led by our commanding general, Ludlow Griscom. I remember particularly the day we piled up a grand total that broke all previous records for New England.

The evening before we held a council of war over the telephone. Griscom had studied the weather maps and the tide tables. He had outlined where we would stop and when, but each of us offered amendments. Even though the trip was planned as precisely as a train schedule, we left some room for flexibility. In migration, birds seem to gather in "pockets." It is a waste of time to linger where not much is stirring.

I got my gear together before I went to bed, so there would be no delay. My trousers were of a sort that could not be ripped easily on barbed wire. I prefer sneakers to boots when the weather is warm for they let the water out as well as in, and they dry quickly. I dug out a hat with a good brim to shade my eyes from the sun. Although I had a pair of 12-power glasses, I decided to use my eights. They had a very wide field and were better for warblers and other small birds than the larger glass. Griscom would have his Zeiss telescope, with its three rotating oculars, so if we saw any shore birds on a bar too distant to identify them with our glasses, we could magnify them as much as forty times if need be.

My alarm went off at two that morning. Although I hate alarm clocks and choose to ignore them, suffering as I do from some sort of compulsion complex, at the sound of the bell this morning I jumped from bed like a fighter from his corner. At the diner, three blocks away, I gulped my coffee and scrambled eggs while little gray mice played among the boxes of breakfast food on the shelf. I do not know what birdmen would do without diners! They are as much a part of early morning bird trips as the robin chorus and the rising sun.

I met Griscom and the others at Harvard Square, in Cambridge. Although it was black as pitch, Griscom said there was no time to lose. We had to reach Boxford, thirty miles down the turnpike, to listen for owls before it got light. We made only one stop. Pulling to the side of the road, we turned off the engine and listened. The sound of the motor still hummed in our ears and at first we could hear nothing. Then Griscom announced, "There it is—number one!" We strained, and faintly above the chorus of the spring peepers came a nasal *beezp!* It was a woodcock, the first bird of the day. A moment later came the chippering whistle of its wings as the "timber-doodle" took off on its aerial song-flight. Higher and higher it climbed against the descending moon; until, reaching the zenith, it spilled forth its ecstatic bubble-pipe-like warblings and twisted headlong back to earth. All was silent again as we climbed back into the car. We did not wait to hear the performance again nor did we search out the singer. A bird heard is as good as a bird seen, and there were other night birds to be recorded before dawn rolled back the darkness.

We turned off the main highway onto a dirt road, went as far as we could, parked, and walked down the narrow path leading to Crooked Pond. Faint lisps and chips dropped from the blackness above us, a good sign that meant there would be a flight. It is almost impossible to be sure of these tiny night voices beyond identifying them broadly as warblers or sparrows, but the thrush notes are quite distinctive. There was no doubt, either, about the whip-poor-will that lashed out with its nocturnal chant. It went down on our list as number two.

Griscom, leading the party single file through the dew-drenched grass, stopped abruptly as a strange call came from the second-growth woodland to our left. Dove-like yet frog-like, we could not place it. "Long-eared owl," Griscom announced finally. "It had me guessing for a minute." The rest of us had never heard that note before, so we could not dispute the verdict. Yet we had not expected the long-ear. The real reason we were walking down this trail was to try for the pair of barred owls that lived near the pond. Owls won't "talk" every morning, but that day we were favored; a few hoots from Griscom in his best strixine falsetto brought a muffled answer. The second bird gave moral support to the first, and we left Crooked Pond with both owls whooping and caterwauling at the tops of their lungs, in defiance of the strangers who had invaded their wilderness.

By the time we reached the car, the east was streaked with light. The robin chorus was in full voice and, although we had not yet seen a single bird, our list had already passed twenty. Song sparrows, field sparrows and catbirds announced themselves. A pheasant squawked. We had to hurry. Marsh birds are at their best around sunrise, and if we did not reach the Lynnfield Meadows early, we might miss the rails.

Dawn on a marsh is the most vocal time of day—even on a New England marsh, which is, at best, a pale reflection of the teeming duck marshes further west. Following the high dry cinder bed of the railroad, the one way in and out of the Lynnfield Meadows, we were soon in the heart of the great swamp. Patches of fog still clung to the sodden earth, or, stirred by the dawn wind, drifted off in milky wisps. Chilled, we could have done with a second cup of coffee, but this would have to wait. Our luck at Lynnfield would have much to do with the success of the day. Perhaps we might pick up a rarity—a king rail, big and rusty, or even the small elusive yellow rail. In this we were disappointed. Lynnfield was particularly poor. We heard the bittern's hollow pumping, and detected both marsh wrens: the long-bill gurgling in the cattails and the short-bill stuttering from the more grassy part of the swamp. We heard the grunting of the Virginia rail but once and missed the whinny of the sora entirely. Usually these little chicken-like birds sound off all over the swamp in the early morning. We laid their silence to the cool breeze that had sprung up, rattling the sabers of the reeds.

We had already picked up a large number of small land birds in the sparse groves at the edge of the swamp, but we placed our biggest hopes for these on Nahant, a narrow-waisted headland that juts out into the ocean. There on the spacious estates would parade the warblers and other migrants, concentrated in this natural bird trap by the barrier of the sea. We found buffy-breasted Lincoln sparrows and smart-looking white-crowns on the lawns, as we had hoped, but we had not expected the flock of ten purple sandpipers that scrambled over a dripping, tide-exposed rock. These hardy junco-colored sandpipers are uncertain enough on these barnacle-encrusted boulders, even in winter. In May, they were a genuine surprise for us. We were doing well, but it looked as though our luck would taper off; it was beginning to rain.

Mount Auburn Cemetery, in Cambridge, was our last stop before starting on the long run to the Cape for shore birds. By the time we entered the wrought-iron gates the drizzle had stopped and the gray clouds were breaking up. This famous old cemetery, where ornithologists have hunted warblers among the tombstones since the days of William Brewster, was full of birds, brought in by the southwesterly wind of the night before. Quickly we rounded out our list of warblers, adding the Tennessee, Blackburnian, Canada, Wilson's and bay-breast. Our warbler list alone was twenty-two, not bad for New England, although twenty-five or even more, is a possibility.

Our total list had reached eighty by 8:00 a.m.; a hundred by 10:00 a.m. But this furious pace slowed down to a walk by noon. New birds were harder to find; our limbs had become weary from the ten-hour grind; eyelids were heavy and heads nodded in the back seat, while the driver doggedly held to the endless ribbon of concrete unwinding toward the Cape. We went by way of Carver to take in a colony of purple martins, one of the few breeding colonies of this big glossy swallow in eastern Massachusetts. A detour at Wareham gave us the hermit thrush, singing beside a cranberry bog in the barrens, and three bald eagles, lured by the myriads of shad that swarmed into the inland ponds to spawn and die.

Nothing is duller for birds than most pine-barren country, so we spent little time on it. The outer Cape was a long haul, and it was late in the day before we reached Chatham, with its white houses and wind-swept silver poplars. There we changed into a hired beach wagon with low-pressure balloon tires for gripping the loose beach sand.

There were not more than two hours of daylight left when we started down Monomoy, the long peninsula of sand dunes and mud flats that stretches southward for ten miles or so into the Atlantic from the crooked elbow of Cape Cod. Here we hoped to wind up the day in a burst of glory. Nor were we disappointed. Shore birds swarmed the flats like sand fleas on a beach. There were a thousand ruddy turnstones all in high rufous breeding plumage with orange legs and harlequin-like head markings. We estimated 300 black-bellied plovers, 3000 sanderlings and countless numbers of the smaller "sand peeps." Our shore-bird list rose to fifteen species.

In the surf bobbed belated groups of those rugged sea ducks, the scoters. All three species were in sight and among them six American eiders, males with white backs, stragglers from the great flocks that make Monomoy their winter headquarters.

Like a magician, plucking rabbits from a hat, Griscom pulled out the two "fanciest" birds of the day. Ordering the driver to stop, he put his glasses on a lone bird swimming beyond the surf. Quickly appraising, he called out "Brunnich's murre." The telescope was brought to bear on the piebald swimmer and without a hint of chagrin, Griscom retracted the first guess. "Sorry!" he apologized, "just an old-squaw." Even Griscom made mistakes, but he was usually the first to correct them.

We had hardly gone several hundred yards further down the beach when another lone swimmer caught our attention. Griscom squinted, hesitated and blurted "Brunnich's murre." We respectfully reserved judgment while he tensely hauled out the telescope again. In a moment he relaxed. "Don't you believe me?" he queried. "Look for yourselves!" We did. There was no doubt about it; the bird was a murre, that black-and-white sea bird that reminds one so much of a penguin. It was in changing plumage and the proportion of the bill and the light-colored mark along the gape showed it to be a Brunnich's! This curious coincidence did much to increase our ever-growing awe of Griscom. No one but he would have dared cry "Brunnich's murre" again so soon after making a blunder.

The pay-off came a short distance further down the beach when a third lone sea bird was spotted, bobbing up and down in the wave troughs. With hardly a moment's deliberation Griscom electrified us with "Atlantic murre!" That was too much! To get both murres in one day was an extremely rare event in Massachusetts even in the dead of winter. It was next to impossible in May. Surely Griscom was getting tired—probably he had too much sun. But the telescope backed him up. The bird *was* an Atlantic murre in winter plumage. The thin pointed bill and the dark line behind the eye left no doubt about it.

At the tip of Monomoy we found the usual great congregation of gulls and terns resting on the high crown of the shell-studded beach. Facing in one direction, into the wind and the setting sun, rested five kinds of gulls and four of terns. Besides the tiny least terns with yellow bills and the familiar common terns with black-tipped vermilion bills, there were a number of roseates with blackish bills, and a few Arctics, grayer than the others, with bills blood-red to the tip. This is one of the southernmost spots in America where the Arctic tern can be depended upon. Indeed, I know of no better place anywhere to study the several most confusing terns side by side. An hour with these birds at the tip of Monomoy is worth months of experience with them elsewhere.

With the sun setting in a coppery haze on the horizon, we sped up the beach, satisfied with Monomoy and with ourselves. We were blissfully pleased but tired—faces windblown, eyes bloodshot and hair filled with sand. Griscom, always a martinet, said we would not stop for food until we had done one thing more—not until we had tried for the great horned owl back in the barrens.

We got not only the great horned, which was obliging enough to hoot once or twice in stentorian tones, but also a screech owl that timidly answered my imitation of its lonely wail. Four kinds of owls in one day was not bad. We had done about all we could, and we were hungry!

Dinner never tasted so good. When the apple pie had been followed by coffee and we had taken out our check-list cards, we counted the day's total. It came to 148! This was a new high for Massachusetts and for all New England.

Riding home, we put our trust in our driver while we dozed and fitfully dreamed of murres with blood-red bills, like those of Arctic terns. At midnight we reached Boston. We had been on the go for twenty-two hours, but we had hung up a record.

For a decade, no one bettered that score in Massachusetts. But on May 20, 1945, after three cold rainy weeks in which the May migrants had become dammed up, a platoon of bird-watchers found 160 species—all in Essex County! Three years later, on May 23, 1948, with identical freak weather conditions in our favor, we nosed out this short-lived record by one species. Late at night the cooperative barred owls of Crooked Pond responded to Griscom's whoops just as they had done on nearly every big day for the past fifteen years, and thus became No. 161 on our list.

Among the most famous of all Big Day trips were those which the late Charles Urner organized in New Jersey. Starting in the swampy Troy Meadows before daybreak, running up to the mountain ridges near Boonton for migrating warblers and down through the pine barrens to the

FROM THE SHADOWS hops the wood thrush to bathe in a fern-lined pool. The thrushes are among our most accomplished avian musicians, at their best for a brief while when the sun sinks and other voices grow silent.

STATUESQUE egrets wander in all directions after their nesting is over. Some travel northward from their southern rookeries and can be seen wading in roadside ponds and streams as far north as the Great Lakes and New England.

southern New Jersey coast for shore birds, Urner's itinerary resembled that of the excursion I have described in Massachusetts. Urner's lists, however, were larger, seldom fewer than 150, once as high as 173. There were more participants, also, sometimes fifteen or twenty; as a result, hardly anyone came within ten of seeing every bird in the day's total. Some of the less experienced men complained it was a dog-eat-dog affair, that once a bird was ticked off no one would wait for the slower fellows to find it.

In more recent years Urner's record has been broken elsewhere in the United States. Connie Hagar and C. D. Brown listed 204 at Rockport, Texas, one April day during a good flight. A single party led by Arnold Small on the California Coast also exceeded the 200 mark in a single day.

A variation of the Big Day is the "Roundup." In this there are no restrictions on distance or number of parties, providing they start from the same point. A number of lists are combined at the end of the day. At St. Louis, Missouri, a "Roundup" recorded 187 species in one day, while the Delaware Valley Ornithological Club checked off 214 between the mountains and the New Jersey shore.

These ornithological sprees do not allow one fully to enjoy the birds or to spend much time watching them. But there are values beyond the excitement of the chase. If exact numbers of each species are kept, a year-to-year comparison gives a hint of increases or declines. Redstart-*common* does not mean much, but redstart-58 does. The conscientious field-man keeps a diary of the outstanding behavior of the birds, his impressions of the sweep and movement of migration and the weather.

No one would want to engage in one of these endurance tests every week end, but once or twice a year it is great sport, a test of the skills acquired by months and years of bird watching. We are waiting for the inevitable day when someone will try it by airplane or helicopter.

Census at Christmas

*I*T IS dangerous to say anything disparaging about the Bronx or Brooklyn—even about their birds. The younger members of the Linnaean Society will hotly defend their boroughs, insisting that, in spite of the apparent aridity, the square miles of apartment houses, tenements and factories in the most completely urbanized area in the world, few places can boast as many unusual bird visitors. If anyone were to say that 100 different species could be seen in the Bronx region at Christmastime, the figure would be thought fantastic. It would seem more nearly correct with one less cipher. Yet this is what the Bronx County Bird Club shoots for each year.

Each December, more than 15,000 bird watchers scattered throughout the United States and Canada select one day during Christmas week for the Audubon Christmas Bird Count. Over a period of more than sixty years, hundreds of thousands of man-hours have been spent taking these counts or censuses, as they originally were called. Charles Rogers of Princeton has not missed a year since the idea started back in 1900. For at least fifty years, Harry B. McConnell of Cadiz, Ohio, editor of a country newspaper, never missed a census. Alexander Wetmore, former secretary of the Smithsonian Institution, took part in the first count when he was a boy in Wisconsin. Although he does not get out every Christmas, one year he helped us break the all-time record for Washington, D. C., by flushing the barn owl from the northeast tower of the old Smithsonian building.

The Count is a sort of cold weather "Big Day," but the rules are somewhat different. Three or four groups, working independently, can pool their lists, although they must stay within a circle fifteen miles in diameter.

There is much plotting with dividers and maps to place the circle so it will include the very best places. Although the whole census scheme was started by Frank Chapman as a game or a sport—a substitute for looking at birds over the sights of a shotgun—the rules have been modified to make the results more useful to ornithology. The weather is noted; the temperature; the wind velocity and direction—also clouds, and field conditions that result from the weather. The habitats visited are estimated—cattail swamps, ten per cent; brushy fields, thirty per cent; second-growth deciduous woodlands, twenty-five per cent; and so on.

In a little pad, the observer jots down the exact number of everything he sees, unless the flocks are so large he can only estimate. Figures must be definite if researchers wish to learn which are the commonest birds and whether they increase or decline through the years. If a rare or unlikely bird is seen, all the substantiating details are given; otherwise the editor is likely to append a skeptical note to the record—for example: Great auk (no details —Ed.). The whole list is put in A.O.U. Check-list order (the order that all bird guides follow) and sent to Audubon Field Notes for publication.

About four-fifths—more than 550—of approximately 650 species of North American birds (not counting the accidental species) have been recorded on these Christmas Counts. The rest winter deep in the tropics, or are extremely rare or accidental. This permanent file is beginning to show us much about winter bird life; cyclic invasions; the center of winter abundance of different birds; increase and decline; and stragglers outside the normal winter range.

Although the census taker thinks vaguely of these things while rushing about, it is not science he is espousing, but the fun of the chase. That certainly was the motive of the boys of the Bronx County Bird Club back in the mid-twenties when they took their first census. Nine sons of brick and concrete, in their late teens, were drawn together from various parts of the sprawling Bronx—Hunts Point Avenue, Woodycrest Avenue and Van Cortlandt—by their common interest. How their youthful dreams took flight on the wings of birds, among the vacant lots, dumps and abandoned estates of this northernmost of New York City's boroughs, is a saga in itself. Typical of the melting pot that is New York, the parentage of these nine lads represented almost as many nationalities—Swiss, English, German, Polish, Jewish, Russian, Irish and Scotch. Later, Swedish was added when I arrived in the big city and was admitted to the club as its first out-side member. Two of the original nine, Allan Cruickshank and Joseph Hickey, are now known to everyone who watches birds.

The Christmas Census brought the club into being and the club in turn brought the census to its highest degree of development. The nine boys represented three competing factions. Some had taken censuses before with their school nature clubs. They noticed that most Bronx lists ran be-tween twenty and twenty-eight. Surely if they forgot their rivalry and pooled their man-power they could do better than that. In their first co-operative effort they reached the unprecedented total of forty-nine. The next year the figure was sixty-seven. On the third Christmas it jumped to eighty-three. That, they thought, would stand as a record. But it did not. The list kept climbing until 1962 when it reached the astounding figure of 124. One hundred and twenty-four species of wild birds at Christmastime sounds like California or Florida. To anyone who knows the Bronx—how built up it is, how limited the places where birds can live—such a number seems incredible. However, the fifteen-mile circle takes in some of West-chester County north of the city.

Each year plans are made weeks ahead; owls are located in their roosting groves; tabs are kept on ducks; and stray half-hardy lingerers such as hermit thrushes and towhees are "staked out." The night before the Count every-one knows within a few birds what the chances are. The grand total for the first four decades of uninterrupted census taking in the Bronx is nearly 200 species. Each year one or two new birds are added. The number of observers has grown from eight or nine to sixty or seventy.

Since my high school days I have taken Christmas Counts in Maine, Massachusetts, Connecticut, New Jersey, Long Island, western New York, Ohio, Pennsylvania, Maryland and Virginia; but I would rather be with the group in the Bronx at census time than anywhere else. There is more spirit and keener competition, even though birding is restricted and the rough heel mark of civilization is visible everywhere. The route I like best is that around Rye where the outer fringes of the Bronx finally give way to bits of rural country. It was there, three weeks after our entry into World War II, that I made the rounds on a memorable census.

Living in Manhattan, I started my day two hours before it was light. I got the car from the garage down on Lexington Avenue, crossed the steel bridge over the murky Harlem River and drove through the deserted streets of the lower Bronx until apartment buildings and tenements gave way to frame houses with milk bottles on their icy steps. In the glare of the head-lights, as I sped along the parkway, I could see patches of dirty half-melted snow.

When I parked the car near the swamp where I was to start the day, the east was just beginning to pale. There would be no bright sunrise; the sky was overcast. It was windless, also; bird voices would carry a long way this morning. Limbering my clammy fingers, I tried several screech owl wails by blowing on my clasped hands. There was no answer. I called a dozen times or more. The first song sparrow announced itself from the cattails with a husky chip, and then I caught what I was listening for—a faint wail among the tall tulip trees and sweet gums on the ridge. The banshee plaint seemed to grow louder and closer. The song sparrows and tree spar-rows were now wide awake. Then a dim form flitted noiselessly across the road and disappeared in a giant sycamore tree. The little screech owl had gone to bed.

Swamp birds are most vocal at daybreak, and if there is a wintering marsh wren or a rail, that is the best time to pick it up. (The first hour is always one of listening.) The best I could do in the marsh this morning were several pheasants which croaked from the reeds and a swamp sparrow. White-throats chinked from the cat brier tangles and the clicking of juncos was audible. A note of dismay in the voices of foraging chickadees called my attention to a sharp-shinned hawk hot on the tail of a frantic red-wing. I did not see the end of the precipitous chase.

Sauntering back to my Studebaker, I was met by a young policeman in a white patrol car. He eyed my 12-power binoculars, took out his pad, and asked me to explain my presence. It was war time, and I had expected something like this. One of the local patriots, glancing out of his kitchen window, had seen me lurking among the cattails. My car, half hidden in a little side road, looked suspicious, too. Credentials were produced—includ-ing my *Field Guide* and a copy of last year's Christmas Count.

He looked at my binoculars. "German glasses?" he asked.

I said, "Yes."

After squinting at a downy woodpecker with them, he offered to take me to a man who kept pheasants in a cage. Thanking him, I replied that

I had already seen four cock pheasants in the swamp and that tame birds didn't count. With an enlightened "Oh!" he stepped on the starter and slowly drove away.

This encounter had cost me valuable time. I would have to skim the estates if I was to meet Irving Kassoy at the appointed hour. My best luck was at a pond on what must have been the estate of the unbelievable Mr. Ripley. I had lost my way on a dead-end road when I arrived there. Scattered over the lawns, I found an odd collection of totem poles, wooden Indians, stone Buddhas and iron storks. A real kingfisher and a real Cooper's hawk made this bewildering place worth-while.

Kassoy was to meet me at ten at the incinerator plant with the tall brick chimney. Covering his route on foot, he had not reached there when I turned in the driveway. Several cowbirds among the starlings on the dump were new. A flock of twelve bluebirds, flying high overhead, dropped their soft gurgling notes just as if it were a day in March.

Comparing scores, Kassoy and I agreed we were not doing badly. Many of our birds were the same but he added to my list a flicker, a catbird, a towhee and several others. Together we combed the small swamp near the disposal plant, but a lone field sparrow, lisping disconsolately, was the only new bird we could find.

We had wisely concentrated on small land birds so far, as they are most active early in the day. We always save the water birds till later when land birding slows down. The pond at Playland, near the Sound, swarmed with hundreds of black ducks. Here and there we could pick out a lighter-colored mallard. The shallow water must have been teeming with fish for all three mergansers were there, including the little black and white hooded merganser with its fanlike white crest. Along the brushy shore we counted fourteen gawky great blue herons standing motionless, hunched and chilly. We always find them about this pond, even in the dead of winter. When the water freezes they probably spear mice.

We were soon joined by the other two members of our party, Richard Herbert and Michael Oboiko. They had spotted, among other species, two sanderlings, the best pick-up so far. None of these little pale sandpipers had ever been recorded on a Christmas Census in the Bronx before. "Firsts" such as this become fewer as the years go on.

"Sir Mike," an Austrian gardener who worked on one of the big estates, is a delightful, Rabelaisian man with a bushy mustache. A Great Dane dog followed him about. Mike had always been our standby in the matter of owls, but this year there were no long-ears roosting in his fir trees. After a soul-warming repast of beans and frankfurters (dozens of them) in Mike's furnace room, and a can or two of beer, we set out to round up what few birds we had missed in the neighborhood.

New birds come very slowly on a winter afternoon. On one of our stops along the Sound, we ran into our old friend John Kieran of *Information, Please!* who was taking his own bird count.. Kieran brought us luck, for presently we spotted a dark bird perched upright on a channel marker. It turned out to be a double-crested cormorant, another census "first" for the Bronx region.

The most exciting bird of the afternoon came just as we were about to call it a day. How Herbert spotted it I do not know, for it was just a tiny white dot on a bush far out on a marshy island. A herring gull would not sit in a bush top, Dick reasoned, so it must be a snowy owl. Oboiko set up his 45-power telescope, and snowy owl it was. Kieran's expressive ears betrayed his excitement. It was the first one of these large arctic owls he had seen in several years.

The day was just about gone, but there was still one more possibility—the barn owls at the Episcopal Church. We arrived just as the congregation was pouring down the wide stone steps. Oboiko, in his rough field clothes, made his way against the tide of the fashionable crowd to the rectory where his friend the minister gave him the keys to the bell tower. We waited self-consciously on the sidewalk while the home-bound parishioners filed by, eyeing us curiously. A flutter of wings and several pigeons catapulting into the gathering dusk told us Oboiko had reached the belfry. But no owls; the chimes, bidding the worshipers to service, had scared them out earlier. This was a bad miss, but there was a chance that someone else would see a barn owl—perhaps at Pelham Bay or the Clason Point garbage dump.

The list for our party was just under fifty for the day. Down in the little restaurant at the end of the Pelham Bay subway line we joined the other census takers. At the long banquet table in the room that had been reserved for us sat over thirty people, mostly young men. Two or three were in the uniforms of the services—others among us would be going soon. This, we were aware, might be the last census for some of the group.

When the comforting effect of the warm room and a good meal had put everyone in a relaxed frame of mind the chairman rose to his feet. In his hand he held a list of all the birds that had ever been seen on a Bronx Census in the previous eighteen years. Using it, we would tabulate the day's total. Each of the eight parties had a spokesman; so the report ran something like this: common loon: Van Cortlandt—none; Pelham Bay—none; Palisades—none; Rye—two; Bronx Park—none; Irvington—none; Westchester—none; Sands Point—five. That made a total of seven common loons. Next came the red-throated loon, with a total of thirteen. The chairman asked if anyone had seen a Pacific loon. (We had seen one at Rye the year before.) One party had seen a suspicious-looking loon, but opinion was divided as to whether it was an ordinary red-throat or the rare Pacific, so it was dropped. And so on down the list. We had seventeen kinds of ducks, nine of hawks, and five of owls.

Names of rare birds of other censuses were read off, even though there was little chance of our finding them twice. Among these were such extraordinary stragglers as a wintering redstart and an oven-bird, both of which should have been in the West Indies, and a magpie which should not have been much nearer than the foothills of the Rockies.

The "firsts" were saved till last. We reported our sanderlings and the cormorant. One party, working a hemlock grove on the Hudson, had discovered an Acadian or brown-capped chickadee. Another group had found a raven, the first known record for the Bronx. Cheers rose from the long table each time one of these firsts was announced, and we eagerly listened to all the small details of their discovery.

We laid a bet of five cents each on the grand total, the closest guess claiming the pot. While we waited in suspense the chairman announced that the day's total was ninety-eight species and about 24,311 individuals.

It was a good list but twice before we had done better. We all agreed it was becoming impossible to reach our old peak because the Bronx was deteriorating ornithologically. Where marshes had once harbored rails and snipe, huge gas tanks reared skyward. The undergrowth had been cleaned out of "the willows" in Bronx Park, and a new super-parkway swept across Van Cortlandt Swamp.

COLD TOES do not bother the tree sparrow that comes down from the Hudson Bay country to feed in the winter weed patches.

WINTER WOODLANDS are enlivened by an inseparable trio. The downy woodpecker, above, climbs up the trunks, the white-breasted nuthatch, lower left, climbs down; and the chickadee, lower right, dangles from the tips of the twigs.

I always like to think that the boys in the Bronx set the standard and developed the technique by which many other groups now get the most out of their regions. Today many Christmas Counts pass the 100 mark each year. Cape Cod usually exceeds 110; Cape May has had 153; Ocean City, Maryland, 142; Wilmington, North Carolina, 165; Tucson, Arizona, 117; and Laguna Atascosa, Texas, 176. The largest Counts ever taken reached 200 at Cocoa, Florida, and 184 at Tomales Bay, California. Inland, especially in the north, Counts are much smaller and there are spots in northern New England and in Canada where four or five species are all an active man can find in a day.

No two winters are quite alike, but now and then we have one so extraordinary that it is talked about for a long time. Such a season closed the year 1946. Almost every year a few half-hardy birds stay further north than they should; catbirds, thrashers, marsh wrens and even yellow-throats. Sometimes an oriole or a warbler, oblivious to the fact that the A.O.U. check-list says it should be in the tropics, lingers very late. They usually succumb to the first bitter snows. But in December, 1946, there had been no weather cold enough to kill these strays. When Margaret Brooks Hickey, editor of the Christmas Count, opened her stack of mail she was incredulous. The Rochester, New York, group reported a Black-burnian warbler. It normally winters in South America. Two observers in Pennsylvania found a Cape May warbler. It should have been in the West Indies. Then Professor Ralph Palmer recorded a second Cape May at Poughkeepsie, and captured the bird to prove it. There was a Baltimore oriole in New Jersey; kingbirds which should have departed from this country were seen in South Carolina, North Carolina and Maryland; and a wood thrush was reported from Cape May.

As if that were not enough, western birds invaded the east. A Brewer's blackbird, the first one for the state, graced our Maryland list. There were western kingbirds and Oregon juncos along the Atlantic Coast. In Pennsylvania, Earl Poole, of the Reading Museum, found a Say's phoebe. This pale phoebe with the rusty breast should have been in Texas or Mexico.

It is a curious thing that most of the western strays that appear along the eastern seaboard turn up in late fall or winter—never in spring. More than half of the records of western tanagers in the east are winter records. One winter there were many scores of dickcissels at feeding trays in the Northeast, yet this sparrow-like bird of the prairies normally spends its winters in Central America. It is as if their compass needles were switched; as if they were directed east instead of south, until stopped by the barrier of the Atlantic.

Any man who keeps a feeding tray outside his window knows that one winter is not like the next. There are always the old standby visitors, of course; downy woodpeckers, nuthatches and jays at the suet; cardinals, chickadees and titmice at the sunflower seeds; tree sparrows, juncos, song sparrows and white-throats at the peanut hearts and scratchfeed; and pheasants and quail at the chaff bed among the corn shocks. But some years there is a deluge of purple finches, the next year none. Then there will be a season of cedar waxwings. Arthur Fast of Arlington, Virginia, thought he had a hundred waxwings or so around his place one winter until he banded 875. Another gentleman, in Connecticut, banded 600 evening grosbeaks out of a supposed flock of seventy-five!

The strange type of bird movements that we call "invasions" or "irruptions" is little understood by naturalists. Unlike normal migration it does not take place regularly. It is peculiar mostly to a handful of northern birds, especially birds of the coniferous forest. After one of their erratic visits, they are often absent for several years. Some say it is the cold, or the anticipation of cold, that brings them down. But often these invasions take place in very mild winters. Another explanation is that lack of food makes the birds move out, but often they go before any shortage actually exists. The most generally accepted idea is that the "irruptions" accompany population pressures—a great increase in numbers.

We think of chickadees as sedentary. Yet every few years the little black-capped sprites swarm south in a flight that dwarfs the exodus of the Children of Israel. In the late fall of 1941 I saw them flying down the stone canyons of New York City—down Fifth Avenue, Sixth Avenue, Seventh Avenue and even the side streets between them. Some of them investigated the fire escapes and roof gardens. One observer estimated that 100,000 chickadees passed through Fort Tryon Park in six weeks.

With the black-caps came a few of the rare brown-caps of the northern spruce woods. Some of these reached Massachusetts and at least two penetrated as far south as the New York City region. One of them was the high point of our Christmas Census as already described. This was the second time in recorded ornithological history that the Acadian brown-cap reached New York City. The other time was, oddly enough, in the winter of 1916-17. Both years, just prior to a declaration of war by Congress, the chickadees came down with their overseas caps on.

Allan Cruickshank of the old Bronx gang is now boss of the Count. After taking part in the top Count around his home at Cocoa, Florida, near Cape Canaveral, he then labors for the next two months editing the mountain of data that is submitted to Audubon Field Notes for publication.

The Christmas Bird Count will continue to give us much information. But even though there are many nuggets that ornithologists can mine from this rich lode of bird information, to me and to my friends it is our way of celebrating the holidays, an ornithological ritual that has come to represent Yuletide more than Santa Claus or the Christmas tree.

Deceiving the Experts

I CONFESS that several times I have played with the idea of planting a fake bird somewhere to deceive the experts. On one of the annual field trips of the American Ornithologists' Union this evil thought again went through my mind. A well-painted wooden bird, a scarlet ibis or something even more improbable, could be placed far out on the marsh along the route of our boat. There it would be identified but because of the treacherous mudbanks that would prevent our landing, no one would be able to check on it. What wild excitement there would be!

It never occurred to me that I might some day be deluded by such a trick myself. But I was. It happened in the Bronx, on a Christmas Bird Count. One of the boys had a score to settle with his friend Danny. He knew Danny was assigned to Bronx Park and that he would spend a half hour looking at the birds on Lake Agassiz. Using a block of soft wood, he carved out a dovekie, the little auk that comes down in winter from the Arctic. He painted it, black above and white below, with the face pattern of the winter plumage. After much work and planning, he anchored it far out in the middle of the lake.

Danny reached the zoological gardens on schedule late in the afternoon, swept the pond with his Deltrinems, but did not spot the decoy. Either he was bleary-eyed from the day's concentration or his mind was on the gadwall that should have been there. A few minutes later I arrived. Bronx Park was not in my province, but I had exhausted the possibilities at Van Cortlandt Park and Riverdale and we could not afford to miss the gadwall. Starting at the right-hand side of the pond and moving toward the left, I scrutinized every tame mallard and every black. Right out in the middle, my glass paused on a small drifting object. My pulse jumped—it was a dovekie! Letting out a triumphant yell that the red howlers in the monkey house could not match, I called Danny. This was the find of the day—not just a new record for the Christmas Census, but the first known record of a dovekie for the whole Greater Bronx region.

Other census takers arrived. We congratulated one another; we were exceedingly pleased with ourselves. There was one thing that bothered us, though. The bird listed slightly, like a leaky toy boat. And it did not move much or dive, but just stayed in one place, slowly turning in the current. I explained to my less experienced companions that its presence so far inland could be accounted for by the heavy wind and fog that had blown in from the ocean two days before. As an afterthought, I added that the bird looked rather sick and probably wouldn't live through the night. Subconsciously one of the other fellows must have questioned the little auk's aliveness, for he cried, "See! See! I saw its head move!" "Yes," we agreed, "its head moved."

We could get no closer without scaling the ten-foot wire fence that girdled the lake. The question in my mind was not whether the bird was alive, but whether it had reached Lake Agassiz under its own power. Perhaps someone had brought it to the park and Lee Crandall, the curator, had released it there.

At the long table that evening, we saved the dovekie till last. It was to be the *pièce de résistance*. We had carefully guarded our secret from the others. They, in turn, gave us no hint that they already knew about it. When the dovekie was announced, one after another of us was asked to stand and give the details. Were we sure the bird moved? We said we were. Then, at a signal from the chairman, the plotters roared in derison and the hoax was laid bare. In our chagrin we consoled ourselves with the thought that we had identified the bird correctly, even though it wasn't alive.

The dovekie experience paid dividends two years later on a field trip to Cape May, held in conjunction with the Audubon Convention. A whole platoon of Aubudonites, eighty strong, led by three of us from the New York office, arose at 4:30 a.m. to watch the morning flight. It didn't come off; the wind was in the southwest. Few places can be as birdless as the dunes of Cape May Point on its off days. Everyone was downhearted until a rumor spread that there was a black-necked stilt on Lighthouse Pond. When I reached there, a crowd had already gathered on the dirt road where it skirts the south side of the marsh. There, at the edge of the cattails on the far shore, stood an honest-to-goodness stilt, its black back, white under parts and long reddish legs clearly visible through 8-power glasses. It seemed to be sleeping, with its slender bill tucked into the loose feathers of its back. Richard Pough, one of the leaders, drawing on his knowledge of New Jersey birds, pronounced that this was the first record of a stilt in the State of New Jersey since the early '90s. But we were running behind schedule, he cautioned, so he advised everyone to take a good look at it and be back in the waiting buses in five minutes.

A species that had not been seen in New Jersey for nearly fifty years ought to be checked further, I thought, even if it were such an obvious bird as a stilt—the busses could wait! Furthermore, there was something about this inactive bird that did not seem right. For one thing, its legs looked too orange. Heedless of Pough's impatient promptings, I plunged into the swamp with a young chap named William Fish. We struggled and fought through the dense cattails and pickerel weed. At one time I sank to my armpits in the slimy mud and thought surely I would collapse from the exertion and sulphurous stench. As we neared our goal, a deep channel we had not seen cut us off. We were close but a thick patch of reeds hid the bird. There was nothing we could throw so we clapped our hands. No result. Looking back helplessly at our audience on the road, we saw Bob Allen poling a leaky rowboat through the pondweed. He would be able to settle the whole matter of the stilt. Passing the mouth of our channel, he rounded the point and disappeared for a few brief moments. When he reappeared he held something aloft for all to see. It was the stilt, stiff as a plank, a badly stuffed specimen that someone had planted.

Two or three in the crowd thought it the poorest sort of humor. I am sure one man held *me* accountable. Inwardly I felt triumphant; it would have been much more humiliating, if, after I had expressed my doubts, the bird had lifted its slim black wings and flown away.

A week later we ran down the story. The Academy of Sciences at Philadelphia had had a house cleaning and consigned a number of birds to the junk pile. Some wit from the Delaware Valley Ornithological Club had salvaged the stilt and set it up across the pond, placing it precisely where the bird watchers would look for gallinules from the road. It was impossible to approach it, except by using the hidden rowboat; it was just near enough to be identified, too far away to reveal its lifeless condition.

A fascinating literature could be built up on this topic of deception. In earlier days, when oology was a fad and museums were not yet glutted with egg collections, unscrupulous eggers palmed off fake rarities on their colleagues. One oologist tells me that bona fide sets of wild turkey eggs are rare because there is no way of telling whether or not they came from a poultry farm. Even the curators at the Smithsonian have had their encounters with counterfeit eggs. Goose eggs have been offered as eggs of the California condor, one of the world's rarest birds. Microscopic examination of the pitting of the eggshell quickly exposed the fraud.

In Britain, where the oologists go to fantastic lengths to get what they want, a story is told about a pair of whooper swans, a species that breeds rarely in the British Isles, in the extreme north of Scotland. A watcher was stationed on the shore of the loch to keep his eye on the island where the birds nested and to head off nest robbers. Nevertheless, an egger swam to the island early one morning; but the guard, biding his time, waited till the thief returned to shore with his loot. While the scoundrel stood shivering with cold, the guard took the eggs from the collecting box and returned them to the nest. But the oologist had planned his strategy very carefully The box had a false bottom, and the eggs which the guard removed were eggs of the mute swan, the ordinary park variety.

Practical jokes like this are embarrassing enough, but everyone knows how easy it is to be deceived by Mother Nature herself. One winter's day I was coming down the rocky trail on Mount Monadnock in southern New Hampshire with a group of teen-aged boys at my heels. My eye caught a dark shape with two ears, nestled close to a hemlock trunk about fifty feet up. I pointed it out to my charges and told them it was a long-eared owl. Here was a good example of natural camouflage, I informed them, and we could easily have passed it by as a piece of bark. One of the boys was not convinced. He tossed a stone at it, but the bird stayed put. We walked over to the tree. Still the bird did not fly. No wonder—it *was* a piece of bark!

Everyone who hunts with a field glass knows how easy it is to make mistakes like that. I remember the bluebird one of the Bronx boys saw on a sand dune. It turned out to be a Bromo-Seltzer bottle. How many times have we put our glass on a tent caterpillar's nest silhouetted against the sky, thinking we had a hawk perched out on a bare limb? Griscom called these aggravating webs "whisker-birds."

Whereas we sometimes see things that look like birds but are not, we constantly pass birds by because they blend with the landscape. Nature attempts to conceal and can be amazingly successful. In a general way, birds of the leafy forest crown—the warblers, vireos and kinglets—tend towards yellowish-greens, while those that rummage about the dead leaves of the forest floor—the thrushes, oven-birds and grouse—run to browns. Birds of the grass country are streaked while those of the beaches are dappled with muddy browns or sandy grays.

The word *camouflage* according to any standard dictionary means "disguise." Although a few birds flaunt such bright colors that they seem to be saying "I dare you," most of them are colored like their surroundings. We call this form of deception "protective coloration." The bitterns not only are streaked with brown like the dead reeds they hide among, but mimic them by standing rigid and pointing their bills toward the sky. It doesn't always work. Once I promised to show a least bittern to a schoolteacher friend. We glimpsed it, as it slipped through the sedge, but it decided to "freeze" rather than fly. The only mistake the little buffy heron made was to freeze in the midst of bright green grass. Sneaking up slowly, I caught it in my hat. Another time I caught an American bittern in the same way, but this indignant bird struck me full in the face. I carry the scar of its sharp bill to this day on my upper lip.

Besides pattern there is another device of natural camouflage that obliterates form. Abbott Thayer, the artist-naturalist, called it "counter-shading." We have two little shore birds that look much alike, the piping plover and the semipalmated plover. One is pale-backed like the dry sand of the glaring beaches where it runs about. The other is dark-backed like the wet sand or like mud exposed by the tide. Neither bird would blend with its surroundings if it were colored the same below as above. The reason for this is that shadow on the under part of a round object throws it into relief and gives it form. These two birds are white below and the shadow cast on their under parts matches their backs, causing the whole bird to disappear. The bright sand reflects light onto the breast of the piping plover, making the shadow lighter, just the color of the bird's pale back. The wet sand reflects less light, so the shadow on the semipalmated plover stays darker, matching its darker back.

Aware as I am of these things, I wonder why I should aspire to be a bird artist. For nothing can be more difficult to paint than birds. This is why: An artist strives with his brushes and his pigments to create the illusion of form. Nature, in coloring the birds, whether with pattern or by counter-shading, attempts to obliterate it. How then, can the artist succeed? First he builds the basic form of the bird. Then he destroys it by superimposing the bird's pattern. He winds up with a score of zero. That is why the most successful bird painters have not attempted to interpret nature literally. Either, like Frank Benson, they had painted third dimensional birds, completely ignoring detail, or, like Fuertes, they have painted feather patterns, overlooking the natural play of light and shade on the bird "in the round."

To get back to the plovers: They have another device that helps make them invisible—the black rings across their breasts. This has been called "ruptive pattern" and it helps to hide the bird by breaking up its shape into smaller pieces.

There are many other things about the pattern and plumage of birds that have set biologists to wondering—the flashy pattern of a willet's wing for example, or the white sides of a junco's tail.

My friend William Vogt, pondering these things, once played a mean trick on a yellow-throat while making a behavior study (behavior to most biologists seems to mean sex behavior). He put a mounted female yellow-throat in the territory of an ardently singing male. The male, as you know, has a black domino through his eyes. The female lacks this; she is just a plain little yellow and olive-brown bird. This male yellow-throat, overlooking the obvious fact that the female was not only inanimate but badly stuffed at that, courted and copulated as if she were the most desirable creature on earth. Two or three times he came back to repeat the perform-ance. While he was away, Vogt slyly pasted a black mask on the female's face. The male returned and was about to resume relations as before when he suddenly noticed the mask. He bounced a full two feet in the air and dashed away as if completely mortified. Vogt concluded that unlike grouse, which use the trial and error technique, yellow-throats can recognize the other sex visually. Dr. G. Kingsley Noble got similar reactions when he pasted black mustaches on female flickers.

So the birds can be deceived as easily as we. In fact, the ducks would not be at such desperately low ebb today if they had not been betrayed by decoys, which they have never been able to figure out. Surprisingly enough, decoys as we know them did not originate in Europe, even though the word comes from a contraction of a Dutch expression *Ende-kooy,* which means a duck trap. The earliest known decoys were found by scientists who were digging in Lovelock Cave, in Nevada. There, in the rubble of a pre-Paiute civilization called "the tule eaters," they found some bundles of tule reeds carefully fashioned into the unmistakable form of canvasbacks. These decoys had been employed over two thousand years ago when the sea that lay in the Great Basin was far larger than the salty fragments that remain today.

Although there is some evidence that the Indians carried the scheme down through the years, the first mention of decoys in the white man's hunting is made by Alexander Wilson, the father of American Ornithology. In 1814, under the mallard, he wrote: "In some ponds frequented by these birds, five or six wooden figures cut and painted so as to represent ducks and sunk by pieces of lead nailed to their bottoms, so as to float at the usual depth on the surface, are anchored in a favorable position."

It was the rapid growth of market hunting about a century ago that brought the wooden decoy into its own and made of its creation an art, albeit a homely one, practiced in between seasons by men with time on their hands. In those days they made "snipe" decoys, too, and you can still find dozens of them hidden under the gear, tarred ropes and paint cans of many a Long Island fisherman's shanty, a reminder of days when shore birds were shot all along the coast. Joel Barber, in his classic book *Wild Fowl Decoys,* shows a photograph of a blue heron decoy once used at Jones Beach. Even crude gulls were made. These were placed at the end of a stool of brant "blocks" just to give the illusion to these small wary geese that "all is well."

Although decoy factories have sprung up, the standardized commercial product has never won the favor of discriminating sportsmen. Recently the hand-carved, hand-painted symbols of our vanishing waterfowl have become part of Americana and are sought by assiduous collectors in antique shops; but probably the best examples still languish in dark corners of shanties on the salt marshes along the Chesapeake, the Jersey Coast, the bays of Long Island or in boathouses along lonely New England shores.

Whether decoys are inexpensive models from Sears, Roebuck or the best examples of the bayman's art, the ducks will be deceived—and so will the experts. On a recent December afternoon I detected a small flock of canvasbacks bobbing on the waves. They were canvasbacks all right, and were as good as on my list. Just then a man rounded the point in a punt and hauled them in—every last one of them!

Billions of Birds

OW many birds are there in the United States? How many robins, how many ducks and how many hawks? Every naturalist has asked questions such as these. Conservationists are always concerned with the relative numbers of birds, especially the scarcer ones, and whether they are increasing or decreasing.

Some years ago I received a letter from Russell Mason, then running the Massachusetts Audubon Society, asking if the National Audubon Society had ever estimated the number of breeding birds in the United States. Somewhere he had read that the avian population was about fifty birds per person. Not knowing of an official estimate, I presumed my figure would be as good as that of the next rash statistician, so I reached for pencil and paper. From my limited experience with breeding bird counts, I took two pairs of birds per acre as my basic figure. By using simple mathematics, and a copy of Hammond's *Atlas,* I arrived at a figure of 7,612,866,560 birds in the United States (or, at our present population, about fifty-two birds per person). I now believe this to be too high.

When Mr. Mason asked this question, I had very little data to work on. Later the question was to come up again. Out of curiosity, I dug out my file of the National Audubon Society's breeding bird censuses. Taking scores of censuses, I found they averaged closer to five birds per acre rather than four, which I had used as my basic figure. However, census takers, being human, like to select "good spots" where there are many birds, areas such as swamps and marshes which boost the average greatly. The total acreage of such favored habitats in the United States is relatively small. I believe three birds per acre is probably more nearly right for the country as a whole.

Very few sections of the world have been evaluated as to their total bird population. One of the best estimates so far has been made in the British Isles. Their latest figure of the number of land birds is in the neighborhood of one hundred and twenty million. This is about two birds per acre. So the average density of birds in Great Britain is probably not much more than one half or two-thirds that of ours. This is contrary to what I had been led to believe by people who have lived in England. Investigating further, I found that their greatest densities of birds are in orchards, gardens and estates. These average about thirty birds per acre, which is far higher than anything except the most extreme densities in this country. On the other hand, two-thirds of the area of the British Isles is taken up by grass country and moorland where the population of birds is extremely low—from less than one (.7) to two birds per acre, depending on the kind of grassland. In our country, a much larger percentage of land is made up of deciduous woodlands and other habitats which have a moderately higher bird population. In the aggregate we come out ahead.

Finland has a more detailed tally of its bird population than any other country. Einari Merikalio, using a technique called the line-strip method, made daily transects of the countryside during June and July for a period of 15 years, from 1941 to 1956. Following a track which enclosed a square measuring one kilometer on each side, he noted every bird within sight and hearing. Sampling his country from end to end he was able to estimate the number of each species (the chaffinch numbers 10.6 million). The grand total for all species in Finland is about 64 million.

What is our commonest bird in America? The robin? Or the red-wing? I would not be at all surprised to find that in the eastern states, at least, the red-eyed vireo is more numerous than the robin. Yet everyone knows the familiar robin and only those interested in birds know the vireo. The reason is that the robin, found around the doorstep, is seen by everyone. On the other hand, it is very thinly distributed in the more wooded sections. Just the opposite is true of the red-eye.

Shortly after I moved to Washington, D.C., a newspaper reporter detained me after a lecture. He wanted a story on birds around the nation's capital. I suggested the teasing thought that the robin, cardinal and song sparrow were probably not the commonest birds in the Virginia-Maryland area, but more likely the red-eyed vireo or the redstart. This brought an explosive reaction in a local nature column. One reader wrote that he seldom saw a red-eyed vireo and that he hadn't seen a redstart in three years. In replying to this correspondent, the columnist provided an alibi for me, saying that Mr. Peterson was new in Washington; and as he had been so busy painting birds he very likely had not been able to get into the field much and was judging this region by other parts of the country.

Fortunately for my ego, I was backed up soon afterward by several breeding bird censuses. One, taken by Chandler Robbins and Bob Stewart in the wooded bottomlands near Bowie, Maryland, showed an extraordinary density of red-eyed vireos, double the number of the nearest runner-up, which proved to be the redstart. The robin was almost absent, except around the buildings. In a census taken along the Potomac by the Washington Audubon Society, the redstart and the red-eyed vireo tied for first place. Another survey, made by John Aldrich in a dry upland woods, several miles away in Virginia, featured the red-eye as the number one bird.

Whereas sample counts indicate that the redstart, oven-bird and red-eyed vireo are the three most abundant species in the wooded hills of much of the Appalachians—undoubtedly running into the high millions—by all odds the most numerous bird of the Great Plains is the horned lark. It is one of the more abundant song birds of the world for countless numbers also range across the grassy plains of Europe and the steppes of Asia and the species nearly encircles the globe.

When birds are very abundant it is possible to take sample counts and arrive at a general idea of their numbers. Species that are very rare can sometimes be counted bird by bird. In January, 1963, only thirty-eight whooping cranes were known to exist in the world. We know there are only about sixty or so California condors left in the United States. We were told by Harold Mayfield and his cohorts that there are approximately 1000 Kirtland's warblers in the world, all in the lower peninsula of Michigan. Hawaiian geese (nénés) numbered about 400 in 1963, an 800% increase in scarcely more than a decade. The Laysan duck, limited to a single small island in the Hawaiian chain has also had a boom, jumping in recent years from a few dozen to more than 600. Eagles, on the other hand, are in a sharp decline and are being censused by the National Audubon Society.

The gannet is one common bird whose world numbers are rather accurately known. James Fisher, that very dynamic British ornithologist, writes: "In 1939, a group of ornithologists, including H. G. Vevers and myself, visited nineteen out of the twenty-two gannet colonies in the world and were able to make counts of all but two per cent of the birds. We believe there are now about 167,000 gannets breeding in the world every year, of which 109,000 breed in Great Britain and Ireland." The world population has steadily increased during the past twenty-five years and now exceeds 200,000. The North American population, in six colonies, is in the neighborhood of 30,000.

On the whole, it is not so easy to determine the numbers of those birds that nest in colonies. They cannot be estimated by samples; each colony must be ferreted out and appraised. In Great Britain, ringed by hundreds of attractive little islets, the sea birds probably equal the land birds in number.

Without question, there are numberless gull and tern colonies and heronries in North America that have never known the prying eyes of an ornithologist. Some of the well-known colonies run into high figures. The sooty terns of the Tortugas number more than 100,000. Rookeries of the white ibis in southern Florida have been known to exceed 100,000 birds and the murres on the Three Arch Rocks in Oregon have been estimated at 750,000.

In early 1947, the United States Fish and Wildlife Service estimated the number of ducks and geese on the North American Continent at 54,000,000. The population was at low ebb, but it was double the estimate at the bottom of the "duck depression" in 1934-35. The greater part of these breed in Canada. Fifty-four million seems like a lot of birds, but remember—it represents over thirty species. Together, they actually make up only a tiny fraction of the total continental bird population. Land birds probably out-numbered them 200 to 1, in 1947. Ducks seem proportionately more plentiful than they really are because they concentrate in large visible flocks while land birds are distributed acre by acre over millions of square miles of American soil.

To get a good idea of the numerical strength of American bird life, we shall first have to know the acreage of the major habitats of the United States. Then, if we have enough censuses of each of these habitats, we can strike an average and multiply by the acreage.

During 1914 and 1915, Wells Cooke, of the United States Department of Agriculture, conducted a survey and found that the average farm harbored about two and a quarter birds per acre. As there are over one billion acres of such land in the United States (including crop lands, pasture lands and farm woodlands), the farms alone would account for at least 2.25 billion birds.

The Audubon breeding bird censuses have tried not to duplicate Cooke's work in farming country. They have, thus far, leaned mostly toward woodland habitats. These show an average of about four birds per acre, in healthy deciduous woodlands. Coniferous woodlands average about the same or a little better, although pine barrens run lower.

From our meager data, the western prairies and plains seem to average less than one bird per acre and will seldom support more than two. These grasslands embrace hundreds of millions of acres, so in order not to run too far astray in our estimate of the birds, we should have more censuses from "the range."

Birds concentrate around wet places. A dozen censuses in bogs, marshes and swamps run between six birds per acre and eighteen, averaging 9.4. There are undoubtedly many places where marsh densities are even greater than eighteen. Everyone who has visited the sprawling Bear River marshes in Utah has wondered at the enormous density of birds there. But the swamps and marshes are only a small dwindling part of our country.

We do not know much about the numbers of English sparrows, starlings or pigeons in the big cities. Nor do we know the density of robins, chipping sparrows, house wrens, yellow warblers and other garden birds in typical communities where the city blocks are made up of frame houses on lots about 50 to 75 feet square. There are at least 50,000,000 acres of urban land in the United States.

There are a great many plant associations, too, that we must know more about if we are to get a good general idea of America's bird life—pine barrens, southern river bottoms, salt marshes, prairies, short grass plains, "pygmy forests" (piñon pine and juniper association), western mountains

MAGNIFICENT. A Merriam's turkey cock struts in an Arizona mountain meadow while an unimpressed hen gobbles the bait before the blind.

HOW MANY? In eastern woodlands the crested flycatcher (with swal-
lowtail butterfly) is greatly outnumbered by the red-eyed vireo, below.
Some believe the red-eye to be the most abundant bird east of the Mississippi.

WELL-NAMED, the white-eyed vireo stares back at the shiny lens of the camera before settling on its basket-like nest beside a Tennessee footpath.

SQUADRONS of tired tree swallows line the wires while resting for the next lap of their autumnal flight southward along the coast.

(from the foothills to the alpine meadows), northwestern rain forest and the desert—to mention a few.

My guess, based roughly on breeding bird censuses, was that there were not less than 5,000,000,000 breeding land birds in the United States and probably closer to 6,000,000,000. Add to this an unknown number of colonial water birds.

I first made this broad statement at a meeting of the National Audubon Society. John O'Reilly, reporter for the *New York Herald Tribune,* sat in the front row of the audience. I could see him feverishly jotting down something. The next morning at the breakfast table I read: "Expert Does Some Calculating, Lists 5,750,000,000 Birds in U.S." Other papers snatched up O'Reilly's story; within a month more than 600 clippings came to me from all over the country. When I asked O'Reilly why he had taken the newspaperman's liberty of making my vague figure exact, he explained that people want things definite. They like to pigeonhole things. Having been told exactly how many birds there are in the United States, they can forget about it, leaving the man who made the guess to worry about its accuracy.

I'm not going to worry much about my estimate. It will be a long time before we will have enough data to test its accuracy. I did, however, receive a very interesting letter from Dr. Leonard Wing, formerly of the State College of Washington, stating that he had estimated the summer population of birds in the United States at about 5,700,000,000. He had arrived at his figure independently, before he had heard of my estimate, by employing a system in which he used both winter and summer counts in a rather complicated way.

In this discussion of bird populations, we must not forget that the numbers of birds in the United States fluctuate greatly during the course of a year. In the fall the birds that nest over the great expanses of Canada and Alaska (larger by a third than the U.S.) come crowding through. Then, also, each pair under average circumstances is responsible for about two young on the southward journey. This doubles the number again. So on a yearly basis the continental population north of Mexico runs somewhere between twelve and twenty billion. Inasmuch as there are five continents in the world, the estimate of one hundred billion made by James Fisher for the global bird population seems reasonable. He writes: "There are about a hundred thousand million birds in the world; that is, there are probably a hundred thousand million rather than a million millon or ten thousand million."

According to the recent estimate by James Fisher, the total of the living species of birds in the world is about 8554. Some systematists, who would call certain subspecies full species, would put the figure at 13,000 or more. Of this world galaxy, North America's share (plus 100 that are accidental) is about 675. The global total of all known species of animals, from the mammals down through the insects and other small creatures to the minute protozoa, is about one million.

In the face of such near-astronomical population figures, it is evident that the small boy with the slingshot or air rifle is a negligible factor in the conservation of bird life. The preservation and improvement of the environment in which birds live is the thing that means most. We swing into action when we see the small boy shooting at a robin which he will probably miss anyway, but we look on resignedly or give a hopeless shrug when we pass a crew of laborers "manicuring" a park, cutting the undergrowth from a woodlot or ditching a marsh. Yet the damage they do is far more wholesale. When a marsh is drained, the population of marsh wrens, swamp sparrows, rails, bitterns and ducks that live there are done away with just as surely as though they had been systematically shot or poisoned.

The breeding bird censuses show the practical conservationist many things. One census, described in the *Journal of Wildlife Management* tells of eighteen birds on an area sprayed for insects, against 154 birds on a comparable plot which had not been sprayed, a decrease of over eighty-five per cent. Many bird censuses have been taken in recent years to see what damage different doses of DDT and similar pesticides will do.

In a sugar maple woodlot, where cattle had been allowed to graze, it was found that there was an average of only one bird per acre and a half. In an adjacent woodlot, where the undergrowth had been protected from the cattle, there were more than three birds per acre, nearly five times the density.

It is the strength of any environment, the food and cover, that determine how many birds can live there. A hundred acres of woodland will have about the same number of birds from year to year. Changes are slow. But farm lands that have been abandoned or woodlands that have been cut change more rapidly. First, low bushes appear, then second growth saplings. Each gives way to the next stage of plant growth until a century later the patriarchal trees become a grand old forest. The birds change as the plants change. Song sparrows give way to chewinks and indigo buntings, while they, in turn, relinquish their home to redstarts, vireos and woodpeckers. This is what we call "succession."

"Territory," another important word in the bird watchers' vocabulary, is also a factor when we discuss populations. People are often puzzled about the robins that flutter against their reflections in dark windows. These foolish birds are not prompted by vanity; they mistake their reflection for that of another robin and are bent on chasing it away. Each male robin is a property owner. By holding territory, birds space themselves evenly over the land. They do not sing just for the delight of singing but to announce to the world their property rights. Song is not only an invitation to a prospective bride, but also a challenge to a rival. The owner is nearly invincible in his home territory, even when he is the weaker or shabbier bird. The man who takes a breeding bird census knows these things. By plotting the singing males on a map and repeating it a few times as a check, he knows just what the population density is.

Birds then, limit their own numbers in an area. The extra birds wander around and are chased from place to place. They form a floating population. If a Cooper's hawk catches one of the established males, his place, his land and perhaps his wife, too, are taken over by one of the "floaters." Nature, like a bank, keeps a surplus to take care of losses.

The Cooper's hawk that eats a robin or the sharp-shin that eats a warbler is a predator, another device in the intricate system of checks and counterchecks that keep bird populations under control. Predators crop the surpluses. They do not eat up the capital. When it gets too hard to catch one thing they try to get something else. Shooting the hawks or the foxes will not, in the long run, result in more birds, for then other checks will act as levelers—catastrophes of weather or migration, disease, parasites, starvation or the birds themselves, through their habit of defending territory.

Just think what would happen if it were not for these checks. If *one pair* of robins, in the spring of 1960, was successful in raising its two broods of four young there would be ten robins by the end of the year. Suppose this pair of robins and their progeny escaped all enemies and ills, had 100 per cent success with their families and all survived. By the end of ten years (the possible life span of the first pair), in the spring of 1970, there would be 97,656,250 robins from this original pair!

Superimposed on all these controls there are "cycles." We know that snowy owls came down from the far north once every four years. As Elton points out, the lemming is the snowy owl's anchor to the arctic; and when these little animals suddenly die off in huge numbers, the owl drifts southward. We know that grouse have an eight to ten-year cycle; they climb to a crest, have sort of an epidemic and then crash. But we are only beginning to suspect that some of our other birds may have cycles too. How else can we explain an increase and decline in nighthawks or a rise and fall in warbling vireos? Some day biologists will know more about these things. They will look back on our times as the dark age of ornithology, but they will admit we had a bright idea when we started the breeding bird census.

Has bird life increased or declined in the last two or three centuries in the United States? Some naturalists believe there are more songbirds, at least, than there were when the continent was a wilderness. But we are not sure. If only we had a few more censuses from virgin areas, we might have some hint. In the center of the lush 1900-acre Santa Ana tract in the Rio Grande delta, Irby Davis found a very high density—nearly twelve and one-half birds per acre. This is unspoiled elm-ash woodland, the only sizable tract of original "delta" woodland left. I have seen few places where there was more bird life than in the Singer Tract in Louisiana, before the last stronghold of the ivory-bill was put to the ax. I was similarly impressed by the numbers of birds in the Santee Swamp, in South Carolina, in spite of the razor-backed hogs that have rooted up the floor of the forest primeval.

Some ecologists have jumped to conclusions by comparing the meager bird life of unbroken second-growth forest, where the trees are of the same age and the canopy unbroken, with the more abundant bird life of woodland "edges." Naturally, a uniform environment would have a lower bird population. It is only when the woodsman, irruptions of insects or drought open up clearings in the forest that the environment is diversified and the bird life increased. In most virgin woodlands the larger trees are comparatively widely spaced and form their own "edges." There is ground growth, with young trees springing up and old trees dying. Birds are distributed vertically as well as horizontally. We do have a good idea of the acreage of the original forest in America and the original prairie. We could easily get some hint as to whether bird life has increased or decreased on the continent if we had a few more censuses in the few remaining primitive areas.

One thing must be taken into account in making such a comparison, and that is the disappearance of the passenger pigeon. If we are to credit Audubon and Wilson, both of whom estimated single flights of these birds at more than a billion, the passenger pigeon must have made a very large part of the entire population of all North American birds. Doctor Friedmann, of the National Museum, suggests to me that they may have kept down some of the other birds, for where the great flocks went they ate up all the food.

On what acre of American soil would we find the highest density of nesting birds? A farm in Maryland had long claimed the record. There, on one acre, fifty-nine pairs of nesting birds were found. However, almost half were purple martins, a colonial species. If we are to include colonial birds, this record will not stand for a moment. Thousands of the gourd-like nests of the cliff swallow have been found clustered together on one small cliff. On the walls and under the eaves of a single barn near Deerfield, Wisconsin, a total of 2,015 nests of these swallows were counted.

The most extreme land bird density would probably be in colonies of the tri-colored red-wing in California. This bird looks like an ordinary red-wing, but has white, instead of yellow borders on its red shoulders. But the biggest difference is in its way of living, for instead of being territorial, it is colonial, and sometimes between 5000 and 10,000 nests are crowded into a single acre of marsh.

The most populated acre of all would be on an island where sea birds nest. Bush Key in the Dry Tortugas would be a strong contender for the title. There, scores of thousands of sooty terns nest so close together that they average three pairs to the square yard; a total of 14,520 pairs per acre. But I suspect the laurels in the United States would go to Three Arch Rocks, in Oregon, if we can credit the estimate of 750,000 murres that are said to live on this seventeen-acre reservation. If this figure is correct, the density would be more than 22,000 pairs per acre, or about one bird per square foot!

Where would we find the lowest density of birds in the United States? There is many an acre here and there where we would find not even one pair of birds. Perhaps the largest area of birdless country would be the Bonneville Salt flats west of Great Salt Lake, in Utah. It is on these flats which cover hundreds of square miles that the high speed records for racing automobiles are made and broken. One can ride for miles across these sun-baked wastes without seeing a bird. Whole square miles are as sterile as an operating table.

Long After Columbus

COLUMBUS was the first American bird watcher. After he left the Canary Islands, birds became the most important entries in his log. As he sailed west into the unknown, his men grew sullen and threatening. At this critical time flocks of birds "coming from the N and making for the SW" gave them heart. Columbus turned his course in the direction the birds were flying and in due time reached the Bahamas. Had he not followed the birds or had he left the Canaries two weeks later, after the heavy fall migration was past, his first landfall might have been the coast of Florida—if indeed there had been a landfall. His men were close to mutiny and the extra two hundred miles might have been the difference between success and failure.

Every ornithologist I know would give his soul to step back into time and walk the continent in the historic year of 1492. It was all virgin country then, with trees centuries old and the native grass waist high on the prairies. The broad distributional concepts—the life zones or the biomes—probably would have been much more satisfactory in those days when most environments were in relatively stable "climaxes," as the old mature plant associations are called. But that was before man set in motion the constant chain of changes that take place wherever he goes. For civilized man is the great disturber. Some would call him a destroyer, but that I think is a harsh term. Certainly he brings change.

There is a vague idea that birds were far more abundant in primeval America than they are now. In 1614, six years before the Pilgrims landed at Plymouth, John Smith sailed down the coast of Maine. He wrote of the incredible abundance of wildlife: "eagles, gripes, divers sort of hauks, cranes, geese, brants, cormorants, ducks, sheldrakes, teals, meawes, guls, turkies, dive-doppers, and many other sorts, whose names I knowe not."

In the early days there were no game laws, but it did not take long to realize that there would have to be some kind of brake on the killing. The first legal regulations were imposed in New Netherlands more than 300 years ago. At the close of the colonial period, twelve of the thirteen colonies had some sort of game laws. Since then restrictions have grown tighter and tighter, for an army of millions of American men now go out with guns each year, fully as many as were pressed into service to fight the greatest war the world has ever known. One to two millions purchase the Duck Stamp. The wildfowlers have grown legion, even though there are alive today only a fraction of the ducks that swarmed the flyways when John Smith cruised the coast.

The ducks may be down, but some of the other birds are well up and still climbing. Let us look briefly at the score sheet and see which way our birds are going.

Most of the waterfowl and the native upland game birds are below par. There has been some restoration in places, but there were many more of them in primitive America. Even twentieth-century America could support more than it does. Hunting often exacts a greater toll than the traffic will bear.

Today all marsh birds, not waterfowl alone, are in the red. Every day plans are made somewhere in this country to drain a lake, a swamp or a marsh. The records show that close to 100,000,000 acres of land have been drained in the United States for agriculture alone. Other millions of acres have been ditched to control mosquitoes. Considering that a marsh or swamp habitat harbors nine or ten nesting birds per acre and most farming country an average of fewer than three, this means that at least half a billion birds may have been eliminated from the face of the continent by the simple process of digging ditches.

The birds of prey—the hawks and the owls—are much reduced. One summer day in 1947, John Craighead, the well-known falconer, and I paddled a rubber boat down the Snake River in Wyoming. There in the dome of the sky that vaulted the breath-taking Teton Valley hawks were never out of sight—circling red-tails and Swainson's hawks, swift-flying prairie falcons, even eagles. It gave me an inkling of what the normal conditions must have been in aboriginal America. Yet the gunner often blamed the growing scarcity of game not on himself but on the natural predators, which had lived in satisfactory adjustment to their prey for thousands of years. He called all hawks "vermin," competitors to be shot and destroyed. And the skies over most of America today are still not empty enough of hawks to satisfy him.

The vultures, on the other hand, seem to be spreading. The turkey vulture, pushing northward in the Appalachians, followed the return of the deer to the Hudson highlands, and can now be found in the Berkshires in Connecticut. Its intelligent, aggressive cousin, the black vulture, has by-passed Washington, D. C., and is invading Maryland.

The gulls and terns were shot and egged almost out of existence by 1900, but in less than fifty years they have made a complete comeback. Most species seem to be as numerous as they ever were. The shore birds, too—"snipe" in the gunners' language—nearly faded from the beaches; but since they have been excluded from the game bags, many of them have returned. The herons are also doing very well. The two white egrets almost crossed the Styx; the pirates of the millinery trade nearly got them all. With protection, these immaculate waders have skyrocketed from a few hundred, perhaps a few thousand, to hundreds of thousands.

And what about the songbirds? In earlier days they were caged; they went into potpies; and boys made collections of their eggs. People no longer do these things. It is easier for most of us to get sentimental about a chickadee or a song sparrow than a duck or a grouse. Inconsistent though it may be, the smaller a thing is the more we want to protect it. I remember the winter day a young ornithologist shot a pine grosbeak. He had a very good reason for doing so, but when he showed his scientific collecting permit to the game protector who intercepted him, the warden's only comment was "I still think it's a damned shame." Yet this same warden killed hawks, even the protected ones, like the red-shouldered, and he always liked to get in a few days of grouse shooting each fall.

Although songbirds are no longer persecuted, a few species have declined because their environment has changed; but for every one of these there must be a half dozen that are more common today than they ever were. The reason for this is logical. Wherever man goes down comes the wilderness. The ringing ax starts plant succession all over again. The majority of songbirds find their niche in the development stages of plant growth; relatively few are obligated to the mature timber.

Audubon found the chestnut-sided warbler only once in all the years he roamed America. "In the beginning of May, 1808," he wrote, "I shot five of these birds on a very cold morning near Pottsgrove, in the State of Pennsylvania. I have never met with a single individual of this species since. Where this species goes to breed I am unable to say. I can only suppose it must be far to the northward, as I ransacked the borders of Lake Ontario and those of Lakes Erie and Michigan without meeting with it. I do not know of any naturalist who has been more fortunate, otherwise I should here quote his observations."

At that time the big timber still covered most of the Northeast. Today the chestnut-side is a common bird. In New England its bright song rings from every brushy slope and clearing. On John Baker's 700-acre farm in Dutchess County, New York, this little sprite with the yellow cap and rufous sides is the most numerous bird at this stage of plant succession, when abandoned pastures are being reclaimed by low scrub. In recent years it has spread down the Appalachian plateau; it has become common in Audubon's Pennsylvania, and, following the scrubby thickets under the blighted chestnuts in the mountains, it has made a spectacular appearance as far south as Georgia. In primeval America, when the trees were big, birds like the chestnut-side must have depended almost entirely on windfalls and lightning-ignited forest fires. These Acts of God were their only chance of survival. In a lumbered America there is much more room for them. But there are all sorts of lumbering practices. Selective cropping of the timber is better for wildlife than the wasteful policy of "cut out and get out."

I am willing to wager there are many more indigo buntings today than there were in Audubon's time. As we drive across the Appalachian hills in July we hear, through the open windows of the car, more of these bright blue finches than of any other bird. True, there were probably more woodpeckers and more vireos in Audubon's day than there are now, but we have far more indigo buntings, song sparrows, robins, catbirds, thrashers, orioles, cardinals, mockingbirds, redstarts, phoebes, kingbirds, waxwings, prairie warblers, chats, goldfinches, towhees and field sparrows.

In brief, the larger birds are down; the smaller birds are doing well.

Gunning, when it has not been wisely regulated, and marsh drainage, have been the two most damaging factors that civilization has imposed on the birds, except for recent pesticides. On the other hand, we believe man's disturbance of the land, for better or worse, has made most of the countryside more suitable for songbirds. But we don't know for sure. Perhaps the virgin forests, by their very diversity, had much higher populations than the uniform second-growth woodlands of today. To offset this, civilization has created enormous amounts of "edge," has scrambled the plant communities, and has kept the green growth in such a constant state of succession that there well may be far more songbirds on the continent now than in the days of the Pilgrim fathers—perhaps more by a billion or two. We can only guess. Let us look at the older countries of Europe, where these processes have gone on longer. In England, as pointed out in the preceding chapter, orchards and gardens average over forty times the number of birds that are found in such wild country as deer forest and ungrazed moorland.

When a land is settled as rapidly as ours, it is harder for the birds to roll with the punch. So we have lost such mainland species as the Carolina paroquet and the passenger pigeon. When the heath hen disappeared we lost merely an isolated race of the prairie chicken that lived along the Atlantic Coast, but evolutionary processes are so slow that it is a sad thing to lose even a subspecies or a local population. We shall, no doubt, lose our last ivory-billed woodpecker any time now, if indeed it is still with us. We shall probably forfeit very few additional species, although birds like the Eskimo curlew, California condor, whooping crane and one or two more are so close to the lethal threshold that they can easily be lost. Once gone, no power on earth can bring them back.

In Europe, settled more slowly than our continent, not a single mainland species has become extinct in historic times (the great auk was an island bird). It would seem then, that birds of continental range can cushion the shock of the invader and survive in the hinterland, adapt themselves, and, given a chance, can even make a recovery. But birds of the islands, when pressed, soon have their backs to the sea. One is astounded to find, as he turns the gilt-edged pages of Baron Rothschild's sumptuous volume on extinct birds, that almost all of them lived on islands.

There is no place for an island bird to retreat while it adapts or changes its rigid patterns. Man and his satellites—rats, rabbits, goats, the mongoose, and introduced birds with their diseases—have swept island after island like a scourge, until fourteen species and subspecies of birds have been wiped out in the West Indies and several scores in the islands of the Pacific. The total of full species lost to the world since the Dodo is seventy-eight.

In 1918, when a ship was wrecked off Lord Howe Island, east of Australia, the rats swam ashore. Three years later a man who lived on the island wrote:

"But two short years ago (1919) the forests of Lord Howe Island were joyous with the notes of myriads of birds . . . They were unmolested save by each other, the residents of the island rarely disturbing their harmony. Today, however, the ravages of rats, the worst enemy of mankind, which have been accidentally introduced, have made the note of a bird rare, and the sight of one, save the strong-billed magpie and the kingfisher (*Halcyon*), even rarer. Within two years this paradise of birds has become a wilderness, and the quietness of death reigns where all was melody."

On Laysan Island, a dot of coral at the west end of the far-flung Hawaiian chain, a well-meaning blunderer introduced rabbits as a source of food for shipwrecked mariners. By doing so, he spelled doom for at least four of the five endemic species of birds. These birds were a flightless teal, a flightless rail, a miller bird and a honey-eater. All bore the name of Laysan, for they were found nowhere else in all the world. In a few years the rabbits ate every bit of vegetation; and when the wind blew, the unanchored sand piled into dunes. Fortunately the little Laysan rail, a stubby red-eyed gnome that picked inquisitively at men's shoelaces and hopped up on tables for crumbs, had been transported to Midway where it took hold. It looked as though it might be brought back to Laysan, now that the rabbits had perished and the vegetation was coming back, but this was not to be. A year after the unsuccessful attempt by the Japanese to take Midway, rats made a landing there and by 1944 it was computed that there were 100 of these rodents to the acre. They were everywhere; in the thickets and down in the burrows of the "moaning birds" (the Bonin Island petrel). Pressed by rats on every hand, the little rail quickly faded into the black void of extinction.

Man is the only check upon himself. There is no higher predator to keep him under control—not since his cave days when he played hide and seek with saber-toothed tigers. He is at the peak of the pyramid. When he goes hog wild in the exploitation of his domain and the ominous writing appears upon the wall, he can look for no outside help. Because of a fundamental decency in his make-up, he seems to sober up at the eleventh hour, so we have ethics, laws, game regulations, soil conservation, national forests, national parks, sanctuaries and wildlife refuges. It is a man's better self trying to rebuild what he has destroyed, to safeguard for his sons what is left of his inheritance.

Today, millions of acres in the United States are bird sanctuaries in name or effect. This started in 1900, the zero year, when the National Audubon Society snatched the last few gull colonies on the Maine Coast away from the millinery hunters. Now the Society patrols a long string of sanctuaries from Maine to Florida, the coast of Texas and California.

Most of the Society's sanctuaries give haven to the large ornamental water birds which have no value as game—gulls, terns, pelicans, egrets, ibises and spoonbills—glamor birds of great aesthetic value which are liable to destruction because they concentrate in large, vulnerable colonies. When you see your next common egret, white against the green marsh, or the little snowy, shuffling in the shallows—take off your hat to the National Audubon Society.

The first Federal bird reservations were set aside in 1903 by executive order of President Theodore Roosevelt. Now there are more than 300 of them—administered by the United States Fish and Wildlife Service. They aggregate about 20,000,000 acres and all forms of wildlife are protected. More than 200 were created for waterfowl alone. I have never visited one of these super-refuges that did not prove to be the best place for birds for miles around, and which was not fully ten times as good after it had been scientifically managed for a decade as when it was established. The smallest of the Federal refuges are islets only an acre or two in extent where gulls and terns breed; the largest is the Aleutian Islands refuge in Alaska which covers 2,900,000 acres.

In addition, the United States National Park Service administers more than 180 park areas where wildlife is protected at all times; and these also are, in effect, bird sanctuaries. The total area of these parks is more than 24,000,000 acres. Besides these, there are the national forests, embracing

176,000,000 acres; and, although hunting is not prohibited, wild creatures find a reasonable haven in these solitudes. Then, too, many states have "wildlife refuges" which are breeding reservoirs for game species, assurance to sportsmen that there will always be enough "seed stock" to insure hunting in the surrounding country.

So, with Federally owned lands, state lands and countless inviolate estates, private parks and sanctuaries, man is trying to take care of wildlife. His conscious acts of destruction and restoration send the fortunes of the birds and the other wild creatures up or down, but no more so than many of the ordinary events that happen every day in a civilized world, where no thought of wildlife is involved.

Aldo Leopold observed that all civilizations seem to have been conditioned upon whether the plant succession, under the impact of occupancy, gave a habitable assortment of vegetative types, or an inferior and uninhabitable assortment. He pointed out that "Caesar's Gaul was utterly changed by human use—for the better. Moses' land of milk and honey was utterly changed—for the worse." Both changes were unforeseen.

But even in civilization's most destructive phases, some birds seem to find their place in the sun. Certainly nothing is more destructive than all-out war. Look at the blitzed part of London near St. Paul's Cathedral. Yet these bombed foundations, chimneys and walls were exactly suited to several pairs of rare black redstarts which were drawn to the rubble as if by a magnet. Rather than return to their rocky cliffs on the continent, they remained to nest in these war-tailored substitutes amid London's noise and clamor, amid the buses and crowds, the starlings and house sparrows.

We don't like worn out land, but horned larks do. They desire their grass short, with bald spots. When the long grass goes and countless hoofs pound the earth into a pavement, meadowlarks go out and horned larks come in. They bid fair eventually to inherit most of the over-grazed grasslands of the northern hemisphere.

Whether we abuse the land or use it wisely, there will be birds—but far more on well-managed land we have good reason to suspect. Whereas many farms average fewer than three birds per acre, this ratio can easily be doubled with good management. Every last one of the fifty or more standard practices of the Soil Conservation Service—strip cropping, hedgerows, gully dams and all the other devices to check erosion—also help wildlife.

This hard-working government agency, whose job it is to insure our daily bread, has undoubtedly increased American birds by millions. As someone wisely said, "Beauty and bread grow best together."

The farmers' fields have favored the spread of bobolinks, meadowlarks, dickcissels and vesper sparrows—in fact, the farms that bridged the Great Plains have been used as stepping stones for western birds now invading the East. Western meadowlarks and western kingbirds have bred as far east as Hamilton, Ontario, and Brewer's blackbirds are already near Lake Michigan. The red-shafted flicker of the West met the yellow-shafted flicker of the East around the ranch houses, and now we see "orange-shafted flickers," or flickers with one red whisker and one black one, suggesting that the systematists were wrong when they called them two distinct species. After all, the birds should know.

More birds have adapted to a changing world than have failed. Very few have the narrow tolerance of the ivory-billed woodpecker or the Bachman's warbler. I have never, in all my years of birding, seen a chimney swift nesting in the old-fashioned way, in a hollow tree. More nighthawks in the Northeast lay their eggs on flat gravel roofs than on the bald ground. Most phoebes today use bridges or rafters. Only a few still favor rocky ledges.

As a family, the swallows seem to be completely won over to man's way of life. Cliff swallows and barn swallows plaster their nests on his barns; martins, tree swallows and violet-green swallows accept his bird boxes; bank swallows and rough-wings live in his road cuts, sand quarries and excavations. The *Hirundinidae* are opportunists. They will never allow civilization to displace them.

At least fifty North American birds have nested in bird boxes. These are the species that in less manicured terrain use second-hand woodpecker-holes or natural cavities. Even the shy solitary birds of prey have been attracted to nesting boxes—barred owls, barn owls, screech owls, saw-whet owls and sparrow hawks. I assume the retired B-29 bomber in the nose of which a friend of mine found a great horned owl's nest could be called an artificial nesting device.

Few nesting devices are as fantastic as the 18″ x 18″ tray put out for peregrine falcons on the 20th-story ledge of the Sun-Life Building in Montreal, or the cartwheels on poles on which the ospreys build their castles of sticks in Cape May County. A variant of the cartwheel idea was tried on Shelter Island, New York, by the electricians of the power commission. They were tired of having ospreys short circuit the wires on their telephone poles with their bulky nests, so they put up some substitute poles nearby. The ospreys readily accepted them.

I think the prize nesting boxes of all are some I saw in Lake Ontario recently—boxes for Holboell's grebes! To begin with, the Holboell's, or red-necked, grebe is a rather rare bird in my experience on the Great Lakes, but a few years ago they began to turn up in increasing numbers along one stretch of shore on Lake Ontario. As many as 1000 have been seen there. Many stay through the summer on the cold deep lake. George North, one of Canada's sharpest field men, took us out on a clay bluff one day in late summer and proudly showed us a flock of thirty on the sparkling water below. Some were in gray winter plumage, others in red-necked summer garb with white cheeks. They preened, they dived, and some gave their strange courting cries. A few miles further along the lake shore North showed us where several had nested. It was, of all unlikely spots, in the boat basin behind the breakwall at Burlington Harbor, not far from Hamilton. In this terrain of bluffs, narrow beaches and deep water, the only place to anchor their buoyant nests was on the wooden floats to which the launches were tied. Whenever the owners came out to use their boats, they had to disturb these nests or break them up. They did not like to do this so several of the men anchored substitutes—floating boxes—out in the water and the grebes used them!

Most continental birds are plastic in their habits. When the buffalo herds were exterminated and cattle populated the plains, the "buffalo bird" became the cowbird. Birds are always ready to fill a new environment. Whenever a favorite woodlot is to be put under the ax or some birdy spot is threatened (perhaps a new airport is to be built on a marsh), the local bird clubs pass resolutions or write letters to the local politicians. They fear for the birds they will lose. Yet they seldom foresee their gains.

A few years ago the bird watchers of western Pennsylvania and eastern Ohio were heartbroken because Pymatuning swamp was to be flooded. It was to be turned into a large lake so as to stabilize the flow in the Shenango River. This swamp was particularly interesting to biologists because a few northern birds still held out in the cold bogs. George Sutton said it had

OLD FASHIONED PHOEBE. Few phoebes nest today in the ancestral manner, on a bank or a cliff. Modern phoebes prefer bridges and barns.

EBB TIDE strands tidbits for expectant gulls whose long shadows make a dark pattern on the sand. Once massacred for their feathers, gulls are now valued as an effective clean-up corps about the wharves and on the beaches.

OPPORTUNISTS. Purple martins were first attracted to hollow gourds hung from saplings by Indians. Today martins reside in elaborate apartment houses like the one above, and we rarely hear of them nesting primitively in tree cavities.

IN AUDUBON'S DAY, the chestnut-sided warbler was so rare that the great ornithologist knew of no one who could tell him where it nested. To-day it is abundant in the brushy slashings of the Appalachian country.

more birds per square mile than any other place of its size in Pennsylvania. In 1932, when the impounded water began to rise in the sixteen-mile-long horseshoe-shaped lake, everyone watched in suspense. The northern water-thrushes, returning to their old territories, flitted forlornly from stump to stump where the trees had been cut. They had been dispossessed. As the water rose, new deep water marshes formed around the edge of the lake. Then a miracle happened. Ducks that wintered on the Atlantic Coast paused en route to their homes in the northern prairies. They liked the place and stayed to nest. Gadwalls and baldpates both bred there; so did pintails, green-winged teal, shovelers, redheads, ring-necks and ruddy ducks—all of them new to Pennsylvania as summer residents. Some of them had never been known to breed east of the Mississippi before. Pymatuning's bird city soon resembled that of a prairie slough in the Dakotas. It was, in truth, a man-made prairie marsh, and the ducks recognized it as such. Ruth Trimble Chapin, in her study of Pymatuning, wisely observed that the breeding of these ducks "prompts me to believe that breeding ranges are not entirely a question of latitude and longitude, but rather selection of a suitable habitat."

When I visited Pymatuning in September, 1938, I saw *fourteen* bald eagles at one time. The attraction for the fish-loving bald eagles was easy to see. Carp had become so abundant at the spillway between the upper and lower lakes, that they boiled up in a mound when bread was thrown to them, and tame mallards walked almost dry-shod over their backs to snatch up the crumbs!

A man-made lake in mountain country is to the birds what an oasis in the desert is to men. Mountainous West Virginia was not reached by the glaciers. The state did not have a single natural lake, so most of the ducks and other water birds were of rare occurrence. Now there are large artificial lakes, like Lake Lynn and Lake Terra Alta, where thousands of waterfowl rest on their flight across the Appalachian highlands to the coast. In Berks County, Pennsylvania there was also a lack of ponds for water birds. In 1929, a dam was built, forming Lake Ontelaunee. Dozens of waterfowl and shore birds have been added to the Berks County list since then. One October day, on our way home from Hawk Mountain, we stopped there and saw, among a flock of noisy killdeers on a mud-spit, a spectacular black and white avocet, fifteen hundred miles off its path.

One would not look for shore birds in the heart of Washington, D. C. Yet, for a few brief weeks in the late summer of 1928 when the ground was being cleared for the United States Department of Commerce Building, shore birds flocked to the muddy pools on 14th Street. The curators of the Smithsonian and the ornithologists of the Biological Survey paused on the way to their offices to see what new shore birds had dropped in each day. Fifteen species were listed, including knots, turnstones and black-bellied plovers. The rain-filled excavation, known at the time as "Hoover's Lake," was one of the best centers for shore birds the District of Columbia has ever known, second only to the golf course in Potomac Park where nineteen species have been recorded.

Golf courses and airports! Who would think they would often be the best areas for rare shore birds? Yet some of them are. A tiny bit of man-made prairie in the eastern countryside is bound to attract a prairie loving bird, off the beaten path.

The rare buff-breasted sandpiper normally flies south across the Great Plains to the Pampas, but now Ontario field-glass enthusiasts find it at Toronto each fall. They do not look for this miniature of the upland plover along the lake shore; they go out to the airport. The Newark (New Jersey) Airport used to be a first-rate spot for golden plovers before traffic got too heavy. These long-distance fliers would drop in just as familiarly as if they were squadrons of transports arriving on schedule.

Hoyes Lloyd, President of the American Ornithologists' Union, once had an arrangement with the man in the control tower of one of the Canadian airports near his home. Whenever large or suspicious-looking shore birds dropped down to the runway, the man in the tower phoned Lloyd and he was out there in a thrice.

When northeasters lash the coast in August and September, the place to look for Patagonia-bound godwits and golden plovers is on the high ground of some golf course close to the sea—one like the club at Absecon or Brigantine near Atlantic City, or some of the courses on Long Island.

Some of the best shore-bird areas I have known have been not on the clean beaches but along the water front at the edge of some city where sewage and other organic waste pollutes the mud. Even pollution, provided it is not chemical waste, can at times be attractive to wildlife. When I lived in Boston we always made one or two trips each fall to look for shore birds at the Framingham filter beds. Similarly, when Allan Cruickshank was stationed in London during the war, one of his favorite haunts was the Slough Sewage Farm. One can imagine what the men in his battalion had to say when he acquired a very legal-looking permit to wander through the area!

Gulls, of course, like such places. They are scavengers; they always have been; but the sewage of the cities, the garbage dumps, and the fish wharves make it possible for more gulls to winter through the starvation months than ever before. On the big city dumps they swarm by thousands; brown gulls, gray gulls, white gulls, young ones, middle-aged and old ones, rising in windrows at our approach and dropping to the rear among the grapefruit rinds, chicken legs and coffee grounds.

But more gulls nesting on the rocky islands to the north often mean fewer terns. On the Weepecket Islands in Massachusetts, where terns had nested for forty years, Sears Crowell found 3500 of the graceful "sea swallows" in 1933; both roseates and commons. Ten years later he could not find one. In their stead, a colony of 1000 herring gulls flourished. What happened? Did the gulls destroy the terns? It is true they do eat some eggs and chicks, but the behaviorist advances a more basic reason: the presence of even a few gulls, though they ignored the terns, would throw these high-strung birds out of adjustment. The interplay between the terns, the posturing and displaying, so important to their mating and nesting cycle, is disturbed by the presence of these big birds which have a different rhythm of activities. As a result, the terns can not concentrate. At first they become nervous when the gulls intrude, then they seem to lose interest in their own affairs and finally they abandon the colony.

The fortunes of the terns go up and down like the stock market. These black-capped, fork-tailed birds are sensitive to every change. Some of the largest colonies of least terns (the little ones with the yellow bills) which I have visited have been on land where real estate promoters had pumped shell and sand over the marsh to lay the foundations for future cities.

When Robert Moses, New York's idealistic park commissioner, dredged the boat channel behind Jones Beach, he extended the range of the black skimmer. Probably he never knew this. For several years a few of these languid black and white birds with the undershot red bills had been seen along the south shore of Long Island, yelping like hounds as they flew by.

William Vogt made the most exciting discovery of the 1934 season when he found their big blotched eggs on the fresh spoil banks of Gilgo Island. Three or four years later there were thirty pairs on Gilgo, but after another five years had passed, I could find only two. The beach grass had reclaimed the sterile fill; the island was no longer suitable for skimmers, and savannah sparrows had taken over. In such unconscious ways man sets in motion the wheel of succession.

In the four and a half centuries since Columbus, the bird life of America has altered prodigiously. The changes in the next four and a half centuries may be equally cataclysmic. There may be more birds as the result of an improved understanding of wildlife. There may be fewer because man has crowded them out.

When George Sutton and I were in the air force in World War II we were assigned for a short while to the same research project to determine just what the new-found panacea, DDT, would do to other things besides mosquitoes. We were witness to a cloud the size of a man's hand; we could not foresee that by 1960 more than a billion pounds of very lethal pesticides would be sprayed yearly over the United States, resulting in the destruction of some millions of birds. The greatest offenders have been the chlorinated hydrocarbons, DDT and its more potent derivatives. Professor George Wallace, who reported on the debacle of robin mortality after the campus at Michigan State was sprayed for elm disease, stated publicly that wholesale spraying was "worse than deforestation, worse than market gunning, worse than drainage, drought or oil pollution."

Rachel Carson in her great book, *Silent Spring,* has alerted the public, and we may see a swing away from the craze to spray. As Roland Clement of the National Audubon Society points out: "Disease, predators and parasites are nature's way of handling overpopulation; we should take advantage of these natural controls and use chemicals only when they do not destroy nature's own regulatory mechanisms."

Modern Noah's Ark

THE story of the deluge, when all birds lived together on the ark, was perhaps in the back of men's minds when they imported exotic birds into this country.

Hundreds of thousands, probably millions, of birds from other parts of the world have been brought here. John C. Phillips wrote in 1928 that about 1000 live birds reach the United States every day. Many of these are cage birds. At this very moment there are probably a thousand species on display in the zoological parks of the country. Once in a while a cage bird escapes. Then we have reports from the field-glass fraternity of a blue tanager in the Brooklyn Botanical Gardens or a Brazilian cardinal at a feeding station in Yonkers. I once saw a big green parrot in a maple tree on our street in Jamestown, New York.

At least 150 species of birds have been deliberately set free in America, released in the hope that they might become a part of the American avifauna. Everything from flamingos to Japanese titmice has been tried, but with all America for an ark, only a handful of species have survived except in Hawaii. Most of this was done before 1900. Ecology was an unknown word then and little was understood about a bird's relation to its environment. Birds of the desert, for instance, were set free in the humid rain forests of the Northwest. But even when some judgment was used, the birds soon died out. It is hard to duplicate in the New World the exact niche a bird has occupied in the Old.

But a city is a city the world over. So is a barnyard. Look down the list of "pests" and see how many of them came from cities and farms across the sea: most of our weeds—dandelion, chicory, orange hawkweed, yarrow and ragweed; the gypsy moth, brown-tail moth, Japanese beetle and cabbage butterfly; the Norway rat, house sparrow and starling. Through the centuries they have adapted themselves to the cities and farms of Europe and Asia. So they have had little trouble here—and almost no competition.

The early settlers found great numbers of game birds here, but they frequently commented on the scarcity of the songbirds, of which they had so many in the homeland. Nostalgic German-Americans imported hundreds of birds from the fatherland: bullfinches, linnets, even European dippers. Transplanted Englishmen, attempting to bring something of their environment, too, imported robin redbreasts, skylarks and nightingales.

In the 70's and 80's "Acclimatization" Societies sprang up. One in Cambridge, Massachusetts, called itself the "Society for the Acclimatization of Foreign Birds," and released all sorts of strange species in Mount Auburn Cemetery. I can imagine Ludlow Griscom's confusion in this favorite stalking ground of his, had he lived at that time. Another group in Ohio, "The Cincinnati Acclimatization Society," spent $9,000 between 1872 and 1874 and liberated 3000 birds of twenty species—but in vain. In the late 80's, The Portland Oregon Songbird Club was established "for the introduction of useful songbirds." It set free thirty species, but none of them took hold, although the skylark did very well for awhile.

To "The American Acclimatization Society" in New York City can be laid the blame for the starling's success. Curiously enough, several previous attempts to get this short-tailed black bird started were complete failures. In 1890, Eugene Schieffelin, leader of the Society, brought eighty birds from Europe and set them free in Central Park. In 1891, he liberated forty more.* These 120 birds have multiplied a millionfold. Their armies have crossed the Great Divide, have successfully laid siege to the fortress of the Rockies, and are now established along the Pacific coast from Canada to Mexico. They have even flown aboard boats far at sea. In earlier years, as I sat at my desk on the sixth floor of Audubon

* Authorities differ on the number of starlings introduced by Schieffelin. The figure ranges from 100 (F. M. Chapman and A. D. Cruickshank) to 160 (E. R. Kalmbach and J. C. Phillips). But the most frequently given number is 120. Perhaps the disparity in the latter two figures can be accounted for by the ambiguity of the statement that "forty pairs of starlings were liberated in 1890 and 40 more in 1891."

House at 1000 Fifth Avenue, New York, on cold winter afternoons, it seemed incredible that the black blizzard of birds that swarmed to the ledges of the Metropolitan Museum across the street could be descended from a mere ten dozen birds released in that very neighborhood hardly more than fifty years before. On several afternoons I put on my overcoat and stepped out onto the small balcony to watch the evening flight. The vanguard straggled in shortly after four o'clock. By 4:30 large flocks began to sweep in. During the next half hour, flock after flock, three or four hundred at a time, poured through the gap in the buildings above me. Most of them had come from far out on Long Island, where commuters see the city-bound flocks twenty miles or more from Manhattan. Other flocks came down Fifth Avenue from the direction of the Bronx. A few arrived from the west. It was like watching a three-ring circus. Yet there was an orderliness about it all. Each flock handled itself with military precision, like a squadron of fast aircraft. When one bird turned, they all turned. When a flock passed in front of another flying in a different direction, the sky was cross-hatched with a moving pattern of birds. I tried counting but the starlings pitched onto the ledges so fast I had to guess at the numbers in each incoming flock. At times the sky was a swirling storm of wings and even the broadest estimate was pure guessing. The first evening when I totaled my figures the count came to 24,000. A week later, when I tried it again, I got 36,000. The din from the thousands that shoved and jostled on the ledges could be heard far into the night. They never seemed to sleep. When I passed by on a Fifth Avenue bus at midnight, they were still squealing.

The directors of the Museum, prodded by the complaints of residents up and down the street, stationed four men on the long flat roof to frighten the starlings off. Each carried a long pole from which cloth streamers trailed, like the tail of a kite. When the starlings were routed from one end of the building they flew to the other, nearly four blocks away. For weeks the uneven battle went on while icy winds whipped down the Avenue. But the birds won out. The Museum directors, unwilling to concede defeat, are reported to have thought of trying the aluminum owls that an enterprising manufacturer had put on the market.

This is a small roost, however, compared to some I have seen. The swarms along Pennsylvania Avenue in Washington must exceed 100,000.

If such a snowballing of numbers were to continue, simple mathematics indicate that in the very near future we would be knee deep in starlings. But, as with all things, there is a leveling off. The house sparrow has actually gone into a decline. Along the Atlantic seaboard there are nothing like the numbers of fifty or sixty years ago. In Boston it is reported that there is only one sparrow today as against twenty at the beginning of the century. Henry Ford, some contend, had much to do with this. Oil droppings from motor cars are a poor substitute for horse droppings. But the sparrows in one town I passed through had turned things to their advantage. At the Greyhound Bus Station they eagerly awaited the arrival of the buses and picked off the insects that were stuck to the radiators—roasted grasshoppers, grilled butterflies and fried bees.

I am not worried however, about the house sparrow. Although one can still see roosts of thousands in cities like El Paso, Texas, it is on the ebb; its damage to native birds has already been done. Furthermore, its food habits are not bad. How many other birds will eat Japanese beetles? The house sparrow must be accepted now and so must the starling. Starlings have put pressure on bluebirds, martins and red-headed woodpeckers, but in the Northeastern states the crest of their tide will probably soon pass.

When a foreign bird is brought in, it usually does one of two things: it either dies out quickly, or, if its new home is like the one it left behind, as in the cases of the English sparrow and the starling, it spreads like wildfire. The rock dove (or park pigeon, if you prefer) is another city dweller that sees no difference between New York and London. Under domestication in Europe it became edificarian, but the original rock dove still nests in the British Isles in caves and fissures by the sea. The only place I know of in America where it reverted to its ancestral way of life is on the headlands fronting the sea at Nahant, in Massachusetts. There among the rocks we could always find several pairs.

It seems to be a paradox that exotics succeed more often on inlands than on continents, while native birds disappear more readily from islands than from continents. Our Hawaiian Islands had thirty-six species of native land birds—*passerines*—when the first collectors went there; sixty if you count the subspecies. These birds were found nowhere else in all the world. To-day fourteen of them are extinct and five others are so rare that few men have ever seen them.

It was not the tribal chieftains who snared the birds for their gorgeous feather cloaks and were thus responsible, although their bird catchers were so efficient that the old chiefs had to impose restrictions. The birds probably reproduced rapidly enough to take care of those losses. It was not because the lush forests were felled to make room for pineapples and cane, although that did affect some species. We suspect the "bird lovers" themselves did the bulk of the damage. Nearly a hundred species of foreign birds have been set free in Hawaii—birds from every continent except Antarctica. At least thirty of them have taken hold!

The road to hell is paved with good intentions, we are told, and the liberators of these imported birds did not know that they would compete ruthlessly with the island birds. Worse still, there is some evidence that they brought diseases—maladies like bird malaria and bird sleeping sickness—diseases to which the invaders had built up a tolerance, but which the native birds could probably not resist any more than the native Polynesians on some of the Pacific Islands could withstand exposure to some of our "harmless" children's diseases, such as measles and mumps.

Sixty years ago the Hawaiian mountain forests rang with the voices of myriads of birds; bright scarlet *iiwi*, red *apapane*, the black and yellow *oo*, and the *mamo*. The *iiwi* and *apapane* still survive but today the members of the Honolulu Audubon Society read about the others in historic accounts. Their feeding stations are visited by cardinals and house finches from America, doves from China and white eyes from Japan. They would gladly trade this polyglot avifauna for the birds of old Hawaii. Their islands can boast the greatest number of foreign birds of any spot in the world, but at the expense of their own species, for in no other areas except New Zealand and the Mascarene Islands have so many birds become extinct.

The starling and house sparrow disasters put an end to free-for-all acclimatization efforts in America. In 1900, the Lacey Act was passed. No one is now permitted to bring in birds from foreign lands without permission from the Fish and Wildlife Service. Although Henry Ford liberated four or five hundred birds on his estates at Dearborn, Michigan, in 1913, songbirds are never intentionally imported nowadays. But there has been one recent introduction that has taken a strong hold—the house finch in the New York City region.

The house finch of the Southwest looks much like a purple finch but acts like a house sparrow. Few American birds are more adaptable and when our West was settled they moved from the deserts and dry canyons into the cities. Perhaps they first learned to nest in the homes of the cliff-dwellers, the adobe huts of the pueblos or in the early Spanish missions. At any rate, a house finch was seen in 1941 at Jones Beach, Long Island. Others were reported the following year, and in 1943 a nest was located. They soon were prospering.

Where did they come from? It seems that in 1940 a great many were sold by cage-bird dealers in New York. They were called "Hollywood Finches," and one large distributor on Fifth Avenue was securing them at $35.00 per hundred. This was illegal under the terms of the recent migratory bird treaty between Mexico and the United States. When United States Game Management agents broke up the traffic, some of the dealers turned their birds loose. Twenty-two years later they were widespread in Connecticut, New Jersey and Pennsylvania.

A number of birds have almost made the grade; they have prospered for awhile and then died out. A few have gained a hold locally but don't seem to spread. The European tree sparrow which looks like a house sparrow with a chocolate crown and a black spot behind the ear was doing well around St. Louis where twelve pairs were set free in Lafayette Park, in 1870. It would have spread, if the stronger and more aggressive house sparrow had not arrived in St. Louis about that time. There are still plenty of European tree sparrows near St. Louis, but you have to know where to look for them.

The skylark, the bird of Shelley, is another species that almost made good. It lasted for twenty-five years around Flatbush, Long Island, until the growing city swallowed the little colony. It was also the one bird that the Portland Oregon Songbird Club nearly succeeded in transplanting. For twenty or thirty years a few skylarks could be seen near Portland. It was introduced around Victoria, in British Columbia, too. The first time it didn't do too well, but the local Natural History Society was not to be discouraged. The people of Victoria are as British as any group on our continent, from the tweed of their jackets to their traditional four-o'clock tea. They longed for the touch of the old English countryside that only the skylark could bring. So they decided to try again. They sent a man to England to find the spot where the climate was most like that of Victoria.

They then imported their birds from that locality. Today there are thousands of skylarks near Victoria, but they will probably not spread beyond the well-kept farms of the southern tip of Vancouver Island. There, on a recent winter's day, several members of the Victoria Natural History Society showed me a flock of thirty. Some of them hovered low over the grass, flashing their white outer tail feathers, pipit-like. While a herd of cows crowded around us in idle curiosity, I gazed open-mouthed at the birds made famous by the English poets. It was late January, but as we watched, several of the larks climbed into the gray sky and sang.

The European goldfinch, a little tan bird with a red face and a yellow wing patch, which we see so often in medieval paintings (it was a symbol of the soul and resurrection) was imported in droves by homesick Europeans. One lot, liberated at Hoboken, in 1878, prospered. They became common around Englewood and in Central Park, and they appeared on Long Island. Then they vanished. Yet during those years there must have been a few holding onto the thin thread of existence somewhere, for in the 30's they again made their appearance; and for a few years many nested in Seaford, Massapequa and other towns along the south shore of Long Island.

Edwin Way Teale and I made a special trip to see them there. We searched about the spot where John Elliott, the local authority on these birds, had seen one the day before. A suspicious bird darted into a maple. I hurried over, and there, its red face peering at me from among the green leaves, was my first European goldfinch—*sitting on a nest!* The species had never been photographed on this side of the Atlantic, so it was worth a try. An old door placed across two sawhorses made a platform for my tripod and Graflex. Standing on a tall stepladder, I focused on the nest and wired a remote control release to my flash equipment. The motorcar patriots driving along the Sunrise Highway that Sunday had reported my suspicious operations to the Seaford police, and a patrol car pulled up just as I was waiting for the bird to come back. In those early war years everyone was nervous about spies along the South Shore. Only a week before several German spies had been captured after landing from a submarine a few miles to the east.

When I told the officer I was after goldfinches he inquired, "British or American?"

"British," I gasped in astonishment.

He then told me he knew all about these birds. He had picked up a man and his wife earlier in the day, and to explain their actions they showed him a book that said Seaford was the best place to look for British goldfinches. The book was a copy of my *Field Guide!*

Occasionally, exotic birds seem to have appeared from nowhere. Some years ago the mynah, a sociable starling-like bird of the Orient, blossomed out in the city of Vancouver, on the mainland of British Columbia. Little is known of how it came, but it spread rapidly until it nested even in the downtown business section. It was another city bird on the rampage. As it approached the U.S. border, mile by mile, there were predictions that some day it might become the most numerous bird on the West Coast. There have been one or two records for Bellingham and Seattle, but so far the prediction has not come true.

As you walk among the exotic plantings in the parks of Los Angeles or the gardens of Hollywood you will see doves. At first, you will pay them scant attention, although they may look a little strange as they mince about on short legs over the lawns. Suddenly you will become aware that they are not just mourning doves. They are Chinese spotted doves, so-called because of a collar of black and white spots on the back of the neck. No one knows how these doves got there. The first evidence of their presence was a dead one picked up in 1917. Now the birds are all over Los Angeles. Another dove, the ringed turtledove, a delicate pale creamy bird with a black crescent on its neck, also seems to have taken hold about Los Angeles. Not as widespread as the spotted dove, it makes its headquarters in Sheridan Square, opposite the Biltmore Hotel.

The mute swan, the big park swan with the black knob on its orange bill, is the only one of all the foreign waterfowl that has taken hold. They were used as ornaments on the big estates on eastern Long Island, in Dutchess County on the Hudson and elsewhere. The young birds, unpinioned, wandered off until now there are thousands of swans of feral stock on Long Island. I have seen 150 in a flock on Shinnecock Bay. The native whistler is almost unknown to Long Islanders. When they speak of wild swans they mean *olor,* the mute swan. The whistler by-passes Long Island on its way from the Chesapeake to the Great Lakes. The Dutchess County birds actually migrate down the Hudson when cold weather comes, so the A.O.U. Check-List has now given the mute swan a place among North American birds.

For the last thirty or forty years most of the birds that have been set free have been game birds. Introduction and artificial propagation seemed to many sportsmen the easiest method of providing more birds to shoot. But it hasn't been as simple as all that.

Some of the birds have been our own game species; the bob-white and the California quail have been carried to every corner of the land. They have done exactly what one would expect them to do. The California quail has not survived in the East, nor has the bob-white done well in California. There are places in the Northwest, however, where the bobwhite has taken hold, places that are enough like the East, where bobwhites would have lived had it not been for the geographic barriers.

Turkeys have been transplanted by the thousands; but in areas outside their original range, they seldom survive. Turkeys set free all over the State of California have disappeared into the air. On the other hand, turkeys released in the shot-out coverts of Pennsylvania, where they had lived in Audubon's day, thrived, and the hawk watchers at Hawk Mountain sometimes see one as it launches from the slope.

There are large turkey flocks in the Chiricahua Mountains in Arizona. They had lived unmolested in the stronghold of the Apaches, for the Indians spared them; but they were soon wiped out, every last gobbler and hen, when the tide of white settlers swept westward. The hundreds of birds living in the Chiricahuas today are the progeny of a small flock brought down from the White Mountains to the north. If the hunting season is ever opened again on turkeys in the Chiricahuas, I doubt that they will last a fortnight; they are too tame, and more afraid of a horse than a man. When in their roost high in the pines, every bird will gobble back when you gobble to them—or even if you clap your hands. When the thunder rolls over the Chiricahuas the synchronized gobbling of the turks sounds all up and down the ridge.

The Cleveland Cliffs Iron Company spent thousands of dollars putting game birds on Grand Island in Lake Superior. They tried the blackcock of Europe but with no luck. They tried the capercaillie, the great game bird of the Scandinavian forests, second in size only to the turkey, but it scarcely lived a season. It has fizzled out wherever it has been tried—in Newfoundland, Vancouver Island, Maine, Algonquin Park in Ontario and in the Adirondacks. Yet when it was reintroduced into the forests of Scotland eighty or ninety years after it had been hunted to extinction there, it made a quick comeback.

In the seventies there was great excitement about migratory or Egyptian quail. Sportsmen thought they were the answer to their depleted game coverts. Here was an upland game bird that could migrate and escape the hard winters. Thousands were set free in the Northeast. A few nests were found the first year, but not a single bird returned the following spring. They completely disappeared. It was reported that some came aboard a ship hundreds of miles to the southeast of Hatteras in November, 1877. The theory went around, and it is logical, that they all migrated to the southeast, the same direction they took from Europe to cross the Mediterranean, and were swallowed up by the Atlantic. In spite of this early history of failure, hundreds of thousands more were raised and liberated in the late 1950's in the central states. They also failed.

But even though the migratory quail (*Coturnix coturnix*) is a vanished dream, its congener in European fields, the "Hungarian" partridge (*Perdix perdix*) can be seen today along the roads in Minnesota and the Dakotas. As it flies from the weeds along the shoulder it flashes a rufous-red tail. This is the common partridge of agricultural Europe. You would expect it to make good here, yet it has never done well on the farms along the Atlantic Seaboard. It was tried out in New Jersey way back in Benjamin Franklin's time, by his son-in-law, Richard Bache. Hundreds of thousands of these feathered immigrants have since crossed the Atlantic. During 1908 and 1909, 40,000 reached our docks. Between 1899 and 1912, the Indiana Game Commission alone spent $62,000 on Hungarian partridges. Today, in the interior Northwest, at least, the "Huns" seem here to stay.

George Washington wrote in his journal, in 1786, that Lafayette sent several species of pheasants to Mount Vernon to be liberated there. They did not do well. In the century and a half that followed this abortive attempt, a dozen kinds of pheasants have been loosed across the land—

Reeve pheasants, silver pheasants, golden pheasants, copper pheasants, Prince of Wales pheasants and others.

Of all this over-gorgeous galaxy, most of which live in the rank undergrowth of Himalayan forests or in the wilder parts of the Orient, only one came through—the ring-neck, the bird of the paddy fields of China. Again it follows the familiar pattern; a bird that had slowly adapted its way of life to civilization in the Old World, transplanted to a similar situation in the New. Centuries of hide-and-seek in the scant cover along the edges of Chinese fields had conditioned the ring-neck for survival here. Today it stands as the outstanding success among introduced game birds. Sixteen million have been shot in one hunting season in twenty-four states from New England to Oregon where the first successful introduction took place in 1881. That puts the pheasant at the top of the game-bird list, now exceeding the yearly bag of *all* wild ducks—more than thirty species. The amount of pheasant meat that reaches the table in a single hunting season is said to equal the meat of 50,000 beef cattle. In South Dakota, where the revenue from hunting licenses exceeds a million dollars a year, 6,500,000 birds have been taken in a season. Still, after the autumnal barrage, enough birds winter through to produce a big crop the next season. Pheasants strut elegantly beside the roads and burst from the stubble of every corn and wheat field, tails streaming like comets. They literally seem to sprout from the black earth of the prairies, but there is reason to believe they have passed their peak, for in some places there has been a population decline.

In some states the game farms turn out enough pheasants each year to replace the deficit caused by hunting, but as a wildlife management practice, this is not as satisfactory as a strong environment where the birds can reproduce themselves without help. Our ring-neck, a blend of the cold-weather races of China and Mongolia, does best in the grain belt, just south of the deep snows. For some reason pheasants do not like the red earth south of Mason and Dixon's line. It is no wonder that none of George Washington's birds lived. You will not find ring-necks today near Mount Vernon.

There is a great difference of opinion among conservationists as to the wisdom of introducing game birds like the pheasant. Some say it eases the hunting pressure on our native game birds. Others insist it creates pressure. Some believe native birds suffer from the competition, or from diseases spread by the foreigners. John C. Phillips, pondering this, wrote: "If sportsmen can procure a new bird without endangering the native species unduly, there is no reason they should not have it. But they must realize that it will take many years to evaluate properly the ultimate worth of any introduced species."

ORNAMENTAL. Its native land unknown, the ringed turtle dove, above, is domesticated throughout the world. Today a colony lives in a wild state in Los Angeles. The mute swan of Europe, below, is now established on Long Island.

A PHOTOGRAPHIC FIRST. To my knowledge this is the first time a wild European Goldfinch has been photographed on American soil. Although introductions of this Finch have failed, a small colony survived until recently on Long Island.

ROMANCE IN CENTRAL PARK. The right-hand bird, a wild hybrid between a mallard and a gadwall has chosen as his lady love a female black duck. Audubon painted such a bird and called it the Bemaculated duck, thinking it a new species.

ITS TRADE MARK is the mark on its bill. Like most other gulls, the ring-bill approves of big cities and finds an easy living along the polluted waterfront.

Birds Among the Skyscrapers

THOUSANDS of birds over Manhattan's desert of skyscrapers at daybreak! Most people are sleeping too soundly at that early hour to be aware of the faint chips, chirps and lisps that shower from the dim but lightening sky. The heart of New York City is hardly the place where one would expect to find large numbers of migrating wanderers. Chicago has its Lincoln Park, and Boston its Public Gardens, but New York boasts the most famous birdtrap of all—Central Park. This two and one-half mile long park, set like a narrow oblong emerald among Gotham's towers, is, at times, an amazing place for birds. More than 220 species have been recorded there.

Most small birds migrate at night. Clear, warm nights in late April or early May are best, evenings with a gentle breeze from the southwest, especially after a spell of poor weather. These are the nights when the small travelers by the hundreds of thousands sweep northward up the globe, unseen. When dawn approaches they drop into the trees nearest at hand. But imagine the predicament of those following the northeastern flyway, when they reach this metropolitan area at daybreak!

What a discouraging outlook for a small, tried bird! By the weak eastern light nothing can be discerned but a vast arid jumble of steel and stone, cut by sterile gorges and steep canyons. In the distance a blur of green becomes dimly visible—Central Park. Some nearly exhausted birds may drop down to the few bushes in Washington Square or even to a scraggly ailanthus in a Greenwich Village courtyard, but most of them struggle on until they reach the more promising oasis of the park.

The park policeman pounding his beat and the homeless unfortunate sprawling on a bench are not the only humans astir at that hour. There are the bird watchers, too; and if it is the month of May, scores of them. To appreciate the force of the attraction, you need only to drape yourself on the rail of the bridge at the head of the park lake on a May dawn. The calls of the birds shower out of the purplish half-light, weakly and from a great height, at first; but as visibility increases the birds drop lower, and an occasional dim form can be seen pitching into the nearest trees. During the minutes that follow, the chorus of song gradually swells until the voices of scores of birds are blended to greet the morning sun as it rises and glows from the direction of Fifth Avenue.

The biggest concentration point is "the Ramble," two verdant acres threaded by winding paths and a trickling stream between 72nd and 77th Streets, near the American Museum of Natural History. Being more remote from the main automobile boulevards and with a heavier growth of trees, it is the logical place for a bird to wander into.

Many people take a turn or two about the Ramble before office hours. Others, less determined, wander in at nine or ten o'clock. These miss half the fun. The binocular is the badge of their brotherhood and anyone with a pair can be confidently approached on a basis of friendship. "Birdmen" (airmen are really "manbirds") are as gregarious as the flocks they follow, although some find more pleasure in foraging alone.

A few years ago a prothonotary warbler, a bird of southern swamps, with burnished gold head and breast, put in an appearance. It remained for days and could always be located by the large ring of admirers surrounding it. Their unabashed enthusiasm had its effect on some of the casual strollers. Because of that one golden bird a number of people took up the study of birds.

The record for Central Park is seventy-nine species in one day. Surely an eightieth must have been around somewhere. A blanket of fog hanging low over the city that dawn had confused a horde of birds that would otherwise have gained Van Cortlandt Park or the woods of Westchester County. Early in the morning, when I left my lodgings in Brooklyn, I could hear and see many small birds flying low in the fog, barely clearing the tops of the buildings. Late that afternoon, after my classes at the Art Student's League, I hurried to the park to find it jammed with birds—not only in the Ramble, but from 59th Street all the way to the north end of the park.

At 110th Street, where they had been stopped in their tree-to-tree wanderings by the forbidding wall of buildings, the branches buzzed with birds. Overawed, the bewildered observers could only look about and gasp. Imagine half a dozen vivid scarlet tanagers in a single tree and four smart-looking rose-breasted grosbeaks in another! In the row of bushes outside the old Casino, now torn down, I saw all five species of brown thrushes. Even the woodcock, that long-nosed recluse, was there. One flushed from a bridle path, and four others were found in other parts of the park.

Rarities often remain for several days. I once saw a dickcissel, a bird of the mid-western prairies, consorting in a patch of ragweed with a flock of English sparrows. The first Bewick's wren ever recorded in New York State was seen in the park. For several days it passed as a Carolina wren (there are many on the Palisades across the river), until its sibilant, song-sparrow-like melody was heard. Few singers have risen to fame so rapidly.

One day an excited woman reported a chicken-sized bird with a purple breast, greenish wings, yellow legs and a red and blue bill. It swam, and climbed along the branches of the willow trees, she said. Investigation proved her fantastic description to be absolutely correct. It was a purple gallinule, a bird of the southern rice fields and swamps—the first one recorded in New York State in forty-nine years. We were so excited when we heard about it at the Linnaean meeting that the whole Bronx County Bird Club hurried up the 110th Street lake, even though it was eleven o'clock at night. We saw the bird silhouetted against the reflections of Harlem's street light on the water, pumping its head as it swam, in typical gallinule fashion.

Not every day is a good bird watching day in Central Park, however. On some mornings the Ramble is almost birdless. Migrants seem to come in "waves." The migration watchers study the high and low pressure areas on the weather maps and try to predict these waves.

During the summer, little more than starlings, grackles, flickers, sparrows and robins can be found in the park. Winter is dull, too, but sometimes an unusual bird strays in. For two winters a barred owl perched every day in the same tree above a squirrel box, near 77th Street. It became one of the sights of Fifth Avenue and bus conductors pointed it out to their passengers.

My best find in winter was among the ducks on the 59th Street lake.

In an ice-free patch of water, roped off from skaters, several hundred wild black ducks gather to share the food thrown to the swans and tame mallards. Sometimes a wild baldpate, pintail or shoveller drops in, creating a striking picture of wildlife against the towering skyline dominated by the Sherry-Netherland Hotel. One January day I noted a strange new duck, something like a mallard, but grayer, with a green crown and tan cheeks. I passed it by as one of the innumerable domestic hybrids that mingle with the wild birds on the pond. Later, I realized this was the same duck which Audubon had painted and which he called the bemaculated or Brewer's duck. Audubon had picked up a specimen that had been shot somewhere in Louisiana, and what he had was a hybrid between the mallard and the gadwall. The bird on the 59th Street pond was Audubon's "bemaculated duck," feather for feather, a hybrid so rare that there is not a single specimen in the vast collection of *Anatidae* in the American Museum of Natural History. The "payoff" came in late February, when the imminence of spring manifested itself in gonadal disturbances among the ardent drakes who would soon leave for more northern ponds. The bemaculated duck, a natural hybrid between the gadwall and the mallard, chose as his inamorata a wild hen black duck. He rushed this way and that, chasing all male blacks away. After much maneuvering, I took the picture of the blissful couple which is printed in this book. What wouldn't I have given to see what their offspring were like!

Strange birds, escaped from zoos, pet shops and aviaries, sometimes roam the park. Brazilian cardinals, waxbills and even parrots have been seen. A few years ago a European chaffinch spent the winter amicably with a flock of English sparrows. One day a curator at the American Museum came across a bewildered group of birders staring goggle-eyed at a pied hornbill from India! On another occasion Allan Cruickshank rushed into my office and announced excitedly that a strange duck had dropped into the small lake behind the Art Museum. In all his twenty years of birding he had never seen anything like it. Together we hurried to the pond. The "duck," which puzzled us both for awhile, turned out to be a maned goose from Australia, free flying, but obviously an "escape."

Birds turn up in odd spots all over the crowded island of Manhattan. Guy Emerson, Edson Heck and other residents of Greenwich Village, have made surprising lists of birds around their homes where hardly anything but a ginkgo or an ailanthus tree will grow. One November there was an invasion of dovekies, the little auk that usually spends the winter far at sea. Easterly gales had forced them inland and several were found swimming in rain-flooded gutters. I have seen a barred owl in a tree outside the City Hall, a tiny saw-whet owl on Riverside Drive, a great blue heron flying down Fifth Avenue and a flock of curlew over Greenwich Village. One morning a woodcock came to rest on a fourth-story ledge of the General Motors Building outside the former offices of the National Audubon Society. Cynical newspaper photographers who had been sent to cover the story, thought the bird had been "planted" for the sake of the publicity. But anything can happen in New York. John Kieran tells of an old-squaw duck that fluttered from under the seat of an inbound Coney Island subway train.

At least a dozen peregrine falcons spent the winter among the towers of New York in former years, taking tribute from the flocks of plump lazy pigeons that befoul the ledges. One winter, a young red-tailed hawk spent two or three months around the Metropolitan Museum, perching above the ornate façade, where I could watch it from my office window across the street.

On some misty evenings hundreds of small birds can be seen fluttering through the brilliant lights that illuminate the tall towers of Radio City. During spring and fall, many birds come to the Gardens of the Nations high up on this modern Tower of Babel. On autumn nights, when the wind is in the northwest, I sometimes take the elevator to the observation platform, sixty-odd stories above the street. There, far below, the city lights are strung like jewels to the hazy horizon, while close about me in the blackness I can hear the small voices of southbound migrants. For a few brief moments I feel as if I were one of them.

On a warm fall day a number of years ago a south-bound hermit thrush, weary of picking its way through the bewildering canyons of New York, descended to the sidewalk on Madison Avenue at the southeast corner of 63rd Street. The display of palms and flowers in the shop of Christatos & Koster must have suggested to the thrush its tropical destination, and it flew in through the open transom, taking refuge in a secluded corner.

All through the winter the bird led a happy existence and finally became so tame it would alight on anyone's hand to secure a meal worm.

Marco, as he was christened for no accountable reason, had many admirers who used to drop in to pay their respects. The following spring he was restless and one day, when the transom windows were open, he departed. His friends hoped that he had gotten safely out of New York and joined his fellow hermit thrushes in their flight to the cool northern woods.

Two years later, during the fall migration, a hermit thrush appeared in front of the very same shop. He allowed himself to be picked up and brought in, and the proprietor and his employees insisted it was Marco who had returned. I myself saw the bird and it really seemed as though it must have been the same Marco, for he had already fallen into his old habits and came to the hand for food. Furthermore, it is well known from banded birds, that many individuals return to the same spot each winter. If this was Marco, why did he skip a year before returning?

The small songbirds, like Marco, that become entrapped by the metropolis, cannot be called normal residents. They are not like the ever-present gulls that have adapted their ecology to the cities along the coasts and the Great Lakes. At any time of day gulls may be seen floating over New York's skyscrapers—herring gulls in winter, laughing gulls in summer—trading between the East River and the Hudson—or merely flying over Central Park to the 86th Street reservoir to take a fresh-water bath.

The very best spot for gulls was the sewer outlet at 92nd Street in Brooklyn. For a number of years the little gull (*Larus minutus*), a tiny European species with smoky-black wing linings, had been seen with the buoyant Bonaparte's gulls, snatching tidbits that well up in the sordid flow. Here in the Narrows, where immigrants get their first view of the Statue of Liberty, I have seen both this and another European, the black-headed gull. Curiously enough, the other place on the Atlantic coast of the U. S. where these two rare *Laridae* from the other side can be depended on is also at a sewer outlet, at Newburyport, Massachusetts. There, for twenty-five years, the black-headed gull, which looks like a largish Bonaparte's gull with a red bill, has been found off the end of the pipe that dumps its waste into the Merrimac.

My first little gull, the first one ever seen in Pennsylvania, I discovered on a cold winter's day at the foot of State Street, in Erie, where warm industrial waste kept the ice open. So if we are to define the preferred ecological niche of these Old-World stragglers in America we might truthfully say—sewer outlets!

Can these transatlantic visitors be birds that came to the great Port of New York as stowaways on ships? Louis Halle tells me he once saw a song sparrow fly aboard a banana boat on which he was traveling while it was off the Jersey coast. It remained on the vessel until it was within sight of Central America, whence it took off for some nearby islands. It was then well within the coastal waters of the Republic of Honduras. If an ornithologist had been on shore when this waif arrived he would have recorded the first song sparrow for that country. This sort of thing must happen often, for during migration nearly every ship carries bird passengers. Perhaps this, rather than the presence of cage bird dealers in the city, may explain some of the occurrences of exotic birds in Central Park.

But the gulls, most likely, make the trans-Atlantic journey unaided. Several black-headed gulls, banded in Europe, have found their way to the New World. Miss May Thatcher Cooke reported that of the many banded birds known to have crossed the ocean, more than one third have been kittiwakes, the little pearly winged gulls whose wing-tips look as though they had been dipped in ink. Kittiwakes banded in the British Isles have reached the Maritime Provinces of Canada, and kittiwakes banded by the Russians on the Arctic Sea were shot in Newfoundland.

This is the froth that makes banding exciting. It is like discovering a flamingo in the Bronx. But there are thousands of less spectacular records, bricks that help build the mansion of ornithology. At least 250,000 herring gulls have been banded on this side of the Atlantic—many thousands with colored bands. In this, the greatest color-marking project ever tried, young gulls were banded in nine different colonies from Long Island Sound to the Gulf of St. Lawrence. The birds of one colony were marked with a black band on one leg and a red one on the other; the birds of another colony with a blue band above a yellow one, and so on. The next year each colony was given a different combination. By the end of the third year it was possible to see gulls with any one of twenty-seven different combinations of colors on their legs.

The first person to spot one of these marked gulls around New York City was John Kieran. On his way to the subway one autumn morning he put his glass on the newly arrived gulls that covered the field at Van

Cortlandt Park and discovered that two of them wore colored bracelets. In the weeks that followed we could always find three or four color-banded gulls along the water front at Fulton Fish Market in downtown Manhattan, and one day in early winter, Joseph Hickey, who promoted the scheme, and I found sixteen, representing six different colonies on the garbage dump at Floyd Bennett Field near Brooklyn.

This was the first time all bird watchers could take part in a banding project. Much was learned about the sequence of plumages from brown young birds to pearly adults and something about the pattern of their migration, too; but, hardly ten years later, not a single colored band could be found. This does not mean that all the thousands of birds were dead, for we know of a captive herring gull (his name was "Kaiser") that lived for forty-nine years. What happened was that eventually the celluloid bands disintegrated. More recently herring gulls have been sprayed with colored dyes to make them conspicuous to bird-watchers.

It is a standing jest among bird watchers along the coast that there is no place like a good garbage dump for birds. Among my favorite sites in years past have been the dumps at Dyker Heights in Brooklyn, at Newark Bay and at Hunt's Point in the Bronx. There have been others, too, but these in particular bring fond, though odoriferous memories. During one of their cyclic eruptions there were four snowy owls at the Hunt's Point dump. Some might say they frequented the place for concealment because they resembled packages of garbage wrapped in newspaper—white with black print—but a more likely reason was the abundance of rats. One winter we had twelve short-eared owls in the marsh adjacent to this dump and that, mind you, was deep inside metropolitan New York, along the bustling East River, with gas tanks and apartment houses crowding in on all sides.

Leonard Dubkin, in his *Murmur of Wings*, has shown that even where the heavy hand of urbanization has locked the green world into a sarcophagus of cement and stone, there are opportunities to watch birds—even if only house sparrows or starlings. But most cities compromise with nature a little more than New York and Chicago do. Washington, D.C., is virtually a city in the woods. John Burroughs wrote of it in *Wake Robin:* "There is perhaps not another city in the Union that has on its very threshold so much natural beauty and grandeur such as men seek for in the

NOCTURNAL BALLET. No bird is found more widely throughout the world than the barn owl. Resident of every continent except Antarctica, this owl hides fearfully from man in his barns, church belfries and old towers.

THREE OF A KIND. These young barn owls will soon be ready
to venture into the black world of the night, where with silent wings
and spring-trap claws they will become the nemesis of all mice.

remote forests and mountains." Theodore Roosevelt, during his term of office in Washington, made a list of the birds he saw on the White House grounds. If anything, there are more birds in the nation's capital now than when these men lived there. Burroughs spoke of the cardinal as a shy bird —an uncommon sight. And the mockingbird was almost unknown in Washington then. Now both can be found among the ornamental plantings of the government buildings in the very heart of town.

I feel certain that as our cities grow older they will harbor more birds, not fewer. As the newness and rawness wear off, species after species that has fled the carpenter and the mason will return to find their niches in the aging trees and gardens, just as the birds in the Old World cities have done. I am assuming, however, that we will learn to curb our misuse of toxic chemicals now so lethal to birds in some suburban areas.

Ghoulies and Ghoosties

GUY EMERSON had not yet seen a white-crowned sparrow for the year. This in itself seemed excuse enough for our drive into rural Maryland that bright October Sunday. As if by appointment, we found our bird, a young one, tan with a pink bill, right where we parked the car outside the Fish and Wildlife Research Laboratories at Bowie. Our objective attained, we sauntered into the narrow brick building where the millions of bird banding records are kept. There we found Joseph Hickey hard at work, as he always seemed to be, day or night, on his doctor's thesis. Emerson, fascinated by the intricate filing system, asked Hickey if he might see the barn owl cards, particularly those from Massachusetts. Joe dumped the stack of barn owl cards into the IBM sorting machine and, with a rapid shuffling motion, the Massachusetts cards dropped out. The first card that popped forth was that of a young bird banded near Emerson's home on Martha's Vineyard. He had seen this very bird, and, by a curious coincidence, so had I, a year later, but not at Martha's Vineyard. The card recorded that the owl was recaptured as a nesting female in an old coal elevator in the Bronx nearly 200 miles away.

The card with its formal telegraphic data evoked memories of a full moon shining on the water among the dark river wharves, on the night that Irving Kassoy took me up the rickety ladder into the tower to see his new owl family. I remember how excited he was when he discovered later that the female wore a band—one that he had not put there! For weeks he tried to catch the owl to read its number. We all offered advice, but it was not until Mike Oboiko set up one of his squirrel traps that the mystery of the bird's origin was solved.

Kassoy was the historian of several barn owls that had lived in the Bronx; he watched these mystery birds for years, and some of his friends in the Linnaean Society said (much to his irritation) that he was beginning to look like an owl. Perhaps his glasses and look of quiet wisdom created this illusion. Like Huxley, Kassoy believed we should "smite every humbug," and over a period of years he dispelled more notions and unearthed more new facts about the barn owl than any man before him.

Kassoy once worked in a midtown Manhattan jeweler's firm. After long days devoted to diamond rings and Swiss watches he would hurry to his owl observatory in the Bronx—in the old Huntington mansion at Pelham Bay. Night after night he kept his lonesome vigil, under the eaves with the "ghoulies and ghoosties, long-leggety beasties, and things that go bump in the night."

I met him one evening after work. He had a necklace to deliver on Park Avenue before we plunged below the street level and boarded the IRT subway for the Bronx. At 125th Street we changed from the lurching local to the Pelham Bay express. While we hung from the swaying straps, shoved and pushed by the evening crush of commuters, Kassoy told me something of the history of his birds. There was a new female, he said. The previous female had been frightened from the building by some workmen. It was daytime, and crows mobbed the bewildered bird. They drove her to the water of Eastchester Bay; then the gulls closed in and finished her off. Apparently even the birds look upon *Tyto* with suspicion, as a bird of ill omen, to be attacked and destroyed. Perhaps that is why barn owls live in church belfries so often, I mused—for, like outcasts of old who sought sanctuary in the temple, they can find refuge there. Certainly, I reflected, they are nonsectarion, for I had seen barn owls in the square tower of a synagogue in Alexandria, Virginia, in a fashionable Episcopal Church at Rye, New York, in a little white Baptist Church on the east coast of Florida and in a famous old Franciscan mission in California.

But whereas some barn owls seek sanctified, holy places, others live in a gloomy, almost evil atmosphere. Such a place was the abandoned Huntington estate, five minutes' walk from the end of the Pelham Bay line. We had long known the place, because it was there that, on the Christmas census, we always saw our night herons, a hundred or more, crouched disconsolately in the somber branches of the Norway spruces inside the wall. We never climbed that wall because into its broad top had been cemented thousands of pieces of broken glass, a jagged hint to trespassers. But now the estate is park property and Kassoy had permission to enter the big house. He flashed a light into the spreading, silvery limbed beech tree where the owls often perched, but they were not there. He swung the bright beam over to the eaves of the house. There was the ventilator hole through which the birds gained access to the ivy-covered building. We could hear the young ones calling for food, a rasping, sucking sound that has been likened to an ill-mannered person imbibing soup.

We passed through the big gate and Kassoy went over to the caretaker's house to get the key which hung on a nail inside the door. The caretaker believed the house was haunted, and I am sure he thought Kassoy was quite mad, sitting up there night after night by himself. We went up two flights, lifted a trap-door and tiptoed across the attic floor. In the corner, Kassoy knelt over a box. He turned a switch attached to a dry cell battery and a tiny light illuminated the dim interior of the box. Huddled there were five of the most grotesque owlets I had ever seen, like little monkeys in fuzzy bedclothes with white caps pulled about their ears. In size they were like stepping stones, for young barn owls usually hatch two days apart.

The top of the box was a pane of glass treated so that the owls saw only their reflections, while we could see them and remain unseen ourselves—a sort of a two-way mirror—the same device that has been used in zoos to make monkeys act natural, unstimulated or uninhibited by their unseen audience. Kassoy is probably the only man who has ever been eye-witness to some of the intimacies of the adult barn owls—even their actual mating. He was amazed to find how closely the courtship cycle was synchronized with the full of the moon. Indeed, he found he could predict within a day or two when the first egg would be laid.

When I called the owlets grotesque, he was indignant. To him they were beautiful babies. Perhaps they were. But no one, seeing an adult barn owl at close range, can deny that it is beautiful. When painting it I have marveled at the soft blendings of rufous and gray, sprinkled with tiny dots, and the liquid brown eyes set deep in the white heart-shaped face. I can see why some people call it the "monkey-faced owl," but a monkey, by contrast, is wizened, wrinkled and homely. If it must have a nickname, I prefer "golden owl."

For many months Kassoy had been climbing up there. His heart would skip faster at the scampering of rats or the sudden thunderclap of a summer storm, but usually all was empty silence broken only by the periodic rumble of a distant train pulling into the station. Night after night, 200 or more, he hunched over his box like some immobile Buddha, his face, reflecting the wan light, the only thing visible in the blackness. A loud rasping cry, like a banshee with laryngitis, told him that one of the old birds was in the big beech outside. In a moment, it would magically appear in the box, like an apparition, a meadow mouse (*microtus*), dangling from its beak, or a rat from the garbage dump out on the Eastchester marshes.

The nest was strewn with bits of fur and bones. Although owls swallow their mice whole, the strong digestive action soon rolls the bones up in a felt-like wad of fur and this the bird coughs up with a struggle. These pellets have a wet, varnished look at first but are soon broken up and trodden into a foul carpet by the young birds. The pellets on the attic floor were the best contact Kassoy had with his pets between seasons when they were not nesting. Like a detective, he would dissect each one for clues. He could tell how well the birds had been eating and how lately they had been roosting in the attic. Most of the pellets held two skulls apiece, nearly all of them rodents with their long curved incisors; but occasionally he found an English sparrow, and once a phoebe.

With no brood of his own at the time, the young owls became to Kassoy as his own family. When two or three of the babies toddled out of the ventilator shaft one night and were dashed to their death on the hard ground below, he was grieved for days. When the owls laid again he built a little porch and railing as a safeguard. One brood was started so late that it was early January before they flew and starvation faced the family. Worried about his charges, he broke track through the deep snow one blustery night with two pounds of raw beefsteak under his arm, only to find that the keeper had locked up his house. He could not get the key, so he scattered the pieces of meat over the snow.

Year by year Kassoy grew to love the old place more and more. While waiting for the owls he spent long hours with his thoughts. There were times, though, when his subconscious seemed to be playing tricks on him.

For example, once he had stayed in the mansion long past midnight. It was probably two or three o'clock but it was a Sunday morning and he could sleep late. He had fallen into a doze when a door slammed downstairs. He knew he was the only one with a key. Footsteps crossed the big empty library. Step by step they came up the first flight of stairs and started up the second. Kassoy's hair stood out above his ears, like the back hairs of a dog at bay. The sounds paused just below the trapdoor. Just then one of the owls popped through the ventilator into the nest, and Kassoy, like a true scientific investigator, put all else from his mind and concentrated on the little drama in the lighted box below him. When the owl left, he listened again. The footsteps had stopped, nor did he hear them after that. He has wondered about it ever since.

The barn owl whose portrait is shown in this book, another of Kassoy's birds, was flashed just as it took off on its first flight. It had been raised in a dovecote, much to the unhappiness of the pigeons who were in a constant state of panic.

All owls are weirdly beautiful, from the big white snowies that come down along the beaches on their cyclic winter invasions, to the mysterious little fellows that live in the desert mountains, but the barn owl is more truly "owlish" than any of the others. At Cape May, New Jersey, lying on my back among the dunes near the boardwalk, I have squeaked them overhead, while their ghostly forms reflected the light from the street lamps. Some day I should like to see a phosphorescent barn owl, a rare but well-authenticated phenomenon. The phosphorescence is not an illusion but is believed to be caused by fungi that impregnate the rotten wood of the cavities where the owls hide in the daytime. The oxidation of the mycelium of these fungi causes the unearthly glow or cold light that has been called "fox fire."

I cannot imagine how such an owl would look, but a barn owl always seems as eery as a golliwog, whether it is hunting amongst the rows of stately palms in southern California where it snatches up the palm rats as they clatter over the dead fronds, or is perched high on the rafters of a rickety ice house along the Hudson (they say that the invention of the automatic refrigerator, and the consequent abandonment of these ice houses, extended the range of the barn owl to Albany).

One of the most widely distributed birds in the world, the barn owl is found on every continent. There are caves in South America, which, to judge by the thick deposits of debris, have probably been occupied by them for centuries, perhaps for thousands of years. In 1934, Sir George Court-hope wrote in the foreword of *The Barn Owl in England and Wales,* by G. B. Blaker:

"There is an old tree near my home where barn owls have bred all my life. Some fifty years ago, my grandfather told me that his grandfather told him that they had bred in the same tree all his life—he was born in 1737."

Two centuries of continuous occupancy!

In Flushing, New York, owls inhabited a church belfry from 1880 to 1926—forty-six years. That is quite a record, but the most famous barn owls in this country are the ones that live in the northeast tower of the old Smithsonian building in Washington. An egg in the National Museum was taken from there one hundred years ago, and barn owls have been in residence ever since. Dr. A. K. Fisher, in making his classic study of the food habits of the hawks and owls, gathered great numbers of pellets that littered the floor of the loft. One small species of rodent, the harvest mouse, was first known to occur in the District of Columbia when its skull was found in a pellet. Alexander Wetmore, formerly Secretary of the Institution, once issued instructions that no one was to clean up the tower. It was to be left just as it is—a permanent haven for owls.

Eagle Man

*W*HEN Charles Broley reached sixty, he retired. He had been manager of a bank in Winnipeg for twenty-five years, and sixty is the traditional age for bankers to quit. It is also traditional for men of means who have passed the three-score mark to go to the west coast of Florida, to towns like Tampa or Saint Petersburg, to enjoy their well-earned rest. En route south, at Audubon House in New York, Broley met Richard Pough, affable host to all the visiting birdmen who stop there on Fifth Avenue. At lunch, Pough suggested he try banding a few Florida eagles. It was only a casual suggestion, but Broley seized on it. He was looking for some project as this. All his life he had been an active man, even though he had been a banker; he couldn't picture himself just sitting in the sun. In the whole history of bird banding prior to this chance visit, only 166 bald eagles had ever been marked. In the active years that followed Broley banded more than 1200.

The first season he banded forty-four eagles. To his great surprise, one of the bands was soon returned from Columbiaville, New York, 1,100 miles away. Ornithologists took notice when other returns came from points equally distant. One bird banded at MacDill Field Army Air Base in Tampa was found shot in the Province of New Brunswick, nearly 1,600 miles away. It had last been seen at the Air Base hardly more than a month before. Another bird reached Prince Edward Island in the Gulf of St. Lawrence.

Broley's banding taught us that Florida bald eagles, like typical American tourists, spent the winter months in Florida (Broley did his banding in January and February) and the summer in the cool north. There are no

OUR NATIONAL EMBLEM, the bald eagle, is more numerous in Florida than in any other state except Alaska. Unlike Alaska, Florida cherishes its eagles, but in the last decade reproduction has been poor.

POWERFUL in its new coat of dark feathers, this young bald eagle defied Broley when he sought to band it. It is one of 1200 young eagles that had been banded by the Canadian ornithologist.

REGAL, even though not yet strong a-wing, is this eleven weeks old youngster. Like all young Florida bald eagles, it will start in a few weeks on its summer trek to the northern states and maritime Canada, as Broley's banding has proved.

TOUGH was eagle man Broley, climbing to an eyrie in a Florida pine, and so was the eleven-weeks-old eagle at the upper right. Broley preferred to band his birds when they were four or five weeks old, like the one at the lower right.

eagles in Florida during the hot summer months. The hawk watchers at Cape May and at Hawk Mountain see these same eagles heading home in September. We always thought this September flight of bald eagles was northern birds, but the bigger, more powerfully built northern birds probably do not come down until much later, perhaps not until winter, when we see them riding the ice floes that choke the Merrimac, the Hudson and the Delaware.

Broley had not originally intended to do the rough work himself. Instead, he hired a boy to climb for him. The lad climbed the first tree; but when he raised himself over the rim of the nest, the large young eagle reared back, ready to strike with its big yellow claw. Frightened, the boy reached for a stick to strike. Broley could not countenance this; he would have to find a way to climb the tree himself, so he devised a system of ropes and ladders.

When I wrote Broley that I was coming to watch him band his eagles he replied:

"Bring your oldest clothes as I always have burnt-over territory to work in and many of the trees are burned and black part way up, and with the pine rosin running on hot days I certainly am a mess. High boots are also advisable. I killed a five-foot rattler last Tuesday and last February I stepped right on a big one. If you intend to climb up to some of the nests with me I would suggest that for three weeks before you come you try chinning a bar until you can go up fifteen times. Work into it gradually— start by chinning yourself three times the first day or two."

We had no chinning bars in our apartment so I used the bathroom door. I struggled up and down its smooth surface and thought, "What a man Broley must be!" Although I was thirty years younger than he, I could hardly pull myself up seven times.

Broley had more than a hundred eyries under his watchful eye in the season of 1946, and we visited forty of them. Many could be reached by little sandy roads that wound through the "flat-woods," but often we had to park the car and pack the forty pounds of cumbersome climbing equipment a long distance through the scrub palmetto and the pines. Most of the nests were in the virile, tortuous-limbed long-leaf pines that give that part of Florida its picturesque, park-like look. I wanted to find an eyrie where I could climb out on a limb and photograph Broley in the nest with a young eagle. Near Placida, in Charlotte County, there was just the right opportunity. A large horizontal branch at nest level would allow me to get out about twelve or fifteen feet from the trunk.

The first big limb was thirty feet from the ground and the thick-set trunk with its rusty scabs of bark was impossible to "shinny." Reaching into his sack, Broley took out a four-ounce lead sinker fastened to a cord. Placing the weight in a spoon attached to a broomstick, he catapulted it over the limb. His accuracy on the first try was explained when he told me that he used to play lacrosse with the Indians in Manitoba. When Broley started eagle banding he pitched the weight over by hand, but one day he threw his arm out, so he employed the broomstick. The weight, falling across the branch, drops to the ground. To the cord is fastened a larger cord; to that a rope, and to the rope is attached a rope ladder. When the ladder is pulled into place it is lashed securely about the base of the tree.

Don't think that a rope ladder is easy to climb. You have to know how. If you climb frontally as on an ordinary ladder, your feet swing forward, and it is very taxing on the arms. The system is to climb the ladder *edge-wise* like a trapeze artist, grasping only one of the vertical ropes and going up "heel and toe" with one foot on either side.

Once up to the first branch, the rest is limb-to-limb climbing, using short lengths of rope to throw over limbs for hoists. Getting over the edge of the nest is often a problem, for the big platforms flare out like huge wine glasses. "Nest No. 23," at St. Petersburg, a "super nest"—twenty feet deep and nine and one-half feet wide—was probably the largest nest in America, exceeding the "Great Eyrie" at Vermilion, Ohio. That famous nest which Doctor Herrick studied was twelve feet deep and eight and one-half feet across its flattened top before it crashed in a storm.

To step up to exceptionally deep nests Broley tossed a short rope ladder over the platform of sticks and secured it. But for most nests he used a sort of shepherd's crook, an iron rod five and one-half feet long with a broad hook which fitted over the edge of the nest. There was a smaller reverse hook at the other end in which to insert his foot.

Our tree was not a hard one to climb and Broley went up first. As his head appeared over the edge of the flight deck, the young eagle, an eleven-weeks-old bird, grew panicky and launched off the other side. As it would have been another three or four days before the eaglet should have flown, it lost altitude rapidly. Broley yelled down to me to watch it. The bird crossed a deep creek and drifted a third of a mile until I lost sight of it in a low spot at the edge of a palmetto hammock.

Broley never left young birds on the ground, for their parents might not feed them there. To save them from predators and from starvation he had been obliged to replace more than thirty youngsters. One day an eaglet jumped out and became tangled in a grapevine. It took an hour to get it back to the nest. Immediately, it hopped out on the stub where its nest mate was perched, then both lost their balance and came flopping into the lake below. They flapped ashore and hid in the dense scrub. By the time Broley got them back up the tree he had spent seven hours. No wonder he had lost as much as seventeen pounds during a single week's banding trip!

This youngster from the Placida nest threatened to be another such problem. We found a way to cross the creek without swimming, but search as we might we could not locate the bird. At the end of two hours, by reorienting ourselves, we discovered it crouching under the fan-like fronds of a saw palmetto. It was a two-man job to get this vinegary full-grown young eagle wrapped up in a piece of cloth so we could transport it back. Broley climbed the tree again and hauled the struggling bird up in its canvas shroud. Replaced in the nest, it calmed down; it had savored enough of adventure for awhile.

I followed up the ladder, reached the nest and, tense and puffing, I edged my way out on the big limb. There was nothing between me and the ground to stop me if I fell. My admiration for Broley's simian abilities grew. He even went out to where I clung nervously and tied me on, so I could use both hands while I took my pictures.

It is exhilarating to perch on *Haliaeetus'* high lookout, usually the strongest and highest tree in the neighborhood. The two or three trees I climbed with Broley commanded magnificent views—great stretches of park-like pine land interlaced by winding tidal creeks or flanked by expansive salt flats, stretching out to the palm-studded shore of the Gulf. The only bald eagle's nest I have ever seen that surpassed these in grandeur was one the Craighead twins showed me on the banks of the turbulent Snake River in Wyoming where the snowy alp-like peaks of the Grand Tetons formed an unbelievable stage backdrop for the King of Birds. But bald eagle nests are rarely seen in the western mountains. That is the realm of the golden eagle.

I have visited eyries in a dozen states and have climbed to a few. When I visited the one in Vermilion, Ohio, Dr. Herrick's famous steel tower had been dismantled, but I did ascend a similar tower that had been erected by C.C.C. boys beside a nest at Bombay Hook, Delaware. The young having flown, I left my camera on the ground; but when I reached the platform, one of the eagles flew over within twenty feet, strafed and dive-bombed by two hot-tempered little kingbirds. This would have been the picture of all pictures, had I not left my camera below.

Very young baby eagles, still covered with pale whitish down, are too small to band since the large aluminum bracelets slip off. Broley banded most of his young birds when they were between three and six weeks old. Then they are easiest to handle and are padded with a heavy dark felt-like down, almost like wool, with the dark budding feathers poking through here and there. Sometimes he had not been able to visit an eyrie until the eaglets were ten or eleven weeks old. These powerful youngsters, sleek in their new coats of glossy dark feathers, were full of fight. Several times they sunk their sharp talons completely through Broley's hands, and he had to employ his banding pliers to force them out. Once a young bird grasped his hand and while he was intent on prying the talons loose, the bird suddenly threw its other foot into Broley's face. Two of the sharp sickle-like hooks narrowly missed each eye, and a third sunk deep into his scalp. With blood streaming down his face, he worked out of that predicament; but he didn't ever quite know how he managed it. So the report was not far wrong that Broley was "scarred from head to foot," or, as one local newspaper stated, through a typographical error, "Mr. Broley is scared from head to foot." Broley learned to avoid the vice-like handshake by certain ju-jitsu tactics which rendered the young birds helpless while he put on the bands.

He was never attacked by an adult bald eagle. Such stories are a part of fiction and folklore. The worried parents flew back and forth at a safe distance, muttering to themselves in a low *kak-kak-kak-kak* or in a high-pitched creaking cackle *kweek-kuk-kuk, kweek-a-kuk-kuk* with the quality of an unoiled castor, hardly the defiant scream one would expect from an eagle.

Great horned owls, on the other hand, were vicious actors. Broley had several scrapes with owls which had taken over eagles' nests for their own use. One of these aggressive silent-winged birds, striking him unawares, left the gashes of every claw in his back, and nearly knocked him from the tree. Every year some of the eyries were appropriated by these big owls which are very plentiful in the flat "piny woods." About five per cent of the eyries, or one in twenty, were commandeered, so the owls were the biggest factor in nest failures, according to Broley, except in those seasons when an autumn hurricane blasted out the nests before the owners returned from their northern tour.

One year, a horned owl was found brooding an eagle's egg with one of its own. Broley told of an even more fantastic situation. As he approached one of his nests the female eagle flew off. When he climbed to the great pile of sticks a great horned owl flew off. There, less than three feet apart he found two eggs, one belonging to the owl and one to the eagle. What fierce looks must have been exchanged by the two stubborn birds as they incubated only an arm's length from each other! Torrential rains flooding the sandy backwoods roads made it impossible to revisit the nest, so Broley never knew what the outcome was.

Broley found that his Florida eagles ate little else besides fish which made up more than ninety per cent of their diet, but one pair—the birds in nest No. 35—were very partial to scaup ducks. This was an exception, however, and not at all typical. Another family with unusual eating habits lived in nest No. 86. These birds had an appetite for brown pelicans and great blue herons! Hardly a year passed that Broley did not find the remains of one of the huge herons in the nest. Both the pelican and the great blue have a wing spread near that of an eagle, but they weigh less, six and one-half to seven and one-half pounds (the limit an eagle can lift) against the eagle's own weight of eight to twelve pounds. Such fare seemed to do something to the young eagles in nest No. 86 for they were by far the toughest and most ornery youngsters Broley had to deal with.

Like other winter residents, Florida bald eagles are great curio collectors. Broley had taken from their nests large electric light bulbs, a clorox bottle, a tennis shoe, a child's dress, a gunny sack, a snap clothespin, corn cobs, whelk shells, silk panties, and a copy of *The American Weekly*. A fish plug and a seventy-foot fishline were probably brought to the nest with fish. In one nest Broley found a white rubber ball which the female did her best to incubate six weeks after her two young were hatched.

The bald eagle's distribution is spotty. Coastal Alaska has the greatest number, the Great Lakes a few score, Maine a few dozen, and there are smaller concentrations in the Santa Barbara Islands, along the northwest coast and elsewhere. In spite of states rights, some commonwealths do not have even one pair of nesting eagles. It is said that there used to be a pair of bald eagles for nearly every mile of shore line in the Potomac-Chesapeake area in Virginia and Maryland, a density of eagles as great as that in western Florida. Bryant Tyrrell, who knew this population well, estimated that as recently as twenty years ago there were probably at least 200 pairs. I knew of three nests within five miles of Washington, D.C., and while taking a Christmas Bird Count I have seen eighteen birds in a day on the ice-choked Potomac. It is appropriate that our nation's capital should be one of the strongholds of the national bird.

There are some who would side with Benjamin Franklin in disputing the bald eagle's fitness to be our national emblem. Professor Francis Herrick, in his brilliant defense, if defense be needed, writes: "He nests high, as near to the sun as he can get, like a true bird of Jove and messenger of the star of day. He is a model parent and probably spends more time—upwards of six months—in rearing his family and giving his progeny a fair start in life than any other bird known to this continent." And, besides all this, the bald eagle is a true native son, found the breadth of the Union, and, unlike the golden eagle or "International eagle," is almost unknown outside, except in the land of our friendly neighbor, Canada.

"Our eagle has been outlawed, robbed, shot, dissected, painted, modeled and mounted for museums, while its comings and goings have been carefully noted by observers for over a century." So wrote Herrick, in his classic monograph, *The American Eagle*. To Charles L. Broley, a Canadian, went the distinction of adding most to the growing accumulation of knowledge of our national bird.

Broley estimated that there were more than 400 eyries in Florida. There was a time when half of them were robbed each year by oologists who traded the eggs off to other oologists. A friend of mine who visited one of these oological kleptomaniacs in Florida a few years ago was shocked when his host drew from beneath a table a bucket, brimful of eagles' eggs, the loot of one season's climbing. And a nesting eagle lays only two eggs! That sort of thing had stopped in Florida, and Broley had lost none of his birds to eggers. He gave the heart-warming news that ninety-five per cent of the residents in Florida liked eagles and wanted to protect them. They regarded them as an asset to the state, a valuable attraction to the tourist trade. In timber lots that have been logged, eagle trees have been left standing, and as evidence of pro-eagle sentiment I saw two or three nests on golf courses. In the center of a colorful gladiolus farm, stood a lone tree, the only one spared when the fields were cleared, because it held an eagle's nest in its grasp. In a nearby town another pair of eagles occupied an aerial castle in a dead tree now surrounded by houses. The town had grown up around it, and the vacant lot where the tall twisted tree stood was for sale, but the man next door, who feared for the eagles if the lot were sold, discouraged prospective buyers by informing them that the land was so low it formed a lake when it rained!

The most remarkable nest of all was one only a hundred feet from the back porch of a house. It reminded me of ospreys' nests I had seen on cart-wheels atop poles near farm houses at Cape May. Directly beneath was a chicken pen, unscreened at the top, but the eagles did not bother the large white leghorns that strutted within, nor the numerous English sparrows that built their trashy nurseries in the sides of the eagles' own great nest.

In Sarasota, I saw two large young eagles standing in a nest in a big pine behind the high school. The boys were weeding their victory garden beneath the tree, and a neat white sign read:

BALD EAGLES
Do Not Disturb
Order of Chief of Police

When Broley first started his work he was arrested several times before the police knew him. Once, while he was climbing to a nest, the defenders of the law received three phone calls from outraged neighbors who thought Broley intended nest robbery. Thereafter he checked in with the police before he started his banding. Local residents came to know him well, and a letter addressed simply to the "Eagle Man," Tampa, Florida, was sure to reach him.

I hope that people elsewhere will follow the enlightened example of

Florida and cherish their eagles before it is too late. Years ago in the British Isles they lost their last sea eagles, the brown-headed European counterpart of our bald eagle which a Russian ornithologist once contended was conspecific with it—merely a race of the same species. In a small country in northwestern Europe, a monument stands where the last pair of sea eagles nested.

Richard Pough, who first suggested to Broley the idea of banding eagles, spent many a sober moment, hoping that he would quit before he had an accident. But Broley was a careful man. He never trusted a rotten limb and tested each branch before he made a move. The tougher the tree the more he enjoyed the problem, even though it sometimes took four or five hours. He was proud that no nest had yet stumped him, even those in cypress trees 115 feet from the ground.

Although he was very reticent about it, he did have one fall. It was at the end of a season of banding. He stood on a chair in the bedroom to put his equipment away on a closet shelf. The chair slipped; Broley hit his head on the bed and was knocked out!

Shortly before his death he noticed a great drop off in reproduction. The last season he banded only a single young bird in Florida. He suspected that the birds were being rendered sterile by insecticides in the food chain. He was dead right. The recent work by the U.S. Fish and Wildlife Service has proven beyond all doubt that our national emblem now faces a danger more serious than any it has known in all its previous history.

Peregrine of the Blood Royal

MAN has emerged from the shadows of antiquity with a peregrine on his wrist. Its dispassionate brown eyes, more than those of any
other bird, have been witness to the struggle for civilization, from the
squalid tents on the steppes of Asia thousands of years ago to the marble
halls of European kings in the seventeenth century.

The peregrine, alone of all the sharp-winged falcon tribe to span the
globe, has been divided into fifteen races in Peter's Check-List of Birds of
the World. They are found on all the continents and on many of the
larger islands. It is unfortunate that our race has been called the duck
hawk, but Alexander Wilson, often acclaimed "the first American ornithologist," did not like the name peregrine (traveler) because he believed
the American bird to be non-migratory. Recently the A.O.U. has voted
to revert to the older name, the one that has always been used in Europe.

We have a second race in America, a very dark one, found in the rain
forest of the Northwest, Peale's peregrine; and the falconers insist that a
third undescribed subspecies, a small blue-backed race from the Arctic
tundra, comes down the Atlantic coast in the fall. I have seen these passage
birds harry the migrating shorebirds. They have a lighter "wing-loading"
than the Appalachian stock, and are so maneuverable that they can literally
turn on a dime.

The most perfect flying machine, the best-constructed bird, the fiercest
(yet, to its trainer, the most gentle), and the fastest bird—all these superla-
tives have been claimed for the peregrine. It may well be the swiftest bird
that flies, but its ordinary cruising speed of forty to sixty miles an hour is
not much greater than that of the pigeons it catches. It is in the "stoop,"

the plunge of several hundred feet when it partially closes its wings and pumps in for the kill, that the peregrine attains the rocket-like speed which has been estimated at between 150 and 200 miles per hour. But swifts in India have been clocked with a stop watch by E. C. Baker at speeds as high as these. On the other hand, a Connecticut farmer reported to Forbush that he saw a duck hawk actually take a chimney swift over his fields. If this observation can be credited, the hawk must be the faster. I have set my Graflex at its top speed, while Luff Meredith exercised his birds on the little landing field at Boonton, New Jersey.. Each time the bird stooped to the lure I tripped the shutter, but all my shots were blurs. A thousandth of a second was much too slow.

Ralph Lawson reports that an aviator whose word he trusts was crusing in a small pursuit plane when he noticed a flock of ducks flying far below him. Turning the nose of his craft toward the flock, he opened the throttle and dived. As he looked to the wing tip to see how great the vibration was, a hawk shot by "as though the plane were standing still" and struck one of the ducks. The plane was traveling at 175 miles per hour, and the hawk seemed to be making twice that speed.

With the use of modern equipment we shall soon learn the exact speed of the stoop. I have been told by two or three of the falconers (who also got their information second or third hand) that during war-time experiments at a Naval Research Laboratory the speed calibrators clocked the stoop of a peregrine at 275 miles per hour. Moreover, when the films were developed, the aeronautical experts were astounded to find that the hawk had been breathing throughout its bullet-like plunge. Some physiologists insisted that this was impossible, that the incoming air stream would burst the bird's lungs like balloons. Closer study of the peregrine's nostrils showed a series of baffles which slowed down the wind from a velocity double that of a violent hurricane to that of a breeze.

I shall long remember the Sunday afternoon when I was shown my first peregrine eyrie on the Palisades. We scanned the dark cliffs with our glasses for the patch of white that splashed the nesting ledge. On a stub to one side perched the bird, its black mustaches and big yellow feet showing plainly. A hundred times since, I have seen the peregrines on the Palisades—so beautifully cut, like giant swallows, with pointed wings, broad shoulders and short necks. I have watched them shoot by with the speed of an arrow, climb upstairs into the blue with rapid beats, wheel on extended wings and drop like a meteor past the nesting ledge. The male can always be distinguished from the female by his size, a third smaller (hence the term, tercel). The two are very noisy around the eyrie, uttering their battle cry, a rapid rasping *cack-cack-cack!*

I always spoke of "the Palisades duck hawk" in those days. I had no idea there were half a dozen between the Fort Lee ferry and West Point. The oologists knew them all, but they kept their secret. The falconers knew, too, but they have long had an understanding among themselves not to molest the Hudson River birds.

It was one of the high points of my quarter of a century of birding to be taken to fourteen eyries in a week-end, the farthest not more than a hundred miles from New York. I even went overside to examine some of the handsome rusty-brown eggs. It takes a good dose of nerve to back off the edge of a 400-foot cliff with nothing but pitons and a half-inch rope for support. The shining river looks so far down, so very far.

The kind of ledge a peregrine likes is high on a sheer cliff, a wall that dominates the countryside, perhaps overlooking a river. I have seen a nest, however, in a ravine so small that you could step down to the ledge with little trouble.

Once peregrines nested in great wind-topped trees along the Mississippi. They still do occasionally. I saw such an eyrie in northern Louisiana, a hundred miles south of any other known nest in eastern North America. The man who directed me to it was nearly blind. He had dimly beheld the silhouette of a sharp-winged bird circling about a tall cypress stub and protesting. He wondered if it could be a Carolina paroquet, but he added that "it sounded just like the duck hawks we have in winter." A week later, Doctor Walter Spofford, who probably has a better understanding of the biology of the peregrine than any other American falconer, showed me another cypress-top eyrie in Tennessee.

Several very odd nesting sites have been recorded. The strangest one of all was on a barrel lying in a marsh near San Francisco Bay. There are recent rumors of peregrines nesting in ospreys' nests, and years ago peregrines' eggs were actually found in a bald eagle's nest in Iowa. In Arctic Russia, peregrines nest on the tundra. Buturlin states that these birds are so fearless in attacking nest robbers, such as gulls and foxes, that ducks and small shorebirds make their homes near them for protection! Falcons strike their quarry from the air, so the ducks and shorebirds take no chances. They *walk* to and from their nests.

In both Europe and Asia, peregrines nest on cathedrals, temples and old castles. It is appropriate that they still nest on the tower of Castel del Monte and other castles of Frederick II of Hohenstaufen. This fabulous ruler of the thirteenth century wrote the greatest of all the 700 known works on falconry: *De Arte Venandi cum Avibus* which has been called "the first zoological treatise written in the critical spirit of modern science."

It was obviously only a matter of time before peregrines would take up residence in New World cities. In winter, pairs lived on the towers of such cities as Boston, Albany, Philadelphia and Washington, while New York's canyons harbored a dozen or more. Among the favorite command posts for peregrines in New York, when I lived there, were the Clason Point gas tank, the George Washington Bridge, the Riverside Church, the New York Hospital, the Lincoln Building and the Chrysler Building. The Riverside Church bird is said to have fallen into disfavor for awhile with the rector because it harried the local pigeons. On the other hand, a pair that lived on the spire of Salisbury Cathedral, in England, became the special wards of the dean.

Once while I was sauntering down Fifth Avenue with a friend he pointed to an ornamental stone shield high on the fashionable St. Regis Hotel. On the ledge behind it, he said, was a peregrine's nest. Although the crowds that thronged the sidewalks below had no knowledge of the existence of this prince of predators in its castle over their heads, the eyrie had been a source of conflict between the hotel management who wanted the eyasses removed; falconers who desired the custody of the dispossessed young birds; and protectionists who thought they should be placed in an eyrie on the Palisades. As befits a bird of violence, the relationship between the men who are interested in the peregrine is fraught with friction.

The main trouble with most modern buildings, from the peregrine's point of view, is that they tend toward simple lines, devoid of gingerbread and suitable niches. When a pair tried unsuccessfully to nest on the *Sun-Life* Building in Montreal, an 18" x 18" tray, filled with gravel, was put out so that the eggs would not roll from the edge. With this help, the birds brought up two young in 1940 and nested there each year until 1952.

Walter Spofford was whacked on the head and bled severely when he visited Mrs. *peregrinus* at her box on this twentieth-story ledge one day. According to Spofford there is past evidence of peregrines nesting, or having tried to nest, in at least five North American cities: Montreal, New York, Philadelphia, Harrisburg, and Baltimore. It is believed that a pair must have nested in Jersey City in 1946, because they attacked and drove to the street two chimney painters who ventured too close to the ledge where the birds lived.

Peregrine eyries are used year after year, and a good ledge has been called an "ecological magnet." Even though birds disappear, others come to take their places. At least fourteen eyries in the East had been in use for fifty years or more, and one for more than eighty. In the British Isles, one eyrie in use today goes back to Elizabethan times. A famous eyrie on the Potomac was long in use, even though, over a period of years, a local pigeon fancier shot successive adults, oologists took the eggs and falconers and natural predators had taken the young. Added to all this, a big sign was painted across the face of the cliff and a railroad roared at its foot. Now the eyrie is abandoned, no one knows why.

At this eyrie two falconers, Jim Fox and Al Nye, had a remarkable experience. One February they trapped the tercel with the intention of training him. They agreed they would release him later if no new male had claimed the cliff. On a cold Sunday in March they returned, but no replacement male was in sight. So they let their bird go. Hardly had the tercel made a reconnaisance of his home cliff than another male streaked out of nowhere. There had been a replacement after all. This created a rare situation. Ordinarily, only one male will occupy a cliff. All others are chased away. Bird behaviorists recognize that in territorial defense the rightful owner has a psychological advantage and only token resistance is put up by the interloper. The owner always wins. But each of these two birds, no doubt, felt itself to be the rightful owner. The greatest display of flying the falconers had ever seen took place—dogfights in the air, plunges across the face of the cliff with only inches to spare, barrel rolls, all the maneuvers at their command. Twice the birds grappled on the ledge and tumbled to the wooded foot of the cliff. For three hours the battle lasted until the pale-breasted bird, the late-comer, departed.

Two thousand years before the Christian era, in central Asia, the very birthplace of man, falconry, the "oldest sport on earth," provided a means to an end. It meant meat for the table, a method of getting game, beyond the range of the swiftest arrow. Today in the dark heart of Asia, a hunting eagle is still worth from three to ten horses. There they are flown even at wolves, and on the snow-capped peaks of the Tian Shan Mountains on the Soviet border of western China, golden eagles not only strike down the white foxes but *carry* them to their trainers! These things sound unbelievable to modern falconers, but even more incredible are the stories of the scale on which falconry was practiced in the past.

Marco Polo, dazzled by what he saw, reported that the Great Khan of Cathay journeyed once a year to the eastern part of his kingdom, to within two days of the eastern sea. He rode on a pavilion borne on the backs of four elephants. Ten thousand falconers and their hawks went along and twelve gyrfalcons attended by twelve officers rode with the Khan in his pavilion. Men on horseback gave the signal when cranes or other birds appeared overhead. Then the curtains of the pavilion were drawn while the Khan, in sensual splendor, watched the sport from his couch.

The Sultan of Bayazid had 7000 hawks and Frederick II of Hohenstaufen built whole castles for his birds. The kings of the East exchanged their birds with the kings of the West until even the Vikings knew of falconry. In fact, in the eleventh century, Greenland was not known by the name Leif Ericson gave it, but was called "the land of the white falcon." These birds, brought back by the sea-roving Vikings, were the first hint to many Europeans that there was a new land across the ocean to the west. Philip the Bold ransomed his son, the Count of Nevers, from the Saracens for twelve white gyrfalcons.

Queens, Tsars, even Popes flew their birds. A knight was as proud of the falcon on his wrist as of the sword at his side. Bishops carried their birds to the church and down the aisle, releasing them as they approached the altar. Hawking was the pastime of an idle gentry, one which was bound to decline with the social upheavals of the seventeenth century.

But falconry has always been carried on, even if at times in a limited way, in some parts of the world. Clubs like the Loo Club in Holland, the Falconers Club in England and the Club de Champagne in France preserved the art in Europe. Most of the birds in later years have come from the little town of Valkenswaard, in Holland, where the Mollens family trapped passage peregrines on the downs for generations. Karl, the last of the Mollens to dedicate himself to the traditions of his family, died in 1935. His son, apparently, has not carried on.

The only place in the world today where falconry is still practiced on a grandiose scale is India. The Craighead twins, noted American falconers, had their eyes opened when they were guests of Prince Dharmakumarsinhji, or "Bapa," as they preferred to call him. The prince and his brother held a falconery meet one day. Each lined up his trainers, thirty-five or forty men on each side, with as many birds! Now that India has her freedom, this pastime of the princes, nawabs and rajahs is becoming a thing of the past.

How many falconers are there in America? One guess is as good as another. Fewer than the fingers on one hand if you mean those who use hawks to take wild game, since most peregrines today are flown at pigeons. Probably not many afficionados train peregrines at this time; certainly not more than a few dozen. It is too difficult to catch passage birds or to scale the cliffs. But those who profess an interest in falconry run into the hundreds. Richard Herbert of New York, who had never kept a hawk himself but who had a fabulous knowledge of these noble birds, said that if you were to advertise in a New York paper, offering a trained peregrine for sale, you would have two hundred takers. But every falconer I know shudders at the thought of selling a hawk or otherwise commercializing his sport.

There has always been a surge of interest in falconry after a war. In the Middle Ages, knights returning from the Crusades brought eastern falconers and their hawks back with them. When the soldiers returned after the First World War, the practitioners of the sport in Europe increased to hundreds, perhaps thousands. The old British Falconer's Club enjoyed a revival, and in Germany, where, so far as we know, only one man, Baron Christoph Von Biedermann, practiced the medieval art during the nineteenth century, men of the fatherland who had been introduced to falconry in the eastern theater of war formed the *Deutscher Falkenorden*.

An even greater increase was expected after the last global conflict, particularly in this country where so many of our men had seen service in the ancient lands of the East. One returning service man had caught the mania from an Afghan prince. Another had attended a hawk fair in India. Still others had watched tribesmen fly their birds along the Persian Gulf and in North Africa. Frankly this surge of interest had the old-line falconers worried, for they feared that the peregrine population could not stand the drain if their use in falconry became too widespread.

Joseph Hickey wrote that "about 400 nesting sites of the peregrine have been reported east of the Rocky Mountains up to the close of 1940, although several times this number are believed to exist." Most of the latter would be in the Far North. Richard Bond placed the breeding population of western North America at 750 pairs. So by all estimates the peregrine was a rarity, numbering in the low thousands, with certainly not many more than 5000 individuals in North America, to make a broad guess. Many songbirds run into the high millions.

One statistician deduced that if more than fifty per cent of the young peregrines were taken from the eyries by falconers each year, the margin of safety would not be enough to keep the species at a constant level. Although Hickey believed that the peregrine had recently declined at least eleven per cent in the more settled regions, it was not a vanishing bird. It had always been limited in numbers. The few eyasses taken from the nest and the passage birds trapped by falconers had been negligible up to then. Most falconers kept only one bird at a time, and some of them were set free within a year. Others refused to return to the lure when their owners were flying them and thus escaped.

On May 19, 1942, I saw a peregrine equipped with jesses flying across Broad Street in Nashville, Tennessee. Doctor Spofford, who lives in Nashville, did not think it was one of his birds, although he had lost one nine months earlier. On another occasion I was watching a sharp-shin flight at Cape May in September. Over the roofs of the houses I heard the tinkle of a tiny bell and looking up saw a merlin with leather jesses streaming from its legs. Writing to Luff Meredith, I found he had lost a Richardson's merlin two days before at Boonton, New Jersey, 120 miles to the north.

A few years ago a falconer who had been in the West brought back a number of prairie falcons to Washington, D. C. These he distributed among his falconer friends. In due time all escaped. They were never seen

ACE FALCONER Luff Meredith has flown peregrines for years and follows the best traditions of the world's oldest sport. Few men, however, are qualified to take proper care of these winged thoroughbreds.

LONG WINGS, cut for speed, and a longish tail mark the stream-lined falcon. The prairie falcon here shown tethered to the falcon-er's block is like a pale sandy version of the glamorous peregrine.

PRINCE OF PREDATORS is the prairie falcon. The high sweeping plains and arid buttes of the west are its hunting ground, where it is said to outmaneuver even its famous cousin, the peregrine.

A STRANGE EGG, perhaps left over from the year before, is found in a peregrine's rocky eyrie by Richard Herbert, in the foreground, and the author. Most peregrine eyries are harder to reach and require expert rock climbing tactics.

again, except for one which haunted the tower of the Bethesda Naval Hospital for six or seven years.

I can hardly regard the rather small brotherhood of falconers as a threat to the birds. More hawk-shooting sportsmen have been converted by the beauty of a well-trained peregrine on the wrist of a falconer than by the leaflets broadcast by conservationists. Some falconers give lectures about the birds of prey and take a protective interest in all the nearby eyries, even though they need no birds for training. In Germany, the *Deutscher Falkenorden* put through many protective laws, and the fact that the peregrine was until recently the commonest of the larger *Raptores* in the British Isles is the result of the fierce opposition of the falconers to the "Scotch gamekeepers" who shot out all the other species.

American falconers recognize that it would be dangerous to their sport if there were too many devotees. But this is not likely; it is almost a full-time job to train a falcon. There is also the equipment to think of such as hoods, jesses, perching blocks and other trappings. Weeks of training follow; carrying the hooded bird about on the glove, breaking it to the hood, teaching it to come to the fist for food, to fly to the lure, and, finally, to hunt. Princes can hire a man to walk about all day with a falcon on his wrist, and boys not yet tied down with a job can spend the necessary time. Falconry is not a sport that can spread greatly except among high-school and college boys who can devote long summer vacations to it. Yet that is where the danger lies. The beginner always wants to start with the glamorous peregrine, but he is not ready for the responsibility. A peregrine's diet, exercise and handling require experienced hands. For this reason the older falconers suggest learning the art with a Cooper's hawk or some other *Accipiter*. These short-winged hawks are not only more numerous but are better fitted for hunting in the wooded eastern terrain. Falcons are better in open country—like the moors of Scotland or our western plains.

If you were to take a poll among the more skilled addicts to determine America's top falconer, you would probably find each ballot marked, first, the man who turned in the ballot; and second, Luff Meredith. Meredith started back in his cadet days at West Point and some of his first birds came from eyries still in use near the Academy. Later, stationed in Washington, he crept daily into the musty clock tower of the old post office building to watch the bird that uses the high ledges as a base for its raids on the pigeons and starlings along Pennsylvania Avenue. Meredith was a pursuit pilot and the tactics of the peregrine were the tactics of aerial warfare—climb above your opponent, cut him down with a burst of speed; if you miss, maneuver quickly and close in. He got many tips about flying from the bird in the tower.

It is perhaps no coincidence that one of the leading falconers of England was Portal of the R.A.F.; Reichsfalconer No. 1 was Herman Göring; and the No. 1 falconer of America was Meredith, who became a brigadier general in the air corps during World War II. There seems to be a symbolic similarity between a falcon and a fighter plane or a dive bomber.

Meredith, incidentally, enjoyed sort of a personal victory over Herman Göring. Before the war, a female gyrfalcon was sent to Meredith from Greenland. His Danish friend who sent the bird would have fallen into all sorts of trouble, had the facts leaked out, because the No. 2 Nazi had a standing order that all gyrfalcons caught in Greenland should go to him.

Although Meredith distributed his birds when his country called him, his heart belonged to the falcons. The story is told that when he was put in command of a western air base, he moved his desk to the foot of a cliff where a prairie falcon was nesting. So falconers haven't changed much. In medieval days, knights attempting to serve both Mars and St. Hubert, took their birds to war with them and handed them over to their squires only at the moment of battle. Frederick II once spent a day flying his falcons before he pressed the siege of a fortress.

In all the four-thousand-year history of falconry, nothing is more fantastic than the short-lived episode that took place at Fort Monmouth, New Jersey, at the outbreak of World War II. The idea is the sort that might well have germinated in the mind of a publicity-seeking second lieutenant attached to the signal corps. Questionnaires were sent out by the hundreds asking for live hawks, preferably peregrines. They were to be trained to intercept enemy pigeons (how they were to distinguish between enemy and friendly pigeons was not explained). The idea had possibilities, but it soon got out of hand. Birds were to be trained to dive at airborne troops, slitting their parachutes with knives attached to their breasts. Newspapers, always eager for un-natural history, went even further. The birds were to be trained to crash into the propellers of enemy planes.

Soon the unit had three birds, a red-tail, a sparrow hawk and one peregrine. Louis Halle, who once kept a pet hawk, was assigned the care of the birds, and an unhappy man he was. Some of his friends who did not understand the anatomy of an army, and how helpless a man can be there, seemed to blame him for the whole program, even though he had only the rank of private at the time. Falconers and ornithologists everywhere protested. They regarded the plan not only as unworkable, but as a threat to the existence of the peregrine if it was developed on a large scale. Meredith, returning from Iceland, went directly to Washington to see the big brass in the Pentagon. Proceedings were abruptly stopped.

However, we learn that the R.A.F. did use fifteen peregrines. "Interception Unit No. 2" patroled the wildest parts of the English Coast and stopped many a suspicious-looking pigeon at the channel. They say that this unit had a real effect on Hitler's cross-channel spy service. On the other hand, some of the wild peregrines living on the cliffs along the channel were such a nuisance intercepting returning British pigeons that they had to be shot.

It is not unlikely that the Germans, always imaginative in techniques of war, used peregrines, too. It is known that in 1939 the German Army had three falcon "studs," where trained hawks were kept, in addition to Herman Göring's *Reichsfalkenhof,* the state falcon center in Riddagshausen.

In a famous old fourteenth-century book, *The Goodman of Paris (Le Menagier de Paris),* we learn that medieval falconers were "traitors and thieves to each other." Six hundred years have not changed some of the practitioners of the art, and several, who cannot be trusted, will lie, cheat and steal to get their birds. On the other hand a high code of ethics prevails among those who are worthy to be called falconers. Most of them follow the ancient advice of the Goodman: "If you wish to be considered a good hawker, think first of your hawk, and then of yourself."

A grim feud of long standing aligned two groups of peregrine admirers in opposite camps. They were the oologists and the falconers. The rarer the bird, the keener the collector was to acquire its eggs. Indeed, falcon eggs were so hard to get that each egg was reckoned to be worth about five dollars in the oologist's illicit rate of exchange; and in England, where oology is still a flourishing hobby, a clutch brought at least five pounds. They were such a challenge that oologists specialized in peregrine eggs. One collector in

Philadelphia showed a friend of mine a cabinet full of them, drawer upon drawer upon drawer. This awesome display represented years when the eyries along the Susquehanna and elsewhere in eastern Pennsylvania fledged scarcely a single young bird. A Boston oologist was reliably reputed to have 180 sets—which means more than 700 eggs! Sixty, eighty and a hundred sets were frequent, and one collector told me that he secured the eggs at one eyrie each year for twenty-nine years, but now, "due to civilization, that site is no longer occupied."

The oologist claimed he caused less damage than the falconer, because when he took the eggs the bird laid again. This they sometimes did, after three weeks or so—a smaller clutch of three eggs—but the eggers were on hand to get those, too. I was shown a cliff in California where a collector pitched his tent before the eggs were laid, so he would be there first.

Although some very important contributions to our knowledge of nesting birds and their ecology have been made by men who began as oologists —Arthur Cleveland Bent, William Leon Dawson and Herbert Brandt, for example—many others have contributed no more to the knowledge of their science than collectors of matchboxes. A distinction should be made between these thoughtful workers and those who merely satisfy an acquisitive instinct. Fortunately the fad is dying—there are scarcely any of the rabid devotees left in the East and they can no longer scale the cliffs. How different seventy-five years ago when it was recorded that thirty men climbed one cliff on the same day for a single set of eggs!

But the falconers' star has been on the rise. Bitter was their feud with oologists. They tell a story of a collector who slipped from a ledge and fell to his death some years ago. His body was discovered later by a group of falconers. They were shocked as they peered over the ledge to see the body sprawled below, even though they recognized that it was one of their hated competitors.

But the oologist had one advantage. Eggs come before chicks. To gain tactical advantage, the falconers climbed the cliffs as soon as eggs were laid and, to make them worthless to oologists, roughed the shells with sandpaper and daubed India ink. "The birds don't mind," one of the Vigilantes remarked, "They would as soon sit on doorknobs." One spiteful oologist, in his annual tour of robbery of the only remaining Connecticut eyrie, got back at his tormentors when he saw what they had done. He promptly threw the eggs over the cliff.

There is a vast difference between some of the irresponsible young men who keep hawks and the few idealists who all but worship the peregrine. The latter had a gentleman's agreement amongst themselves about taking young ones from nests along the Palisades and insisted that nests near big cities be left strictly alone. They even took a special interest in seeing the young safely on the wing. Heaven help the egger they caught, particularly on the New York side of the line where the peregrine was protected by state law. They even enlisted the aid of the park police who patrolled the highway along the cliffs.

But all this changed by 1960. Shortly after 1950 Richard Herbert noticed that the Hudson River birds were laying eggs that failed to hatch. At eyrie after eyrie the birds disappeared. The famous Sun-Life birds in Montreal raised their last family in 1952. Today no one can tell me of a single active eyrie anywhere in the northeast although passage birds from the far north still go through. Some believe that ornithosis contracted from their pigeon prey may have swept through the peregrine population. My own conviction is that this species is a casualty of pesticides, residual chlorinated hydrocarbons that are passed through the food chain. The recent history of the peregrine has been the same in England and there is just enough evidence to point to the subtle but deadly sprays.

The Sky Is Their Highway

*I*T IS a clear cold Sunday in October. Three hundred men, women and children cluster among the rocks on the top of a mountain in eastern Pennsylvania. On another bald outcrop, sixteen miles to the northeast are a dozen others, faces skyward. Scores more stand watch on the bluffs of the Kittatinnies in northwestern New Jersey, along the Watchung Ridge near New York City and on the Goat Peak fire tower atop Mount Tom in Massachusetts. All stare fixedly at black specks in the blue sky. Some use high-powered binoculars. They are not plane spotters; they are hawk watchers, devotees of a new facet of the sport of bird watching.

It was not long ago that the field glass fraternity discovered that the way to see hawks is to watch the ridges in the fall. There, on the right day, they can see far more hawks than they can find elsewhere in a year. Today, most active bird watchers make it a point to get out on two or three hawk days each autumn, just as they make trips specifically for ducks in March, warblers in May or shorebirds in August. When the pumpkins are ripe, corn is in the shock and jugs of cider appear at the roadside stands, then it is time for Easterners to head for the Blue Ridge—the long hazy blue wall that rises out of the Pennsylvania-Dutch farm country, where every barn is protected from witches by the hex signs of its owner.

The Blue Ridge, a recumbent giant 175,000,000 years old, is the easternmost rampart of the Appalachian system in Pennsylvania. Extending unbroken for many miles, from northeast to southwest, it is the last great barrier to the cold autumnal winds blowing out of the northwest toward the Atlantic. To the east the land falls away toward the flat coastal plain which fades into the hazy horizon. The hawks riding the invisible updrafts are loath to leave the mountains. Thousands of generations of sharp-shins, Cooper's hawks, goshawks, red-tails, red-shoulders, broadwings, falcons and eagles have followed this express highway south. Even gyr-falcons from the far north have been recorded. Along these same ridges men have piloted their experimental gliders, making flights of more than 150 miles without power. A glider, after all, is nothing but a wood and fabric replica of a hawk.

At the end of the long forested ridge, not far from Hamburg, Pennsyl-vania, rises a rocky promontory known as Hawk Mountain, the most famous hawk observation point in the eastern mountains. The gunners dis-covered Hawk Mountain long before the bird followers heard about it. At least seventy years ago they climbed the wooded trails to the summit on cold, windy days. They knew the mountain was a bottleneck for hawks. The backbone of the ridge was narrow here, and the stronger the wind, the closer to the jutting knob the birds would fly. On some Sundays as many as 200 gunners assembled among the lichen-covered boulders of Tuscarora sandstone and the slaughter was frightful. It has been estimated that 3,000 to 5,000 birds were blasted off the mountain yearly. Listen to Richard Pough writing in *Bird Lore:* "My mind ran back to the day when I first discovered the spot. On that day, over 100 men armed with shot-guns and rifles were seated among the rocks. Every hawk that came by was greeted by a barrage of shot. Many suddenly collapsed, to travel no more. Others went into dizzy spins and dropped among the rocks on the moun-tainside far below.

"A long scramble took me down to where the hawks were dropping, and I found that a large percentage were not dead but only 'winged' or wounded in some other way. Many showed signs of having suffered for days before starvation and thirst claimed them. Those still alive—and there were many—would try to hide among the rocks . . . in a small space, on that day, I picked up over 100 birds, and the total dead easily ran into the thousands."

But today all that has changed. Instead of 100 guns on an October Sunday, there are hundreds of pairs of binoculars—sometimes 1000. Through the efforts of its president, the late Mrs. C. N. Edge, the Hawk Mountain Sanctuary Association now posts the land and keeps a warden there. Maurice Broun, while fulfilling his duties as guardian, has probably seen more hawks than any other man in America. His total for his first ten seasons at Hawk Mountain was more than 150,000. Nearly 400,000 have passed through up to 1963. His vivacious wife tabulated human visitors. Her score up to 1947 was 35,000. Steadily, year by year, annual attendance has climbed to about 18,000. These pilgrims have come to this bird watchers' Mecca from nearly every state. On one Sunday, in the parking space at the foot of the trail, I counted eleven different car licenses. There have been visitors from at least a dozen foreign lands. Before the war, a young Japanese couple on their honeymoon engaged a taxi as soon as they docked in New York City and instructed the driver to take them to Hawk Mountain!

I have never gone to the mountain on a Sunday without seeing several dozen people whom I knew, mostly from Philadelphia, but always a few from New York and some from as far as Washington, Boston, Buffalo or Cleveland. Two or three trips to the mountaintop during October are as profitable in gossip as an ornithological convention. I have been there on days when the human visitors outnumbered the hawks five to one. On such days Maurice Broun seems nervous and unhappy, as if he were personally responsible for the failure of the flight. Hawk watchers who are in the know, do not go to the mountain when the wind is in the south or east.

But if the hawks are flying, there is little time for chatter. Everyone sits on his boulder and glues his eyes to the sky. To our left, a thousand feet below, flows the Little Schuylkill River, born of the coal country, winding like a thin black snake through a patchwork of farms and woodlots. Tiny cows cluster about the great red barns, which from our Olympian lookout seem like toys in a terrain model landscape. The long ridge, ablaze with October's reds and yellows, extends before us to the northeast. A sharp-eyed youngster is the first to spot a hawk. It is an accipiter, one of the short-winged bird hawks, and it is above one of the four knobs on the horizon. The boy calls out, "Hawk over hill No. 3!" but he leaves it to more experienced eyes to identify. All glasses soon pick up the traveler. It rides the ridge, reaches our cliff, mounts higher and slides by. It is a sharp-shin, small, with rounded wings and a square-tipped tail. Broun clicks it off on the small counting watch he carries in his trousers pocket. Sharp-shins are in predominance today, so they are ticked off on the me-

THE NORTHWEST WIND brings the hawks and eagles to Hawk Mountain, above, and Cape May Point, below. From 12,000 to 15,000 raptores are recorded yearly at each of these vantage points by hundreds of hawk watchers.

SURVIVAL of the osprey along the Atlantic is helped by people who like to have this fine bird about. Cape May farmers erect cartwheels on poles for the nests, but inland ospreys have fared badly at the hands of fish hatcheries.

UNDERTAKER'S CONVENTION. Well fed after officiating at the funeral of a white-tailed deer killed by an automobile, turkey vultures bask in the warmth of the late afternoon sun before leaving for their night roost in the swamp.

MASTERS OF THE SKYWAYS. The young red-tailed hawk, above, will soon join its circling parents over Michigan's pine barrens. The black vulture, pictured below, was grounded during a Maryland hailstorm.

chanical counter; the other species are jotted into a notebook. Even the novice soon learns to tell the sharp-shins by their peculiar butterfly-like flight, several quick beats and a sail.

Blue jays straggle through the saddle below, and small nondescript warblers, darting into the hemlocks down the slope, momentarily divert us from the earnest business of hawk watching. Occasionally a Cooper's hawk shoots by, larger than the sharp-shins, with a rounded tip to its tail. The large, easy-going *Buteos* with broad wings and fan tails are on the move, too —mostly red-tails, no trick to identify if they are rufous-tailed adults—not so easy if they are young birds. Arguments flare up: Is it a red-shoulder, a broadwing or a rough-leg? If Broun is not near by to put an end to conjecture, there is always some seasoned hawk watcher in the crowd who knows all the answers.

It is a poor day when eight or ten species of birds of prey do not sail down the ridge. The real prize is the golden eagle, which for years was thought to be only a straggler in the east. At Hawk Mountain it outnumbers the bald eagle some seasons. During the fall of 1939 Maurice Broun counted eighty-three of these regal birds, southbound from an unknown breeding ground to an unknown wintering place, perhaps in the Great Smokies.

Migrating birds of prey can travel quite well under their own power; in fact, the sharp-winged falcons are rather like pursuit planes. But on the journey south most hawks save energy when they can, using the tactics of gliders, taking advantage of rising air currents. There are two kinds of these lifting currents—thermal and deflective. The *thermals* develop when the hot sun warms blobs of air close to the earth, causing them to bubble up into the cool atmosphere above. Often these invisible columns of air are capped with a billowy mass of clouds. It is under these heaps of cumuli that we look for hawks, often so high we cannot see them without our binoculars. Slowly the tiny specks wheel round and round, staying within the supporting shaft of air. We cannot see these thermals, except as a shimmer above the pavement, but the circling hawks feel their ballooning influence in their wings. Warm still days are best for these winds "that blow straight up." Hawks are on the move over a broad aerial front, but we cannot expect to find them concentrated anywhere. No one goes out for hawks on such a day, for there is not much satisfaction in seeing a few speck at the limit of vision.

Deflective currents are produced on windy days. When a wind strikes a ridge or mountainside it is deflected upwards, like water flowing over a boulder. The hawks travel at a good clip on these updrafts, cutting their sail surface down enough to balance the lifting power of the wind. They can glide for miles along the face of a ridge with only a few strokes to correct their course. Maurice Broun and a helper, Ben Goodwin, using a telephone, a stop watch and an anemometer, an instrument for measuring the force of wind, timed 152 hawks over a measured course at Hawk Mountain. They found that most of the hawks travel at speeds of twenty to forty miles per hour—occasionally up to sixty or more. Assuming that they fly for five or six hours out of each day, they cover from 100 to 250 miles between dawn and dark.

The flights seem to have a definite tie-up with meteorological disturbances. The best movements are almost always preceded by a low pressure area passing across the Appalachians to the north. The hawk watcher, studying the weather maps, sets out the following day or the day after, when clearing weather starts the hawks on their way. The birds move southward regardless of which way the breezes blow, but it is the wind direction that determines on what hill slopes and mountainsides they will concentrate. Northerly or northwesterly winds are best at Hawk Mountain. The birds scud past on half-furled wings, riding the updraft along the west face of the ridge. Mile after mile of autumn landscape slips by below as effortlessly as if the hawk were stationary and the world was doing the traveling, or as if the bird were carried along on an invisible conveyer belt.

Not long after they had discovered Hawk Mountain, the hawk watchers began to find other good places from which to watch the sky parade. They located one or two other vantage points in Pennsylvania, and at least two more in northwestern New Jersey. Field students, scouting around New York City, found an abandoned traprock quarry on the Watchung Ridge in New Jersey where they could see as many hawks on some days as they could at Hawk Mountain. To the east of this low ridge a vast urban plain extends like one great sprawling city to the skyscrapers of Manhattan, fifteen to twenty miles away; to the west rise the New Jersey highlands. Here, over the Watchungs, the hawks fly higher, but for the sky gazer lying comfortably on the flat of his back with a good pair of 12-powers, it is as good a place as any to watch them.

One hundred and forty miles to the southeast of Hawk Mountain, as the sharp-shin flies, lies Cape May. At the southern tip of New Jersey, wedged between Delaware Bay and the sea, it is land's-end for the migrants traveling southward through the Garden State. Cape May is flat for miles around; there are no hills higher than the dunes that have been piled up by the winds along the bay shore, yet this antique summer playground of Philadelphians is as much a bottleneck for hawks as Hawk Mountain. Here the broad flight of the birds of prey is focused by the sea to a lane as narrow as the hawkway down the Pennsylvania ridges. I have counted a thousand sharp-shinned hawks in a morning from the concrete highway where it passes through the point woods.

The little sharp-shins are the dominant hawks at Cape May as they are much of the time at Hawk Mountain. The big, easy-moving *Buteos,* the red-tail, red-shoulder and broadwing, are much less common here than on the ridges, but we see many more falcons—the peregrine, sparrow hawk and pigeon hawk. Theirs seems to be a coastal flight, less dependent on buoyant winds. They are power fliers, sped by quick deft beats of their sharp-pointed wings. I have seen twenty-five peregrine falcons in a day over the Cape May marshes, and, on an afternoon when squadrons of migrating dragonflies filled the air, a hundred pigeon hawks. One can see more falcons on some days at Cape May than he can in a whole season in the mountains.

These concentrations of a variety of migrants, not only hawks, but all sorts of small birds, seem to be largely the result of the same wind condition that makes the ridges so good, a northwest wind blowing across the traditional lanes of travel of birds moving southward along inland routes. The birds drift southeastward in the moving mass of polar air, and if the wind is strong enough, the night migrants are carried out to sea in the darkness. At daybreak, near the Cape May Light, I have watched small birds, weak and tired, beating their way in over the surf, tacking into the stiff northwesterly breeze that had carried them offshore.

Birds seem to evaporate into thin air on other days when the wind is in a southerly or easterly quarter. Dr. Witmer Stone told of working the woodlands along the bay for five miles during one of these lulls. He recorded only ten species of birds. That night a northwester set in. The following day, over the same ground, he listed eighty-three.

Between flights, Cape May can be as dull as any place I know. How exciting, after a dead spell of several days, to wake in the night to the uncertain *quoks* of night herons flying over the rooftops! The lesser voices of thrushes and warblers fill the air, hundreds of them, almost as incessant as the sloshing rumble of the surf. These bird sounds, distinctly audible indoors, accompany the cold drafts from the north and northwest, and are as stirring as the roll of drums, eloquent of the whole magnificent pageantry of migration.

A movement of small birds at night usually means a flight of hawks the next day. A few years ago we watched the birds from the highway where the hawk hunters did their shooting, but we now have a better lookout—a huge dune a mile north of the lighthouse and close to the bay shore. We call it Sunrise Hill. Trudging through the loose sand in the darkness, we try to get there before the morning flight begins. Clothed with bayberry bushes and a few low persimmons and oaks, it is a grandstand seat with a fairly clear view in all directions. The number of birds that pass by some mornings is incredible—ten thousand robins, five thousand flickers, several thousands of myrtle warblers; blackbirds and meadowlarks by the hundreds. The hawks arrive as the passage of the small birds subsides. The first is usually a sharp-shin. Sometimes a score are in sight at one time. All are traveling northward—*northward into a northerly or northwesterly wind.*

Why, you ask, should a bird be going northward when it is migrating south?

The birds, funneled by the tapering peninsula of southern New Jersey, arrive high over Cape May. Confronted by the barrier of the broad, glistening waters of Delaware Bay, they reverse their direction, drop to a lower level near the lighthouse and beat their way through the town of Cape May Point and *north* along the bay. From Sunrise Hill I have seen robins, and sharp-shins, too, arriving very high, headed south, while at a much lower level other robins and other sharp-shins were returning, flying north.

On a clear day one can discern the tremendous sand dune southward at Cape Henlopen in Delaware. The hawks obviously, then, can see Delaware from their point of vantage in the sky, but will not attempt the crossing on the northwest wind that has borne them to Cape May. It is a long flight and there is too much danger of being carried out to sea, like a swimmer trying to breach a wide inlet in a strong ebb tide.

It is thought that the birds backtrack along the bay until they reach a point where the Delaware River is narrow enough to cross. I have followed them for seventeen miles, but have discovered no concentrated crossing place.

The pioneer exploits; later generations conserve. So the hunter has always preceded the aesthete and the ornithologist. At Cape May, as at Hawk Mountain, the hawks were slaughtered for years before anyone became concerned. A concrete highway runs from east to west through the groves of Spanish oaks just north of the town of Cape May Point. Here the local gunners formerly lined the road and waited for the hawks to come over. You could depend on the three boys who lived over the grocery store to be there, and the old Italian who ran the taxi from the railroad station, and "Pusey," the colored man who owned a boat over on the bay. Sometimes sportsmen came from as far away as Trenton and Camden. One September morning in 1935 I watched 800 sharp-shins try to cross the firing line. Each time a "sharpy" sailed over the treetops it was met by a pattern of lead. Some folded up silently; others, with head wounds, flopped to the ground, chattering shrilly. By noon 254 birds lay on the pavement.

That evening, in a Cape May home, I sat down to a meal of hawks—twenty sharp-shins, broiled like squabs, for a family of six. I tasted the birds, found them good, and wondered what my friends would say if they could see me. Like a spy breaking bread with the enemy, I felt uneasy. I could not tell my hosts I disapproved, for their consciences were clear—weren't they killing the hawks as edible game and at the same time saving all the little song birds? It would have done no good to explain predation, ecology and the natural balance to these folk. Having lived at Cape May all their lives, they had a distorted idea of the abundance of hawks. They did not realize that a single season's sport by the Cape May gunners could drain the sharp-shins from thousands of square miles of northern woodland.

Shooting has now been prohibited from the highways in New Jersey, and shooting from the sandhills in the woods at Cape May Point has been largely eliminated through the creation of the Witmer Stone Wildlife

Sanctuary by the National Audubon Society. The sanctuary has now changed hands and is guarded by the New Jersey Audubon Society. As at Hawk Mountain, the binocular has replaced the gun and hawks now enjoy a relatively safe passage.

Southward along the coast nearly one hundred and fifty miles lies Cape Charles. Spearheading the long "Delmarva" peninsula, it lies like a thin wedge and splits the broad waters of the Chesapeake from the ocean. One of the Audubon men who spent part of a season there reported that the flight was four times as heavy as at Cape May. Fortunately the point is private property where the hawks are safe. These birds double back and fly north along the Chesapeake, past the lawless Hooper Island district (where some residents shoot anything that flies) and apparently cross the Chesapeake below the Choptank—nearly 100 miles north of Cape Charles.

In the East then, hawks concentrate in two kinds of places—along the ridges where they ride the air currents, and on peninsulas where water becomes sort of a psychological barrier. On the Great Lakes there are several of these land funnels: Toronto Island in Lake Ontario, Point Pelee on the north shore of Lake Erie; Whitefish Point in Lake Superior; and a number of others that have only recently been investigated.

In the heart of the continent where the short grass plains shelve slowly from the Mississippi basin to the foothills of the Rockies there is a third type of flight—caravans of red-tails and Swainson's hawks over open country. These flights have been seen all the way from Winnipeg to Texas —but not too much is known about them yet. Their story remains to be told.

Warbler Waves

*L*EE JAQUES, the bird artist, once remarked: "The difference between warblers and no warblers is very slight."

Jaques likes the big birds, the ducks and geese, birds that are large enough to put into a landscape when he portrays them. It is difficult to introduce third-dimensional activity into a painting of a creature that is only five inches long.

But what the warblers lack in size they make up in numbers. There are fifty-four species north of the Mexican boundary, which is about equal to the number of waterfowl (*Anatidae*) if we include all the strays; but the brightly colored mites enjoy a population many times that of the ducks and geese. A *billion* would be much too conservative an estimate, for in most of the wooded country of the United States during the summer months one bird in six is a warbler of some kind, while in parts of the great conifer forest that stretches across Canada, warblers make up more than half of the breeding population of songbirds.

Although the vireos, flycatchers, orioles and tanagers make the long journey from the tropics along with the wood warblers, we usually speak of the tides of birds that flood the countryside on certain days in May as *warbler waves*. One can see twenty-five species of warblers or even more in one morning. In fact, it is possible to see that many in a single tree back of the tourist cottages near Rockport, Texas, when a "norther" pins down the migrants along the edge of the Gulf.

If it were not for the warblers, birding would lose half its fun—in the East, anyway. One who lives in the West cannot fully appreciate what a real spring "wave" is, for it is fundamentally an eastern phenomenon. In

.165.

the states west of the 100th meridian, songbirds in migration seem to drift in and drift out. Their comings and goings stretch over a longer period of weeks. There is none of the spectacular effect of the flights that occur in the Appalachians or in the Mississippi Valley.

Warblers make their journeys at night, reassuring themselves with faint lisps and zips as they pass overhead in the dark. When the tiny notes fill the sky, it usually means a wave in the morning. If we put a low-powered telescope on the moon on such a night we can see the silhouettes of the small transients passing across the luminous disc.

Two of our best students of migration were at swords' points not long ago over the path that the night migrants take between the tropics and the Gulf states. George Williams, of Houston, believes that the "trans-Gulf migration" is much over-rated, that most of the migrants *go around* the Gulf of Mexico and through his state of Texas. George Lowery, of Baton Rouge, disagrees, contending that there is a big flight *across* the Gulf, to his state of Louisiana (state pride is probably involved here). Bitter has been their battle in the staid ornithological journals, The Auk and The Wilson Bulletin. But controversy is a healthy thing. When I spoke to Lowery about it he told me that he planned to spend the spring on a reef off the tip of the Yucatan peninsula with his telescope trained on the moon, counting the birds that fly over and noting the direction they take. Williams confided to me that he intended to spend his nights in the same way on the coast of Texas.

Regardless of how the migrants enter the continent, all of them have to pass through the southern tier of states. Some warblers, like the Bachman's, which I have never seen, and the Swainson's, the will-o'-the-wisp that hides in the cane patches, are content to stay in the deep south. They go no further. The yellow-throated warbler that creeps about the moss-covered live oaks and the Kentucky warbler, the one with the sideburns, barely cross Mason and Dixon's Line. The other "Carolinian" warblers venture to the edge of the Great Lakes. There are swamps in southern Michigan and western New York where blue-gray and gold prothonotary warblers can be seen carrying nesting material into abandoned downy woodpecker holes, just as they do in Tennessee. Louisiana water thrushes teeter along ravines that empty their water into Lake Erie; and yellow-breasted chats, the most unwarbler-like of all the warblers, clown and catcall from

ON A FIFTY-FIFTY BASIS, two prairie warblers who live in Maryland carry out their domestic responsibilities. Resident of pine barrens and dry scrub-oak slashings, this misnamed species neither lives in prairies nor does it warble.

WARBLERS ALL. The ovenbird, above, whose chant rings through the woods, looks more like a thrush than a warbler. At the left a blue-winged warbler bathes. To the right is a bay-breasted warbler, a Canadian member of the family.

LICHEN LOVER is the bluish parula warbler, above, which has tucked its nest in a tuft of usnea hanging from a fog-drenched spruce branch. Below is a family of black-throated green warblers.

JEWEL CASKET. Somewhere back in the shadows the male hooded warbler sings his bright whistled notes while his mate, *sans* hood, inspects her eggs in a dogwood shrub.

Connecticut brier patches. There are places in central New York and else-where in the Appalachian highlands, where north meets south—where deciduous trees give way to evergreens—and twenty or more species of warblers breed in a single county.

The hardwood forest has its own warblers: the cerulean that forages in the forest canopy throughout the Mississippi River bottoms; the black and white warbler, more adapted to the life of a creeper or a nuthatch than that of a warbler; and the redstart, the most numerous of all the family in the Appalachian plateau, exceeding in number even the ovenbirds that shout from the leafy understory. In a woodland in northern New Jersey I have found as many as four pairs of redstarts on a five-acre plot.

But the warblers that climax spring bird watching are the ones that stop only briefly on their way north—the ones that live in the "Canadian" zone, if you wish to use that term. Not that they are rare, for most of them are not. They are the most "warblerish" of all the warblers, brightly colored and satisfying in their variety. But whereas they will forage in the apple trees or even in lilac bushes when they are traveling through, to really know them go to the Hyperborean realm where they spend the summer—to the Adirondacks, or the "strong forest" of the Ojibways near Lake Superior. Or go to a place like Hog Island, Maine, where the spruces come down to the ocean. There, in an open glade, sit upon a rock among the bracken and watch the show. Magnolia warblers (inappropriately named, as so many warblers are) flash the white bands across their wings and tails as they dodge into the small Christmas-tree-sized balsams at the edge of the clearing. The myrtle warblers, showing their yellow rumps as they fly, also like the young trees. But the black-throated greens, lisping *zee-zee-zee-zee-zoo-zee,* the dreamiest sound in the woods, prefer the lower branches of the bigger trees. Higher up, the Blackburnian, its throat ablaze, throws back its head and scrapes out its wiry notes. Each has its preferred niche.

Here on the Maine coast where the usnea hangs in wispy beards from the fog-drenched branches, parula warblers are as numerous as you will see them any place. The tiny little blue and yellow sprites, hardly larger than kinglets, are everywhere, sizzling the air with their song.

Frank Chapman once said that the finding of a parula warbler's nest should be marked on the calendar as a red-letter day. During the summer of 1936, we had thirteen such red-letter days at Hog Island. One nest was nearly fifty feet from the ground, another less than four. All were suspended in the hanging *usnea*. I have also seen nests of the parula warbler in Florida and the Carolinas. These were in Spanish moss, an epiphyte not even related to the lichen *usnea* but in looks very much like it. But when I first went to Washington, D.C., I was puzzled, for the parula was common along the Potomac, and neither *usnea* nor Spanish moss grew there. Later I found the answer. The birds were nesting in the tangled tufts of trash lodged in the trees along the river by the high spring floods. One nest was tucked under a strip of burlap that had been draped over a branch by the receding water. The parula warbler is a beautiful example of a bird whose distribution cannot be shown to fit either the Life Zone or the Biome concepts of the biologists. Rather, as with so many other birds, its distribution seems to be determined by the "life form" or the physical appearance of the plants that provide its proper niche.

There are parulas from the Gulf of St. Lawrence to the Gulf of Mexico; and if we were to include the Sennett's warbler, which sings exactly like it and, for all I can see, is just a well-marked race of the parula, they are found all the way to the Argentine. When a bird has such a wide distribution as this, or as the yellow warbler which nests from South America to Alaska, we wonder at the limited breeding range of the Kirtland's warbler, confined within the State of Michigan.

When I first visited Hog Island, in 1936, bay-breasted warblers sang their high sibilant squeaks from the tops of the spruces, and so did the tiger-patterned Cape Mays. There were numbers of both about, and it was the furthest south the Cape May had ever been known to nest. The next summer there were fewer of both species. In three years the bay-breast disappeared from the island and in five the Cape May was gone. The Blackburnian warbler, relieved of competition, trebled its numbers and the golden-crowned kinglet doubled. What was the reason for the disappearance of the bay-breast and the Cape May? It is possible that an outbreak of some insect had been responsible for their presence, and when the epidemic waned they disappeared. Dr. S. Charles Kendeigh, of the University of Illinois, who spent the summer of 1945 north of Lake Superior during an outbreak of spruce budworms, found ninety-two pairs of baybreasted warblers in 100 acres of forest, fifty-nine pairs of Tennessee warblers and twenty-eight pairs of Cape Mays. These warblers seem to prosper during the outbreaks, perhaps to the disadvantage of some of the other species, according to Dr. Kendeigh. This may explain the scarcity of Cape May warblers in the northeast for a few years, followed by several years when they are common.

The numbers of warblers marked by the 1700 bird banders are no index to their abundance. More than 13,000,000 aluminum bracelets have been fastened to the legs of North American birds, but the largest numbers of bands have been put on birds like the junco and the white-throated sparrow, species which can be baited with grain in the backyard; or colonial birds, such as herring gulls and common terns, where several banders using assembly line methods can band great numbers of birds in a short time. All these species have been banded by hundreds of thousands. The chimney swift has more than a half million entries registered in the files of the United States Fish and Wildlife Service. These speedy fliers can be trapped by the thousands as they leave their roosting chimneys in the morning. Yet of all North American birds, these little jet-propelled rockets withheld their migration secret longest. It was not until the summer of 1944, when thirteen bands were returned from Peru, that their mystery was solved.

Warblers do not eat birdseed, nor can they be trapped in chimneys. Finding their nests and banding the young is slow work, but some banders have discovered that a trap placed at a little pool of water works wonders, especially if a can of dripping water is suspended above it. The slow drip, drip, drip, attracts the birds' attention.

What would the north woods be like without the wood warblers? About like the evergreen forests of northern Europe, I suspect. At the Audubon Nature Camp in Maine, Cruickshank and Cadbury found nearly five birds per acre; three out of five were warblers. In the Lake Nipigon region of Canada, Kendeigh found more than six birds per acre; better than four out of six were warblers. Subtracting the warblers from the bird population of these coniferous woodlands, we have left slightly less than one pair of birds per acre—about as many birds as there are in the spruce forests of Finland. In Finnish forests, thrushes sing from the shadows, titmice and kinglets hang upside down from the twig-tips, and woodpeckers test the dead branches, just as they do in our woodlands. But Europe has no wood warblers.

However, they do have a group of birds that they call warblers (*Sylviidae*) in Europe, but they are more closely related to our gnatcatchers and kinglets. The wood warblers (*Parulidae*) are strictly an American family and if we include those in the tropics there are 115 species. South of the border there are such incredibly beautiful forms as the red warbler, vivid as a tanager, with white cheeks, a flaming coal that flashes among the dark pines of the Mexican highlands.

Systematists believe that the ground-nesting warblers of the genus *Vermivora*, (birds like the Nashville, orange-crown, blue-wing and golden-wing) originated in Central America, while the tree-nesting species of the genus *Dendroica* (myrtle, yellow, Cape May, etc.) came from the West Indies.

At any rate, they are a tropical tribe, and many of them seem to come north solely for expedience—to enjoy elbow room enough to raise their families. Yellow warblers travel to Newfoundland and even Alaska, yet by the middle of July, some of them are already leaving the United States for the West Indies or Central America. They much prefer the tropics and spend at least two-thirds of their year there. Other yellow warblers, or at least birds that the museum men tell us are conspecific with the yellow warbler (even though some of them have rusty caps), do not make the long journey. They stay in the West Indies and even in northern South America, where, in lieu of willows, they live among the mangroves.

They used to call these tropical races "golden warblers," and I myself took part in the discovery of one of them in the Florida Keys in 1941. Earle Greene, who was then manager of the Key West Wildlife Refuge, and I had pulled our boat up to the lee side of a small mangrove key off Key West about noon one hot June day. We were looking for the nests of great white herons in a group of islands called the Bay Keys. While we were eating our lunch a bird sang from the dark mangrove tangles a song that we could not place. It had the bright opening notes of a yellow warbler, but it ended differently. We hunted for half an hour through the almost impassable thickets before we found the singer. It looked to us just like an ordinary yellow warbler, but we knew it must be something different, for the nearest breeding yellow warblers lived in the hills of Georgia, seven hundred miles to the north. A month later, Greene collected the bird along with a female and a nest which contained an addled egg. Word came back from John Aldrich at the National Museum in Washington that it was the Cuban golden warbler, *Dendroica petechia grundlachii*.

The next year others were found in the Bay Keys. Probably they had been there all along. True, the birds are common in Cuba, and might have been expected in the Keys, with their West Indian flora, but ornithologists had completely overlooked them for more than a century.

Now that the golden warbler of the tropics was officially a North American bird, Aldrich became interested in its relationship to the yellow warblers of North America. After examining them carefully, he decided that they were all races of one plastic species, and that the two groups were linked together in Yucatan.

It is not often that one adds a new bird to the A.O.U. Check-List of North American Birds, yet Earle Greene and I found a second bird new to the United States on the very day that we discovered the warbler. It was the Cuban nighthawk. The warbler was a new species for the check-list; the nighthawk a new subspecies. Several years later the warbler had been reduced to a subspecies and there was talk of elevating the nighthawk from a subspecies to the rank of a full species! If neither had been taken within the United States, they would not have fallen under the scrutiny of the experts of the United States Fish and Wildlife Service, and both would have been left as they were. In such ways do political boundaries often influence our thinking.

Warblers, of course, do not observe political boundaries. Nor do they bother with passports. Their residence in the north country is short. Song is silenced by mid-July, and on quiet nights you can hear the first southbound migrants as they navigate the starlit void.

Most of us know the warblers well in the spring, but we throw up our hands in perplexity when they return in August or September. The blackpoll warbler was easy to tell in May when it had its black cap and white cheeks, but now, on its return from tree limit in Canada and Alaska, it is an obscure little yellow-green bird. And the bay-breasted warbler, so very different in spring, now looks so much like the blackpoll that it could be its twin.

Fortunately, some, like the myrtle warbler, retain their basic field marks.

A myrtle warbler always has a yellow rump and it says *check*, just so there will be no mistake. But the myrtle is an individualist, anyway. Many myrtle warblers do not leave the United States in winter, and where bayberries grow I have seen them as far north as Lake Erie and Cape Cod on the most bitter cold days of January.

One autumn, many of the myrtle warblers that wintered along the outer beaches of the New Jersey coast arrived on a foggy night. Thousands dashed themselves to death against the dazzling lenses of the Barnegat Light. For several years one could notice the reduction in numbers. There are many such hazards during migration. On nights in September, when the wind was in the northwest, I have watched thousands of birds passing the tall granite shaft of the Washington Monument, and I have seen scores killed. Although, on such nights, the birds are coming from the north, the unlucky ones, caught in the backdraft, are killed on the south side of the monument. Vireos hit with a thud, warblers buffet the wall until they suffer a concussion, but the thrushes, big eyed, and more at home in the dark, seem to get by safely.

The Fugitive Warblers

URNING the elephantine pages of Audubon's fabulous *Birds of America* to Plate 60, we find two small yellowish birds. Their black caps and streaked sides give them a puzzling, unfamiliar look. The round full script at the bottom of the page informs us they are "carbonated warblers."

Out of curiosity we turn to Audubon's own account of this "species" in his *Ornithological Biography*:

> "I shot the two little birds here represented, near the village of Henderson, in the State of Kentucky, in May, 1811. They were both busily engaged searching for insects along the branches and amongst the leaves of a dogwood tree. Their motions were those common to all the species of the genus *Sylvia*. Upon examination, they were found to be both males. I am of the opinion that they were both young birds of the preceding year, and not in full plumage, as they had no part of their dress seemingly complete, excepting the head. Not having met with any other individual of the species, I am at this moment unable to say anything more about them. They were drawn, like all the other birds which I have represented, immediately after being killed; but the branch on which you see them was not added until the following summer."

The carbonated warbler, like several other mystery birds described by Audubon, has not since been found by any naturalist. Was it a creation of Audubon's vivid imagination or did such a bird actually exist in North America more than 100 years ago? Or could it have been a chance hybrid —between a blackpoll and a Cape May warbler, perhaps? The bird does not have the appearance of a fabrication; it looks very convincing—less obscure than those other *"Aves ignotae,"* the Blue Mountain and small-headed warblers, which were figured by the great bird artist. However, the A.O.U. Check-List committee has shelved it in the hypothetical or doubtful list of American birds, with the remark that "as a large number of his drawings of birds obtained about this time were later destroyed, it is possible that the published plate might have been based to some extent upon memory." Perhaps, but I prefer to keep an open mind about it. Are there not several other warblers with a curious history?

Four or five species of North American birds have become extinct since the colonization of the continent, and three or four more have been brought to the border line. They are all rather large handsome species. But ornithologists seem to consider small songbirds of continental distribution immune from such total annihilation. Obviously they are not as vulnerable as the big showy species, or those that flock or nest in colonies. Indeed, bird students are so firm in this belief that until recently all but a few failed to notice the virtual disappearance of one small bird within our times. This is the Bachman's warbler, a little yellowish, black-throated bird discovered by the Reverend John Bachman near Charleston in 1833. Audubon described it to the world and gave it the name of its discoverer.

Curiously enough, Audubon portrayed this fragile warbler on a plant with an even stranger history—the Franklinia—where the large white blossoms and narrow dark leaves, suggestive of a magnolia, make a lovely decorative setting for the two small birds. This tree was discovered back in 1790, by the pioneer botanist, William Bartram, who found it in groves covering an area of two or three acres along the Altamaha River in Georgia. No botanist has ever found the plant growing wild since. Expeditions have combed the swamps along the Altamaha for it, but they found no trace of those almost mythical groves. The Franklinia, named in honor of Benjamin Franklin, would probably be doubted like Audubon's Carbonated warbler, except for the fact that Bartram carried several slips of it in his saddle bag to his father's gardens in Philadelphia. Today, a few Franklinia trees can still be seen there and in other arboretums, lineal descendants of those which Bartram transplanted. It is said that Miss Maria Martin of Charleston painted the blossoms from plants that had come from Philadelphia, while Audubon put in the birds. Time may prove the bird to be

ONLY 1000 Kirtland's warblers exist on earth. Nesting exclusively in the pine barrens of Michigan, it might well have been chosen as Michigan's state bird. It crosses the mountains and strikes out to sea to reach its winter home in the Bahamas.

THE PINE BARRENS must be swept by fire and the young trees that reclaim the burnt soil must grow several feet high, like those above, before the rare Kirtland's warbler, shown below, will take up residence.

an even more irretrievable loss than the tree, for plants can be perpetuated in cultivation, warblers cannot.

For fifty-three years after its discovery, Bachman's warbler dropped from sight in the United States; then, in the spring of 1886, one was taken in Louisiana. During the next several years a flood of them reached museums and Chapman later wrote:

> "The efforts of collectors now being especially directed toward this species, it proved to be an abundant migrant in Florida and Louisiana."

Abundant it must have been, for we find such figures as these: thirty-one taken in March, 1888, near Lake Pontchartrain in Louisiana; forty taken at Key West in 1889, by J. W. Atkins; twenty females and one male picked up after striking the light at Sombrero Key in one night, in 1889; forty-six taken on the Suwanee River in Florida in March, 1889, by Brewster and Chapman; fifty collected along the Suwanee in March, 1892, by Wayne; etc. These were migrants, taken while traveling to and from their winter home in Cuba.

Several years later the summer home of the bird was sketchily outlined. Nests were found in South Carolina, northern Alabama, western Kentucky and in the sunken lands of southeastern Missouri and northeastern Arkansas. On this slender basis, bird books stated that Bachman's warbler was well distributed in the river bottom swamps of the South. But the picture has changed.

Today, only in a single locality in South Carolina might one see this songster. Earle Greene, who lived at Key West while he was manager of the refuge there, never saw one in that region, where it was so common in migration a half century before. So far as I can find out, there has been scarcely a record of it for the whole State of Florida since 1909. There have been only four or five records for Louisiana since 1900.

The bird has disappeared from nearly every locality on which the 1931 A.O.U. Check-List based its breeding range. Only near Charleston has it been seen with any regularity during recent decades. Observers in recent years have looked in vain for it in the St. Francis basin of southeastern Missouri and northeastern Arkansas. One spring I searched for it where it had once nested in a swamp in western Kentucky, but found that even the swamp was gone. In its stead stretched fields of potatoes and corn.

What it sums up to is this: Bachman's warbler was a common bird at the close of the last century, but has faded like a ghost. Once in a while one is still seen, and a nest was found in Alabama as late as 1937, but these may prove to be among the last tag ends. Just why this distinctive little warbler has disappeared would be hard to say. I doubt very much that it was because of museum collectors. Could it be associated with the changes that pushed the ivory-billed woodpecker out—the cutting of the river bottom forests? The peak of this deforestation—around 1900—coincides closely with the disappearance of the warbler. Or is the bird too specialized in its needs? It likes wooded swamps where the trees stand in pools of stagnant water. Nowhere were more nests found than in southeastern Missouri and northeastern Arkansas. These sunken lands were probably just right for Bachman's warblers for awhile. The species could have built up a sizable population there, perhaps reaching its peak in the eighties and nineties when so many were taken in migration, only to decline and disappear when the land promoters drained off the water.

If a small bird occupying a fair-sized portion of the United States can disappear, what about one with a specialized environment in a very small area? What about the Kirtland's warbler?

This largish warbler, gray above and yellow below, with a few sparse streaks on its sides, nests in a belt scarcely sixty miles wide, stretching across several counties in north-central Michigan. Even there it is confined to groves of young jack pines where the trees range between five and eighteen feet high.

For years the bird was something of a mystery to ornithologists. They knew it only from a few specimens taken in migration, and in its winter home in the Bahamas. They did not know where it spent the summer. In 1903, a fisherman, who was also a keen field naturalist, while casting his flies on the Au Sable River, heard a bird song new to him. Leaving his rod and reel on the bank, he searched for the singer. It was a male Kirtland's warbler and the riddle of this elusive *Dendroica's* summer home was solved.

Several years ago, when I drove through the jack pine barrens near Grayling, I anticipated no trouble in finding Michigan's most famous bird. Arriving late in the morning, I allowed several hours for the quest. But I had not realized that even in suitable territory the Kirtland's warbler is hard to find. It exists in little isolated colonies of from two to a dozen or more pairs. In addition to pines of the right size, it must have the proper ground cover—blueberries, bearberries or sweetfern. It shifts and disappears from time to time and seems dependent on searing forest fires to regenerate the young growth. Driving slowly along the dirt roads of Oscoda, Crawford and Roscommon Counties in the car, I listened carefully, stopping at every grove of young jack pines that looked promising. According to the accounts I had read, the bird has a loud, brilliant song, audible from one-third to one-half a mile. Although many other warblers sang, not once did I hear anything that I suspected of being Kirtland's. So, late in the afternoon, I gave up my search.

The next time I went there, I sought out Dr. Josselyn Van Tyne, who had spent years documenting the Kirtland's warbler. He knew where the little colonies were tucked away and how to get to them on the backwoods roads. In a single day he showed me, not one nest, but ten! Some of the adults were so tame that they came to my fingertips to feed the newly fledged young which I held in my hands. These big gentle warblers, with their throaty voices, lower than those of any other *Dendroica,* reminded me a little of myrtle warblers, but they wagged their tails with all the persistence of the prairie warblers with which they share the barrens. If it would be possible for two species to hybridize and give rise to a population that eventually bred true as a distinct species, the myrtle and the prairie would seem to be the Kirtland's logical ancestors.

Harold Mayfield and a corps of helpers in a recent survey were of the opinion that approximately 1000 of these warblers existed on earth. Paradoxically, the increasingly efficient system of controlling forest fires may some day seal its fate. It is so specialized that large mature jack pines won't suffice. The Department of Conservation, conscious that no state but Michigan can boast of Kirtland's warblers, and that many people make long pilgrimages to see them, has seriously considered "controlled burning" for the sake of this species and for other wildlife. But that may not be necessary for there continue to be enough large fires, ignited by lightning, to produce the proper habitat.

In contrast to the waning star of the Bachman's warbler and the uncertain one of the Kirtland's, two warblers have dropped from the heavens into our laps in the last several years, birds that were not known to exist in America before.

One of them is the Cuban golden warbler, the discovery of which I have described in the preceding chapter. But the finding of this attractive race of the yellow warbler in the Keys meant just an extension of known range, and only a subspecies at that. The other discovery, Sutton's warbler, was far more exciting, for the like of it had never been seen in the long study trays of any museum.

On May 30, 1939, two student ornithologists, Karl W. Haller and J. Lloyd Poland, were exploring a mixed woodland of Virginia pine and oak in the eastern panhandle of West Virginia when they heard a strange song. It sounded like the familiar sizzling buzz of the parula warbler, but was double—*zeeeeeeee-up*—*zeeeeeeee-up*. When they collected the unorthodox singer they found it was not a parula; it looked more like the yellow-throated warbler, a bird not found in West Virginia. Closer scrutiny showed it was not that species either; for one thing it lacked stripes on its sides. It was different from anything they had ever seen. Raking their memories for other places where they had heard parulas, Mr. Poland remembered a spot about eighteen miles away. There, two days later, they took another specimen, a female.

The discovery had the effect of a bombshell amongst the systematic ornithologists who tend the study collections in the museums of the country. They pulled out the flat insecticide-reeking trays in their dimly lit quarters and searched the orderly rows of carefully labeled yellow-throated warblers for one that might closely resemble the new bird. Not one out of 825 available specimens fitted the description. This was news indeed! The last previous new species of bird described from North America had been the Cape Sable seaside sparrow, discovered in 1918 on a few square miles of isolated salt marsh in southern Florida. Ornithologists then predicted it would be the last *nova avis* to be found on our continent north of the Mexican border. America was too well known, they contended, for any further discoveries. It seemed incredible that a warbler could have escaped notice in the Appalachian Mountains. The new bird was named the *Sutton's warbler* in honor of the well-known bird artist.

There has been a great deal of discussion about this puzzling bird. The resemblance to both the yellow-throated warbler and the parula warbler suggested to some that it might be only a hybrid. West Virginians point out that the yellow-throated warbler is not found in their state, hence hybrids are unlikely. Others argue that yellow-throated warblers *are* found commonly in Washington, D.C., only seventy-five miles away and that a stray bird which had wandered too far upriver might very well mate with a parula if it could not find one of its own species. However, the fact that a second Sutton's warbler was deliberately located miles away from the first, by the same men, is one of the best arguments against the hybrid theory. It seems more than a coincidence—contrary to the laws of chance. Because of these contradictions, naturalists decided to stay judgment until time had shown whether others would turn up.

Three years later, on May 21 and 22, 1942, Maurice Brooks and Bayard Christy made a search for the Sutton's warbler. Scarcely expecting to find it, they believed that even failure would prove something. But the amazing thing is, they did not fail! They write of their experience: *

"We made Martinsburg our headquarters, as Mr. Haller and his companion, Mr. J. Lloyd Poland, had done before us; and, following Mr. Haller's directions, we endeavored to cover the same ground. The weather was execrable; it could hardly have been more hostile to the enterprise. Thunderstorms with heavy downpour succeeded one upon another. There were, however, intervals in the mornings of both the two days when there was little or no rain, and even glimpses of sunshine. Our field of investigation was to the south of Martinsburg.

"After some scouting about on the first morning, we came, a little before noon, upon a grove of Virginia pine (*Pinus virginiana*) surrounded by a mature forest of hardwoods. It was on high ground. The pine grove covered a northward-leading shoulder of the hilltop. To east and west the land fell away in gullies, and the little streams, gathering there and uniting, flowed through a ravine northward and then eastward to Opequon Creek. On the farther slopes of the gullies rose the hardwood forest.

"It was raining a little, and the birds in the pines, though active, were all but silent. . . . There were black-polls about, and presently Brooks caught in his field of view a warbler with a dark head, striped with white, that for an instant he thought to be a black-poll. But this bird, flitting to another perch, revealed a slate-blue back, white wing-bars, and intense and glowing orange-yellow throat, and, most important of all, the diagnostic character

* "Sutton's Warbler Again" by Brooks and Christy in *The Cardinal*, July, 1942, pp. 187, 188.

—its sides lacked the heavy markings of the yellow-throated warbler. Christy also, his attention directed to the bird, saw clearly the orange throat bordered with black. A second flitting and a second view confirmed the first, and established indubitably the identification; here was the duplicate of the male bird that three years before, and in perhaps identically the same place, Mr. Haller had taken."

Brooks told me later that Christy had a look almost of transfiguration when he saw the bird. His face lighted up that same way when we saw the ivory-bills in Louisiana. But this adventure was closer to home, at the very back door of Washington, where I lived. It was too exciting to miss. Twice I made the trip and combed the locale where the birds had been found, but my treasure hunts did not turn up anything suspicious, other than a pine warbler that sang an unusual song.

But others were more fortunate. During the five years following 1942, the year Brooks and Christy saw their bird, Sutton's warblers were reported four times—twice in the eastern panhandle of West Virginia, and twice outside the state. But even though the observers in each case were careful, there is always the possibility of error in sight records.

Mrs. E. G. Brownsey showed me a crayon drawing she made of a bird she saw near Tampa, Florida, on September 28, 1944. It could very well have been Sutton's warbler, but several ornithologists to whom I showed her sketch agreed that most of the markings could be duplicated in an immature female parula warbler—except that the eye stripe was a bit too long.

In August of 1947, Georg Sigel telephoned one night, to invite me to go birding the next morning at Fort Belvoir, Virginia. But I had just moved to Maryland and the phone had been disconnected. That day, he and Captain Jackson Abbott saw a bird that they took to be a Sutton's warbler. Abbott, who is an accomplished artist, made a water color of the bird. The drawing is very convincing, but here again we are disturbed by a trace of doubt. Was it really Sutton's or could it have been an aberrant yellow-throated warbler? Warblers are tricky in the Fall.

The truth is, we are grappling with a will-o'-the-wisp. That there is such a thing as Sutton's warbler cannot be denied. The two specimens kept under lock and key at the museum in Ann Arbor are proof of that. But just what it is, is another thing. Ornithologists are still abuzz with conjecture and opinions. Is it only a hybrid such as the Brewster's and Lawrence's warblers? If so, we may expect all sorts of variations, and thus the slight inconsistencies in the two drawings could easily be explained. Is it just a well-marked subspecies of limited range, and was it there in the mountains all along? Or can it be a new species in its own right, coming into being before our eyes? Is it, as Dr. Sutton suggests, a species that has arisen *per saltum,* at a leap or at a bound? Students of speciation recognize that some species may mysteriously appear in this way rather than by the slower processes of evolution.

Will ornithologists see this pretty little wood warbler spread dominion over larger and larger areas of the West Virginia mountains until it is commonplace, or will it disappear? However, the general consensus of opinion today is that the bird is merely a hybrid that might pop up again at any time.

Cities in the Wilderness

IN THE winter of 1811-12, the New Madrid earthquake shook the northwest corner of Tennessee so that the ground sank and the Mississippi, a few miles away, rushed in like a tidal wave. The shocks, the noise and the semi-darkness convinced many that the day of judgment was at hand. Some swore they detected a sulphurous odor. When it was all over, a lake had been formed, filled with a chaos of dead and dying trees, their trunks tilted crazily, their branches interlocked.

This sprawling body of water was named Reelfoot after a club-footed chief of the Chickasaws who lived on the bluffs of the Mississippi. This legendary aborigine defied the Great Spirit when he and his party of raiders rode into the territory of the Chocktaws and carried off the young daughter of the chief. During the wedding rites the rhythm of the tom-toms was caught up by the earth. The rumbling ground shook convulsively, split wide and the water swept in mountainous waves over the village of the Chickasaws. There, on the sunken floor of the lake, it is said, lie the bodies of Reelfoot, his bride and his people.

Today, Reelfoot is surrounded by a fairyland of cypress, the northernmost of the true southern swamps in the Mississippi Valley. The dead stubs that choked the lake have rotted away above the surface of the water, but the forest of submerged snags, lurking places for crappie, bass and bream, is an angler's paradise. A feud exists between the fishermen near the spillway at the lower end of the lake who desire to lower the water level, expose the snags and improve their fishing, and the "sloughbackers" who live on the upper arm of the lake, along the Bayou de Chien (Bayou of the Dog) in cabins perched on stilts. They want the water high.

CRANETOWN'S SUBURBS are occupied by ebon-hued cormorants. Their sinuous black forms contrast strikingly with the snowy white robes of their elegant neighbors, the egrets.

EVERGLADE SKIES form a cobalt-blue backdrop for a white ibis as it balances in the top of a mangrove. In some Florida rookeries the numbers of these "white curlew" with red faces have been known to exceed 100,000.

BRIDAL PLUMES adorn the graceful common egret stepping to its nest of twigs, high in a cypress in Reelfoot's Cranetown. Rare at the turn of the century, many large colonies exist throughout the south today.

SACRED in ancient Egypt, the ibis was ranked as a god, but our white ibis (above) often went into the cracker's stew pot before wardens were employed to guard them. Below is a dimorphic pair of reddish egrets at Green Island, Texas.

By virtue of its lush swamps and teeming waters, Reelfoot is one of the best bird resorts in the heart of the continent, a Mecca of the bog-trotting ornithologists of the surrounding states. In spring, warblers swarm through the willows in bewildering numbers, and waterfowl crowd the bays and marshes during their season of passage. There the snakebird finds its northernmost nesting place. One of two or three known tree eyries of the peregrine falcon in America is hidden there in a huge broken-topped cypress, its location a secret to all but a few.

But the real drawing card at Reelfoot is "Big Cranetown" where the egrets and cormorants colonize back in the cypress. The guides will tell you it is no use trying to find "Cranetown" by wading into the swamp; you had better go with them in their boats if you do not wish to get lost. We knew how to reach the rookery by following an old fence line into the swamp, but we yielded to their suggestion, more to see the full beauty of the lake from the water than through fear of losing our way.

We were a strange flotilla—seven rowboats, towed in a string by an outboard. The boats, each of which carried one passenger and a guide, were of a sort I had never seen before, with curious oars, jointed in three sections like the tri-partite legs of some huge water insect. The reason for this device was clear when our convoy reached the half-hidden channel through the swamp. Oars of normal length would be useless in the narrow passages between the trees; these jointed affairs take up less room and offer the same leverage. Trying them out, I swung around and blocked the channel. I gave a stroke forward; the boat went into reverse. Everything worked opposite to what I had been accustomed to. To use one of these grasshopper-legged swamp boats one must learn to row all over again.

We passed scattered cypresses standing knee-deep in the water, their feathery branches alive with dozens of migrating kingbirds, stuttering and bickering. It was odd to see them in a habitat where red-wings looked so much more in keeping. Beyond stood thickets of willows, fresh green with new leaves. The water, like clear thin coffee, was iridescent where shafts of sunlight played on the thin film of plant pollen floating on the surface. One of the men in our party, Professor Mayfield of Vanderbilt University at Nashville, gave most of his attention to warbler songs, glibly calling off parulas, ceruleans, Tennessees, prothonotaries, bay-breasts and a score of others. He was rightly proud of his trained ear. A photographer, who had come all the way from Ohio to photograph Cranetown, made a pictorial record of our progress through the swamp. We poled through pockets choked with pickerel weed and yoncopin lilies, pushed our boats over shallow bars and pulled them around snags, keeping an eye out for moccasins basking on the half-submerged logs which drifted by like miniature floating gardens. We rowed, poled, pushed and tugged through an almost interminable maze before we heard the muffled clamor of Cranetown.

The first nests silhouetted against the sky were those of cormorants. Their owners, sitting gaunt and black upon the blasted limbs, looked strangely out of place to one who is used to seeing cormorants on rocky ocean ledges. The egrets occupied the heart of the colony, big common egrets, all of them, like ghosts among the misty green of the cypress. There were four hundred, at least, and more than a thousand of the cormorants.

Several years before our visit, Karl Maslowski, one of America's most accomplished bird photographers, had singled out one of the tallest trees in the heart of the colony and built a blind in its top, eighty feet from the ground. The improvised ladder of sticks he had nailed to the trunk was still there, but it was a struggle to reach the flimsy wooden platform and I do not believe many more made the climb after we did. At least two of the weathered sticks were already broken and another snapped under one of the men in our party. Only a firm arm-lock around the trunk saved him from a nasty drop. The photographer stayed below, confessing that high places made him dizzy.

With our feet dangling into space, we had a heron's-eye view of the bird city. Prothonotary warblers darted like golden flames over the reddish-black waters below us, and pileated woodpeckers marched up the giant cypress boles. The egrets paid little attention to us after our first appearance in the treetop, soon returning to the scraggly nests that cluttered the branches. Some of the flat piles of sticks held four or five pale chalky-blue eggs, weathered and soiled. In other nests small young begged hungrily with feeble voices. This clicking and rasping from the throats of hundreds of young egrets created an incessant background of sound that was punctuated by the loud, raucous squawks of the incoming parents. Cormorants added their coarse grunts to the din and throb; great blue herons their basso profoundo discord.

In a rookery, all is activity; birds come and go; there are violent squabbles between rivals, fencing matches between neighbors, even arguments among small young in the same nest. They learn to spar early, striking savagely with movements that are suggestively reptilian.

As we watched, an egret swung over the colony and pitched into the big cypress on our left. It stepped stealthily along the limb to one of the half dozen nests clustered there. Pulling its snaky neck into a comfortable S-curve, it contemplated the four pastel-blue treasures lying in their rough cradle. Then it raised the sweeping bridal plumes on its back, and let them fall gently into place. Squatting on its collapsible legs, it placed the warm bare skin of its brood patch in contact with the eggs. One would have said offhand that it could tell its own eggs from the others near by, but Bob Allen, who perhaps understood heron psychology better than anyone else, once tested this in a Long Island night heron colony. He painted stripes on the eggs but it didn't seem to surprise the birds. He then placed four square wooden blocks in a nest and removed the eggs to a makeshift nest less than a foot or two away. Although the heron could have touched its own eggs with its bill, it reacted purely to location, went directly to the uncomfortable wooden blocks and tried to adjust them under its brood patch!

Allen also found that night herons develop bright coral legs during their courtship. At first these pink-stockinged birds sit around in the trees as if waiting for something to happen—which is literally true. A few males, each on his own territory, commence to "dance," a set routine of treading and bowing. Soon the whole colony is caught up in the spirit of the thing. Females approach the displaying males, to be accepted or rebuffed, and thus is the mating consummated and the egg-laying started. I am sure the egrets must have some such marriage ritual; and their plumes must play an important part, for they are bridal plumes, discarded when the flush of mating is over.

With such loveliness about us, we overlooked the slight fishy odor that hung over Cranetown. It was not bad. Two weeks later it would be intolerable when the knee-deep water at the foot of the trees had receded, exposing the mud. The accumulation of droppings, the stinking half-digested fish disgorged by nervous young, and the dead bodies of some of the young birds themselves would retch an uncertain stomach.

But on that day we saw no dead young lying about; such mortality would be more noticeable later when the restless half-grown youngsters started to clamber about the branches. Those that miss their footing and fall to the ground are abandoned. They are a typical sight in all heron rookeries. It always grieves me to see these scrawny half-starved birds sitting hunched and dejected on the ground, waiting for death to end their hunger. This mortality is normal; allowance for it is made in the ruthless ecological bookkeeping of nature.

In over forty years of birding, I have visited scores of heron rookeries, more than I can easily recall. I have seen colonies of American egrets in cactus on islands along the Texas coast; in tall eucalyptus trees in California; in dense willows bordering the St. Johns River in Florida; and high up in swamp maples in New Jersey; but Reelfoot's Cranetown is by all odds the most beautiful. It has the Chinese print quality with which I had vested my early preconceived visions of what an egret colony should look like—graceful alabaster birds in a wonderland of tall cypress.

That there are today bird cities like Cranetown is a tribute to the National Audubon Society and other conservation-minded people, for a half century ago egrets were rarely to be seen in Tennessee, or anywhere else for that matter. Today there are scores of rookeries of them in the South, and they have actually become familiar birds in summer months all the way to the Great Lakes and New England. But in the far South the little snowy egret is the commoner bird. Hundreds can again be seen walking on golden slippers over the black muck along the St. Johns River and hundreds, even thousands at times, can be seen from the Tamiami Trail without even leaving the car. All this is reflected in their growing colonies to the north—as far as tidewater Maryland and even New Jersey. In fact, as I had confidently predicted, their gurgling love notes can now be heard in heronies on Long Island where they bred in Giraud's day.

Yet fifty years ago, a friend of mine journeying down the St. Johns saw but one egret. The plume hunters had been very thorough. When we hear about the prices that were paid for "aigrettes" we can understand; they brought $32 an ounce, twice their weight in gold. In a few months, at the London Commercial Sales Rooms alone, nearly 200,000 plumes were auctioned off. That meant not only 200,000 egrets but all their young besides, for the adults bore the nuptial spray only during the nesting season.

It is revolting to read the eye-witness accounts of bodies rotting on the mud, young too weak to stand, and parentless birds staggering to their feet and vainly trying to attract the attention of every passing heron. One plumer testified that wounded egrets were propped up where they would attract the attention of others, until ants ate out their eyes.

The first Audubon warden in South Florida, Guy Bradley, was shot near Cape Sable, in 1905, as he boarded a boat to look for plumes. A marker stands today where his body washed ashore. In those days they knew no law along the Everglades coast. One sly character, who was said to have killed more than fifty men, even kept a record of his victims. For their own protection his neighbors banded together and did away with him one dark night, lest their own names be entered in the ledger. Until recently people of the southwest coast and the Shark River system were a tough lot, close to the edge of subsistence and even more out of step with the times than their Anglo-Saxon brethren in the Ozarks, or the "pecker-woods" in the mountains of Tennessee. For years the only law and order they were aware of were the wardens of the National Audubon Society. Recently, the part of the Everglades where they live, the last truly wild remnant of Florida, has become our newest National Park.

In the spring of 1937, when I first visited this sub-tropical wilderness, it was as wild as it was when Ponce de Leon sailed past its southern capes. As we poled our skiff through the tea-colored channel from East Lake to Cuthbert Lake, the mangroves formed an interlacing arch overhead, making a weird tunnel. To all appearances it might have been ten thousand years ago—or a million, for mangroves have looked the same since the Eocene. We peered into the gloomy labyrinth where the tangle of roots, projecting several feet above the water, propped up masses of leathery green foliage. It was easy to imagine that ancient reptiles or primitive birds or at least the extinct Florida rhinoceros could still exist there.

Our guide, an Audubon warden, was an amateur herpetologist and had recently taken a water-snake new to science not far from this place. There were crocodiles around, too, he said—not alligators mind you, but the rare Florida crocodile, the one with the nasty temper. We half wanted to see one, but half hoped we wouldn't.

Mullet by the dozen raced from the shallows as we rounded the bends, and, impatient to reach safety, skipped clear of the water. Several slapped the side of the boat in their haste to get away. A huge tarpon left its wake in the narrow channel ahead; an alligator, its eyes protruding like two knobs above the turbid water, suddenly submerged, and a cotton-mouth moccasin slid away among the roots. This was primordial country, slowly being created from the ooze by that builder of land, the red mangrove.

At the end of our Amazonian tunnel we broke full upon the broad green water of Cuthbert Lake, which took its name from a plume hunter who was the first to find his way there. When he left he carried with him $1,800 worth of egret plumes. As we looked out upon the lake we could see an island white with birds, the very island that Cuthbert saw when he fought his way through the mud, the sawgrass and the mangroves. The dominant birds were wood ibises, and they crowned the skyline of the island like huge white blossoms.

There were a few white ibises, too, very much smaller, with just a touch of black on the four outer wing feathers. The bright scarlet faces of these "Spanish curlews" are very different from the naked wattled gray visages of the "flint-heads," as the crackers call the wood ibises. The latter is a true stork, and not an ibis. Most Americans do not know we have a native stork.

As our skiff approached, a host of white birds, a thousand or more, swirled out of the trees and spiraled upward. A few wood ibises stayed behind and balanced awkwardly on the topmost branches, but one by one they left to join the milling throng soaring in wide circles in the thermal of warm air that rose in an invisible column above the island. Some were at least half a mile up, seemingly right under the clouds, and we had to look them over carefully with our 12-powers, for white pelicans were up there, too. The white pelicans do not nest in Florida, however.

As the blizzard of ibises and egrets swept over us, a dozen breathlessly beautiful shell-pink birds with tawny tails banked against the dark green of the mangroves, like flamboyant tropical orchids that had taken wing. They were my first roseate spoonbills. Later we found several nests, but most of the young were already flying—all except a few half-grown well-padded white babies, very much more cuddly and appealing than the scrawny, homely young of the herons and egrets. Their stubby spoon-shaped bills, which reminded us of the lip ornaments of the Ubangis, snapped at us harmlessly.

I hauled my ponderous 4 x 5 Graflex about with me through the rank growth; and, although I located several young spoonbills in the top of a dead mangrove, it took all my will power to keep both hands on the camera while I focused. Clouds of mosquitoes swarmed over my bare arms, particularly just above my elbows where I had been sunburned a week or two before, and where the new tender skin had become badly burned again on this trip. The little brown vampires settled by the hundreds, while I was impotent to brush them off. I got my pictures, but I carry a memento of that ordeal to this day in a band of heavy freckles on each arm—produced, I suppose, by some alchemy of the poisons of sun and mosquitoes.

Somehow spoonbills, swinging their bills rhythmically like metronomes through the muddy shallows for the little pot-bellied minnows, (*Cyprinodon*) and other killifishes look as though they belong among the mangroves. There are always a few back in the shadowy "Auger Hole" on the southwest coast of Florida, and on Bottlepoint Key where Bob Allen lived like a hermit among the "pinks" which he described so captivatingly in *The Flame Birds*. But in Texas, where they nest in a setting of prickly pear cactus and mesquite, there are ten spoonbills today for every one that lives in Florida. They have never made a real comeback in the peninsula since the days when their wings were sold in St. Augustine for fans.

Today most of the big glamorous waders are a bit more secure. Reddish egrets again dance their fantastic ballet in the shallows along the Texas coast. We know about how many of them there are, and how many spoonbills, but we can only guess at the numbers of some of the more widespread species—great blue herons for example. We should have to search out each colony and appraise it.

The largest rookeries are those of the white ibis. Some years there may be nesting aggregations of 100,000 and even more. In 1937 it seemed as though every white ibis in Florida had gathered in the "jams" on the St. Johns River north of Lake Washington. The birds were well protected that year, too—by the Audubon wardens and by the weather. Seven of the eighteen miles of road that we traversed from Lake Washington to Turtle Mound, where we kept the boat, had been flooded by torrential rains, and it was the only time I have ever seen fish swim down the road in front of the car! The river was swollen, too, and when we reached the square mile of willows and buttonbush where the birds congregated, we could stand in our boat and look into the nests. Long goose-like strings of white birds, converging from every quarter, twisted down out of the blue sky in snaky streamers. Some who saw the colony that year calculated there were half a million birds; but others, more cautious, put the figure at 200,000. The following year the site was abandoned. Ibises, like herons are mobile. They shift with the varying waterlevels, especially in the State of Florida.

Those who damn the herons because they eat fish, have often noticed that the best fishing grounds are down current from an established rookery. They insist that the herons choose the place because of that. Biologists are now convinced that the reverse is true. The fish are numerous because of the birds. Dr. Herbert Mills, of Tampa, Florida, firmly believed that the protection of the fish-eating waterbirds is not just an aesthetic and educational principle, but an *economic* one, which will insure Florida's multimillion-dollar fish industry.* A few years ago when several islands in Tampa Bay were put under guardianship, about 2700 birds nested there. In less than a dozen years they increased spectacularly to 215,000! At the time the colonies were taken over, fishing in the bay was so poor that the local extinction of the mullet was predicted. But as the bird colonies grew, the bare white sands in the water near by and for miles around gradually turned green with algae, grass and water weeds. Small mullet became numerous again and each year they grew larger. By 1944, mullet were again caught in Tampa Bay in the fabulous numbers of a half century before. Dr. Mills estimated that the rains and tides washed the excrement of the herons into the water at the rate of fifty tons a day. Just as we manure the land to better the crops, so do the birds fertilize the watery pastures from which they exact tribute. Some day mariculture will take its place beside agriculture.

A visit to any rookery, whether it be that of the dainty snowy or the clumsy great blue, is an odoriferous experience. But one expects fish-eating birds to smell fishy. It would not be so bad if it were not for the habit they all have—especially the young ones—of losing their meal so easily. This is probably nervousness, but it almost looks as though there were some intention to it when a person is whacked on the back of the head with a half-digested mud-puppy.

* "The Log of Whiskey Stump" by Herbert R. Mills in *Florida Naturalist,* October, 1944.

The most trying afternoon I ever spent in a heronry was in a colony of little blue herons near the Stone Harbor Lighthouse on the New Jersey coast. The grove of trees where the birds nested was as nearly impregnable as any rookery could be. It was virtually a fortress. I hauled my equipment, the camera, tripod, jointed pipes for the blind, burlap and camp stool through a clinging, clawing, catbrier entanglement, then across a rank poison ivy thicket through which I could discover no easy path. The last few yards were negotiated on my hands and knees under the nests while the fish rained down. Hot, exhausted and sticky, I set up my blind and relaxed on the flimsy camp stool. Two or three large young birds were silhouetted against the sky. On these I focused. After a long hour in which I became acutely aware that I had forgotten the flit gun, a blue-black adult heron flew by with a *wof, wof, wof,* of its wings, swung around and landed. It looked disapprovingly at the expectant young birds, whose parent I presumed it to be, and momentarily raised its hackles and plumes. I pressed the shutter release. At the loud *ka-lump!* when the Graflex mirror flipped up, the bird bolted and headed, so far as I could tell, straight for Cape May. But I had got my picture. I waited for another shot, but the trees blocked off the sinking afternoon sun, so I dismantled my blind.

Again with the bundle of heavy pipes and my camera equipment I struggled out—through the fish, the poison ivy and the catbriers. Tired, sweaty and not much interested in birds, I reached the car.

An hour later, when I walked through the streets of Stone Harbor, a half dozen mongrel dogs followed me for several blocks. I was probably the most interesting-smelling visitor they had met in some time!

Trailing America's Rarest Bird

THE mud flats at the mouth of the Merrimac were swarming with shorebirds that autumn afternoon. A northeast wind whipping over the sea had forced in some of the flocks that take the short cut from Nova Scotia to the southern beaches. A lone curlew flew over. It looked small and my glass showed its sickle-shaped bill to be very stubby—shorter than the bill of any young Hudsonian whimbrel should be. Could this be an Eskimo curlew, at last? Silhouetted against the low sunlight, it showed no color, nor did it call. It kept right on traveling until it was out of sight, and I had the uneasy feeling that I had muffed the chance of a lifetime.

The Eskimo curlew is still being reported; in the last few years field ornithologists have spotted several in Texas. They have been well seen too, so I have no doubt that a handful of these almost mythical shorebirds still make the long and hazardous pilgrimage from the arctic to the pampas. I would like to make its acquaintance before it joins the spectral company of the Labrador duck, the great auk, the passenger pigeon and the Carolina paroquet.

Any tourist can see trumpeter swans if he will make the trip. One can watch them without getting out of the car where the road skirts the elk refuge at Jackson Hole, Wyoming. There are others further up the Teton Valley at Jackson Lake and a few pairs float like miniature icebergs on lakes in the Yellowstone.

The California condor, the huge vulture with the ten-foot wing spread, is not so accessible as it was in 1936 when I stopped in Los Angeles with six hours between trains. Five young members of a Junior Audubon Club took me to Sespé Canyon, showed me my first condors soaring high in the blue like mammoth prehistoric birds, and hustled me back to the railroad station with four minutes to spare. Lately the area has been closed for it was found that even bird photographers and field glass students are a disturbing factor in the precarious life of the six score giants that still survive. Most bird watchers are good sports about the restrictions and are willing to make the sacrifice.

Whereas the trumpeter swan and the condor will probably not disappear within our time, and may hold on indefinitely, we cannot be so sure of the whooping crane. There are only about three dozen left—which is not much capital to build on. Whereas the condor has the greatest wingspread of any North American bird, and the trumpeter swan the greatest weight, the whooping crane is the tallest. Size is a lethal handicap in the modern world. Bob Allen, however, was optimistic when I saw him in Texas in early January of 1948. Six of the whooping crane families that spent the winter on the Aransas Refuge had returned from the north with one young bird each. Allen, who was engaged in a three-year joint research project of the National Audubon Society and the United States Fish and Wildlife Service, proudly showed me his charges. He could tell each pair on sight and knew where they went each day. There were thirty-one whoopers in Texas, he said, and one in Louisiana. One wild one, that is, for there were two captives in the New Orleans Zoo. The Louisiana bird could, he said, be written off the books if it continued to live alone.

On New Year's day in 1948, when Bob Smith, the Mississippi flyway biologist, took me out over the vast coastal marshes west of the Delta in his two-seated patrol plane, we invaded the lonely realm of the last of the Louisiana whoopers. There had been ten of them prior to the high water in 1940. When the floods receded, only three birds returned from the back country where they had sought high ground. The others were casualties. As Smith put it, "they had probably gone into the Gumbo." Since 1942 there has been but one bird and Smith tells me it is so wary that he has never seen it on the ground.

As we flew west from the Rainey, Smith leaned back in his pilot's seat and pointed ahead. Over his shoulder I saw a white speck against the golden marsh, a huge white bird flying, not one of the numerous snow geese that were scattered like white flakes among the blues. It was a mile or more away when we first saw it, but as our speedy little plane shortened the gap we could see the great black primaries stroking the air with the deft upward flip, so characteristic of cranes. We could even see its bald red crown. The big bird towered and veered to the right and for a brief moment we were flying not more than two hundred feet apart. I cursed the broken lensboard of the graflex that rested idly across my knees. The bird was bugling I was sure, for we could see its bill open, but the roar of our motor drowned out its challenge.

With the probable exception of the Eskimo curlew, which looks so much like the Hudsonian curlew that we can merely guess at its status, there is only one North American bird rarer than the whooping crane—the ivory-billed woodpecker. A few years ago Lester Walsh and I spent ten days trying to settle rumors that were being whispered amongst ornithologists —rumors of ivory-billed woodpeckers in the wilderness of the Santee Basin of South Carolina. A well-known turkey hunter whose word was considered good had seen them there. As if that were not enough, he swore the Carolina paroquet was there, too. Several times small green parrots had come to the bait before his blind while he was waiting for turkeys, he said. This sounded incredible, as the last good record of Carolina paroquets was a flock in Florida in 1920.

Even if the paroquets were not there, the ivory-bills were worth trying for. The Santee Swamps are extensive; hundreds of square miles of cypress, sweet gum and pine embrace the muddy yellow stream with its tortuous oxbows, swamps known to few men besides a handful of hogherders and trappers since the historic days of Marion, the "Swamp Fox." Should we go straight to the spot where the turkey hunter had made his discovery? One or two other parties had searched the woods there without success. Might it not be possible that the birds were elsewhere in this vast area— perhaps somewhere upriver? After consulting maps with Alexander Sprunt, who knows the Carolina low country well, we decided to put a boat into the stream at a point far inland in the state, and drift down toward the coast—a distance of about 100 miles. It was an exciting thought —penetrating this virgin territory. Walsh and I would be the first bird-men ever to cover this section of river.

Unpacking our folding boat, we stretched its vulcanized rubber hull over the skeleton framework, made the fastenings tight and eased the trim eighteen-foot craft into the water. Food, enough to last five or six days, was stowed fore and aft, and with double-bladed paddles flashing, we slipped into the silty flow.

It was late in the day when we made our start, and our better judgment should have held us until next morning, but we were eager to be on the river for at least an hour or two before making camp. The exhilaration of floating between walls of moss-hung cypresses and verdant tangles crowned by large white Cherokee roses and yellow jessamine obliterated all thoughts of time and caution, and darkness found us without a camping spot. We welcomed this excuse to make a night of it on the river, loafing in the current, listening to the night sounds.

With paddles across our knees, ready for quick action should a riffle betray a snag, we floated along. Several times the sudden slap of an alligator's tail, or a leaping carp, made us jump. We pierced the darkness with the thin beam of our flashlight in the direction of strange animal voices, but could do nothing. Occasionally a white-throated sparrow sang in the blackness, as if disturbed from fitful slumber. We drifted into little parties of wood ducks concernedly uttering their soft finch-like *jeee*. At the stabbing flash of the light they fled, the females almost screaming their terrified *who-eek!*

The real bird of the night in the Santee is the barred owl. From everywhere came their baritone hootings—*Who cooks for you, who cooks for you all?* Two owls "talking" to each other in mellow southern accent, would work up to a pitch that reverberated back and forth through the swamp. Although we saw the dim form of but one of them that evening, we counted fifty-five of them hooting in the course of a few miles!

Rather than pass by too much of the river country at night, we pulled up to the right bank, wedged the prow between two logs, and waited for morning. People trained in the art of sleeping under adverse conditions can get their forty winks anywhere—in the rear seat of an automobile, on the floor, or even standing up, hanging to a subway strap. We had never before tried sleeping in a sitting posture in a narrow, unstable boat, but we eventually dropped into a sort of coma that certainly could not have been called slumber. Daylight seemed interminably long in coming. For hours we imagined we could see the sky lightening toward the horizon. Awakening from a long doze, we heard a cardinal sing. That time we knew it was the real thing. In a few minutes the air was ringing with the chants of cardinals, Carolina wrens and titmice. The lesser voices were drowned out, but in half an hour, when the first burst of song had subsided, we could hear the weak sibilant jargon of gnatcatchers, the sweet song of yellow-throated warblers and the ascending buzz of the parulas.

The plain-colored Swainson's warbler, which plays hide-and-seek in the cane patches, had not yet arrived, but the striking blue-gray and gold prothonotary warbler was there, singing its emphatic *tweet-tweet-tweet-tweet-tweet* in the sepulchral cypress sloughs. We heard the Wayne's black-throated green warbler lisping its *zee-zee-zee-zee-zoo-zee,* identically like the sibilant song of its brother subspecies in New England.

During the first five days we saw more than 1200 wood ducks. From every bend of the river they flew, usually in pairs, the drab females always just in front of the exquisite males, as if by some inviolable rule of wood duck etiquette. A few birds had brought their fluffy newly hatched young from the hollow boles in the forest through the dried-out swamps to the river's edge, where they hugged the banks in close convoy at their mothers' tails. The swiftness of the current in parts of the river is a hazard to young ducklings, and several times we saw lone babies, wildly peeping, borne downstream far from their broods. Alligators probably gobble up some of them.

The "gators" prefer the low muddy banks on which to drag themselves. There are not many on the Santee, and they are extremely shy, because shooting parties from time to time cruise the river at night with jack lights, spotting the coal-red eye-shine of the armored saurians.

Although the swamp forests extend almost unbroken over hundreds of square miles, much was cut over years ago, as the old stumps testify. But we found large tracts that had never known an ax. We were awed by the tremendous size of some of the forest giants—sweet gums fourteen feet in circumference and loblolly pines with a girth of sixteen feet. Some of the cypresses had swollen buttresses that measured over thirty feet!

Early morning was, by far, the best time of day. Turkey cocks could be heard gobbling at daybreak, a fatal habit that poachers take advantage of. Woodpeckers of half a dozen species rolled out their tattoos. An eagle overhead, a glimpse of a swallow-tailed kite gliding above the live oaks and ghostly egrets in a dark "gum slough" contributed to a picture of primeval beauty. The only false note was the great number of scraggly hogs we encountered. These swamps in spots are virtual pigpens with soil rooted up and countless interlacing hoofmarks in the soft mud. Perhaps this is the reason we saw so few moccasins away from the riverbank.

Four days we traveled down the yellow-brown river, stopping where the trees were biggest to hunt for ivory-bills; at night we dragged the kayak ashore over the slippery mud and slung our hammocks between cypress saplings. We saw hardly a soul, except for two or three Negroes fishing for mudfish. On the fifth day, sunburned and without water, we reached "the bluff." Here where the ivory-bills were originally reported, we were joined by two friends from the north, John Baker and Bayard Christy.

During the next four days we covered the swamp for miles around by dugout and on foot. We concentrated on Wadmacaun Island, the best-looking spot we had seen yet; but if we had known as much about ivory-bills then as we know now, we would have passed the cypress by and spent more time on the drier ridges, among the sweet gums and pines.

But our mission failed; we saw pileated woodpeckers wherever we went but no ivory-bills. It is quite possible that the ivory-bill reports were authentic, as the amount of virgin timber along the Santee would probably have supported at least one pair. No one has had further evidence that they were present, other than a few suspicious-looking diggings. However, we are convinced that almost anything might hide in these swamps successfully for years.

As for the paroquets—we had never quite believed the report in the first place. Holly Shokes, a native who had lived all his young life at the edge of the swamp and had never even visited Charleston, forty miles away, showed us the clearing where the paroquets were seen. It was an open sedgy field between the pine woods and the swamp. We agreed that if paroquets would resort to such a spot they could just as well turn up in a thousand similar places in back-country Carolina.

On the night before our return to New York, we listened in fascination to Holly's father, Old Man Shokes, as he told stories of the "ha'nts" which prowl the abandoned rice plantations of the low country. Blowing out the candles past midnight, we climbed into our bunks. Chuck-will's-widows chanted monotonously in the live-oak woodlands outside. It must have been well after one when I heard Holly mumble excitedly in his sleep,

"See! See! There 'tis!" I am sure it was not of "ha'nts" he was dreaming but of ivory-bills or paroquets.

Few living naturalists have seen a live ivory-bill. Twenty inches long, it is exceeded in size by only one other woodpecker in the world—the imperial woodpecker—a giant that lives among the pines in the mountains of Northwestern Mexico.

Audubon wrote about the ivory-bill, so did Alexander Wilson, but it began to look as though the last remnants of its clan would disappear from the earth before its life history and ecology could be properly recorded. In what might prove to be the twilight of the species, the National Audubon Society set up a research project in collaboration with Cornell University to study the bird and to see whether anything could be done to save it. For three years James Tanner devoted himself to the study and when his painstaking work was completed he was awarded his doctor's degree. Tanner travelled 45,000 miles by car, train, boat, horseback and on foot, searching for ivory-bills. He spent months in the swamps, following the birds around, recording their every action. He found out many things about them; that each pair requires a territory of no less than six square miles of primeval wilderness to live in; that an average of thirty-six pairs of pileated woodpeckers could subsist in the same piece of woodlands, and that at least 126 pairs of red-bellied woodpeckers could also find their living there. The ivory-bill feeds mostly on trees that have been dead two or three years. It takes about that long for decay to set in and the first insects to attack the wood—the fat whitish grubs of borers that tunnel just beneath the tight bark. These grubs are the staple food of the ivory-bill. In another year or so, these subsurface borers disappear. Decay strikes deeper into the heartwood, but the ivory-bill is no longer interested. The tree now becomes fodder for the pileated, which continues to rip open the tunneled wood until the tree, blasted and crumbling, falls to earth.

When Audubon voyaged down the Mississippi he found ivory-bills common enough. He began to notice them at the point where the Ohio joins the Mississippi, and recorded more as he progressed southward. He wrote, "I have seen entire belts of Indian chiefs closely ornamented with the tufts and bills of this species."

It was not the Indians who eliminated the ivory-bill nor the collectors

CLOSE TO EXTINCTION and second only to the ivory-billed woodpecker in rarity, the whooping crane is doomed unless the few surviving birds can raise young yearly as this alert pair has done. There were thirty-two wild whoopers in 1962.

SWAMPS KNOWN TO FEW MEN surround the Santee River in South Carolina where we searched the primeval forest for a rumored ivory-billed woodpecker.

who came later (there are between 200 and 250 ivory-bills in museums and collections in this country); it was the logging of the southern river forests. These specialized birds were not able to adapt themselves to second-growth woodlands as the pileated has done.

Tanner points out that the disappearance of the ivory-bill in different sections of the southeast coincided with the timber cutting. By 1940 there was good evidence of the presence of ivory-bills in only three states, South Carolina, Florida and Louisiana. Tanner estimated that there could not be more than twenty-four left in the whole southeast—the remaining environment would not support more. However, in three years of hard work he had seen only *five*—all of these on the Singer Tract in northeastern Louisiana.

The Singer Tract! It had become a legend to me. It was the largest piece of virgin timber left in the east; the only spot that still retained nearly all of its original fauna—wolves, panthers, turkeys, even ivory-bills —all except paroquets. Eighty thousand acres of low-lying wilderness; it would not last long. Already the axe was ringing against ancient buttresses, and large blocks of marketable timber had been stripped away. If I was ever to see an ivory-bill I would have to act, and so it was that in May of 1942, at the little hotel in Talullah I again joined Bayard Christy. Five years had passed since we slogged through the swamps of Wadmacaun; this time we hoped for better luck. Mr. Christy, just turned seventy, said the ivory-bill and the flamingo were the two birds he most wished to see before he died.

We had permits from the State of Louisiana to trespass on this forbidden ground where outsiders are jealously excluded. But 80,000 acres is a big territory in which to locate a pair of woodpeckers. To insure our success, we searched out a local woodsman by the name of Kuhn, a modern Daniel Boone of great integrity, who had helped Jim Tanner with his work and who probably had seen as many ivory-bills as any man living. Kuhn knew every foot of the great woodlands that extend along the winding Tensas (Tinsaw) River. When we asked what our chances were, he replied, "Well, gentlemen, I've got good news. One of the colored boys was down on the west side of John's Bayou two weeks ago and he saw four—a whole family."

We were in the swamp before daybreak while the barred owls were still rolling their baritone hootings across the cypress bays. Waiting only until it was light enough to see our way through the trees, we struck out from the dirt road where we had parked the car. Setting the pace with his long swinging stride, Kuhn led us toward a section where a pair of ivory-bills had roosted the year before. He urged us to step along because the best time to locate ivory-bills is when they first leave their roosting holes in the morning. "Then they talk more," he explained.

It was not as hard going as I had anticipated. The vistas between the widely spaced forest giants were quite open, and the tangles of cat brier and poison ivy that barred our way were easily circumvented. We were in the higher, drier part of the swamp, "the second bottoms." The trees whose massive crowns towered 150 or more feet above our heads were sweet gums, Nuttall's oaks and ash, while the lesser trees were mostly hackberries and pecans. In the lower parts of the swamp grew the pale green cypresses, their knobby "knees" emerging from the dark coffee-colored water. Never, said Kuhn, had he seen an ivory-bill on a cypress.

A primeval forest is not like a second-growth woodland with its uniform growth and closed crown. The ancient forest giants are separated by smaller trees and tangles of undergrowth. In spots, the sunlight even reaches the ground. Seldom have I heard more bird song than filled the air in the Singer Tract that May morning. Cardinals, chats, white-eyed vireos, hooded warblers and Carolina wrens sang from the low tangles; Acadian flycatchers, gnatcatchers, redstarts and yellow-throated, parula and cerulean warblers poured their contributions into the cauldron of song from higher perches.

We had gone half a mile from the road when Kuhn stopped short. He had caught a note on the edge of his sphere of hearing. I thought I heard it, but it could have been the versatile chat. We had been told to listen for a voice that sounded something like a nuthatch. But there were plenty of nuthatches in these woods, too, to confound us. We found ourselves starting at strange unfamiliar notes that turned out to be squirrels and red-bellied woodpeckers. Kuhn assured us that when we heard the ivory-bill we would know it all right. "Nothing in the whole woods sounds like it."

Striking off in the direction where Kuhn had heard the suspicious note, we walked a hundred paces, then listened in silence for several minutes. This procedure we repeated again and again. Red-bellied woodpeckers seemed to be in every huge tree, calling *chiv, chiv.* Of pileateds there were any number, and we found a nest with a brood of young, buzzing like angry bees. We crossed and criss-crossed the best part of the swamp where the John's Bayou birds once ranged. Deer leaped from our path and stood watching, wide-eyed, from the shadows. The tracks of turkeys and 'coon laced the soft mud, and we even found some large round prints that Kuhn said were made by a panther. At least one or two of these large animals still ranged through the Singer—Louisiana cougars—survivors of a nearly extinct race of these big cats. Later, when I hung back to investigate a Swainson's warbler in a tangle of cane and palmetto, from the corner of my eye I caught sight of a large tawny form as it bounded silently across the wagon trail over which we had just passed. It was the panther, I knew, for no deer has a tail three feet long. It had probably not noticed me as I stood, half hidden, waiting for the warbler to sing. Hoping for a better look, I searched after it; but the wily cat had gone.

By early afternoon we must have covered fifteen or twenty miles within a block of woodland less than two or three miles square. Kuhn said it was possible to go for days without finding the ivory-bills. "You might take one direction and the birds the other," he explained. As proof that they were around he pointed out some diggings made by ivory-bills and showed us how to tell them from the squarish holes made by the pileated. The ivory-bills chip off the tight bark in great flakes, sometimes almost peeling a tree. We saw many trees where ivory-bills had been at work.

Late in the afternoon we found a hole that looked suspicious; it seemed much too large for a pileated. We planned to watch it that evening, suspecting it might prove to be an ivory-bill's roosting hollow, but our hopes were blasted, when at dusk, a fox squirrel entered it.

The next morning we started out on our own. Except for a small magnetic compass, we were unguided, but we had a good mental picture of the layout of this part of the Singer Tract; we knew that the road extended from east to west and that John's Bayou crossed it from north to south. With this knowledge, we picked our way over the same ground as the day before, alert for rattlesnakes, camouflaged by the dry, silt-covered leafage. Our luck was no better, so we waded the turbid waters of John's Bayou and tried the woodlands on the west bank. We found wolf tracks in the yellow mud along the margin of the stream. It was here that the colored boy had seen the ivory-bills two weeks before. There were signs about; many trees had been peeled, but we saw no birds. We were beginning to give up hope.

By noon, we were back at the spot, down the road, where we had seen so many diggings the day before. We would make another sortie before throwing in the sponge. Hardly had we gone a hundred yards when a startling new sound came from our right—an indescribable tooting note, musical in a staccato sort of way. For a moment it did not click, but then I knew—*it was the ivory-bill!* I had expected it to sound more like a nuthatch; it was much more like the "toy tin trumpet" described by Alexander Wilson or the "clarinet" of Audubon. Breathlessly we stalked the insistent toots, stepping carefully, stealthily, so that no twig would crack. With our hearts pounding we tried to keep cool, hardly daring to believe that this was it—that this was what we had come fifteen hundred miles to see. We were dead certain this was no squirrel or lesser woodpecker, for an occasional blow would land—*whop!*—like the sound of an axe. Straining our eyes, we discovered the first bird, half hidden by the leafage, and in a moment it leaped upward into the full sunlight. This was no puny pileated; this was a whacking big bird, with great white patches on its wings and a gleaming white bill. By its long recurved crest of blackish jet we knew it was a female. We were even close enough to see its pale yellow eyes. Tossing its hammer-like head to right and left, it tested the diseased trunk with a whack or two as it jerked upward. Lurching out to the end of a broken-off branch, it pitched off on a straight line, like a duck, its wings making a wooden sound.

The other bird was a female, too. We had no trouble following the two, for as soon as they landed after a flight, they betrayed their location by their curious *henk, henk*. Whereas a pileated might call once and then remain silent for a quarter of an hour, an ivory-bill, once heard, is easy to find. Audubon wrote: "These (notes) are heard so frequently as to induce one to say that the bird spends few minutes of the day without uttering them, and the circumstance leads to its destruction."

These were the "kints" of the Bayou country; the white-billed "kates" we had heard about from Holly Shokes and old Sam who tended hogs up in the Santee. We had a feeling of unreality as we watched them. They looked downright archaic, completely unlike any other birds—unlike even the pileated.

We followed the big woodpeckers for nearly an hour before we lost them. During all that time they were in a partly logged section of the forest where some trees had been taken out but others, less marketable, were left standing. These birds, most likely, were the same two females that Tanner had seen in this place six months earlier. As mated ivory-bills accompany each other throughout the year, it could be surmised that there were no males about and these females were forced to resort to their own sex for companionship. Six months after our visit, John Baker saw only *one* female in this spot. The other had disappeared. One ivory-bill was seen in the Singer Tract as late as December, 1946.

Alleged sightings elsewhere have persisted right up until 1962, but they need verification. Even if the species is still with us, it is doubtful whether more than half a dozen individuals still exist on earth. Unlike the last passenger pigeon, which officially expired at the Cincinnati Zoo at 1:00 p.m. Central Standard Time, September 1, 1914, no one will know the exact time of the ivory-bill's passing.

Wings Over the Marsh

IN MY boyhood, on January evenings when I trudged home over Beckerink's fields, after making the rounds of my feeding trays, I often heard the whistling of wings in the dark, as golden-eyes flew over, headed for the Chadakoin. Later, I found small groups of them swimming on this little wooded creek that drains Chautauqua Lake in western New York. By crawling on my belly through the loose snow that blanketed the frozen swamp, I could reach the up-turned trees on the creek bank undetected. My 4-power LeMaire field glasses, which I had bought in response to an advertisement in *Bird Lore,* plainly showed the round white face spots on the drakes that swam attentively around the gray females. In fascination I watched them throw back their heads and sound their strange nasal courting cries. Near by floated big white American mergansers, with dark glossy-green heads and a peach-colored bloom on their breasts. From time to time reinforcements scaled over the elms and plowed into the icy water with a splash, using their big webbed feet as brakes. When all had assembled at the bend of the river where they would spend the night, there were nearly fifty golden-eyes and twice that many mergansers.

In early March, when a patch of water opened up at the lower end of the lake, migrating ducks of other sorts dropped in. Scaup, "black at both ends and white in the middle," were the most numerous. Among them were redheads and canvas backs, and a few ring-necks. I had no idea the water birds were so much fun; like most bird watchers, I had started with the songbirds, but now I had discovered the ducks. Little ruddies, their tails cocked like wrens, and diminutive buffleheads with white head patches floated like toy ducks in a gigantic bathtub. The water was deep, so most of the species represented were diving ducks, although a small flock of baldpates, which are surface feeders, made a living by robbing the coots when they came up with waterweed in their bills.

Just before the big spring breakup, when the ice went out of the lake, there were four or five hundred waterfowl in the open lead near the amusement park. That, we thought, was a great many ducks, and indeed it was for most places in the Appalachian plateau, for the hill country is ill-adapted to waterfowl. The *anatidae* follow the drainage pattern of the continent, reaching their greatest concentrations along the larger rivers, the Great Lakes, and the ocean. I have seen 100,000 canvas-backs on the Susquehanna flats in Maryland, and nearly that many pintails in the air over a marsh owned by a California gun club. Beyond the surf at Fire Island Inlet, on Long Island, I have estimated 30,000 scoters at one time, and at Montauk more than 50,000 of them. Once, on the shoals off Monomoy, on Cape Cod, our small boat plowed through a mile-long flock of American eiders, which Ludlow Griscom estimated to contain 60,000 birds. Griscom had once seen a gathering five times that large. The greatest single flock of ducks I have ever witnessed was on a federal refuge in the Illinois River bottoms——two-thirds of a million mallards.

People who live near these large concentrations have a distorted impression of the numbers of waterfowl. They cannot understand why some conservationists are so pessimistic about the future of these birds. But ducks are either as thick as bees about a hive or there are none. The distances between the pockets of birds are great, and actually the waterfowl make up only a tiny fraction of the total continental bird population.

Ducks of a feather flock together; and although it is often possible to see a dozen kinds at one time, each species has its traditional stopping places. One pond is a favorite resort of ruddy ducks, another of redheads. This is particularly noticeable on Long Island where it is possible to run up a list of thirty *anatidae* on a single trip, a feat that cannot be duplicated anywhere else on the Atlantic seaboard.

In making the Long Island tour, one of our first stops as we drive eastward from New York City is Hempstead Reservoir. Among the baldpates there, are often found two or three rusty-headed European widgeons, perhaps raised in Iceland, as is indicated by the seven recoveries on this side of the Atlantic of European widgeons banded on that bleak island. For many years we could also find a European teal or two there whenever we chose. Once when I showed a visiting Dutch ornithologist both of these European species in the field of his glass simultaneously, he commented that it looked just like a scene in Holland.

Further out on the island the highway crosses little creeks and inlets. Many of the small ponds, nearly devoid of plant life, are of no more interest to a duck than a cement-lined swimming pool, and scarcely a bird of any kind is to be seen save for a few mute swans which were bred on the big estates and have now gone wild. In contrast to these barren ponds and inlets, the fertile water at Carman River, a private sanctuary where we peer through a high wire fence, is swarming with pintails, black ducks, mallards and American mergansers. Among them are always a few gadwalls and shovellers, two species which are almost unknown elsewhere on Long Island.

And so, as we continue eastward, scaup, redhead, ruddy duck, goldeneye, bufflehead, old-squaw and others are added to our growing list, until we reach the headlands, where Long Island, shaped like a fish, terminates in one of the points of its tail. There stands Montauk Light, looking out over the water, and in the shelter of its lee wall we scan the thousands of scoters bedded offshore. There are American scoters, velvety black with bright orange noses; surf scoters or "skunk heads" with white head patches; and white-winged scoters. If we are lucky our telescope may pick up an eider. The ducks bob about like corks, far beyond the push and pull of the crashing surf, and smoky clouds of them trade back and forth on the horizon. The North Atlantic wind bites through double layers of clothing and our eyes water until it seems that the distant specks at which we are squinting do not merit the discomfort. If we stay over, however, we will see the morning flight, the great mass movement past the point. The scoters will be much closer then. An hour on the windswept bluff is all we can take at one time, yet the hardy birds are exposed to this bitter buffeting day and night.

In contrast to most ducks, whose pattern of life is filled with hardship, uncertainty and danger, the scaups that swim and dive around the municipal pier at St. Petersburg, Florida, don't have a bad time of it, nor do the pintails that flock to Lake Merritt in Oakland, California. They spend the summer in Western Canada where it is cool, and the winter in the sunny

PATTERNS are woven against the California sky by wavering skeins of snow geese. Conservationists fervently hope that our land will never become so crowded that there will no longer be room for great flocks of geese.

LORDLY CANVASBACKS ride at anchor. Large flocks still winter on
the Susquehanna Flats, on the Gulf Coast and along the Pacific, but with
a duck hunting pressure of 1,500,000 guns their future is precarious.

INTELLIGENT AND WARY, the black ducks survive the autumnal barrage better than do other more trusting waterfowl. Their dark bodies and silvery wing-linings are part of the picture in every salt marsh along the Atlantic seaboard.

DABBLERS. The European widgeon, upper left, visits America yearly. This one was photographed on Vancouver Island. The mallard, upper right, is our most abundant duck but in the Atlantic states the black duck, below, outnumbers it.

south, and they need not worry about their food problem, either, for they have been bribed with a daily handout of corn until they have become as trusting as puddle ducks. But except for the sheltered few that live on the dole, the life of a duck is a precarious one—the number of eggs they lay is an indicator of that. Whereas a hummingbird lays but two eggs and a gull, three, a duck must produce a dozen or more to maintain its population level. The odds against a duck are much greater than those that operate against hummingbirds or gulls.

No one knows what the original duck population of the continent was. Some put it at 500,000,000; others say it was probably not even half that. More than a century ago when Jim Bridger paddled his buffalo-skin boat through the gorge of Bear River where the stream meanders across the sprawling delta marshland before pouring its fresh mountain water into Great Salt Lake, the sky was darkened by a million wings. That was long before the market hunters came. But eventually, when competition became too great in the east and the flocks along the seaboard and in the Mississippi Valley were dwindling, these despoilers brought their methods to the Bear River country. In 1887, one gunner shot 1880 birds. Another bagged 335 in a single day, quite a contrast to today's legal limit of four birds. But the greatest drain on the ducks was a biological one, unwittingly imposed by the settlers who diverted more and more water from the upper reaches of the Bear River for irrigation. The marshes dried out, and tens of thousands of waterfowl died each year from western duck sickness, a form of botulism, a food disease that runs rampant when water becomes stagnant.

Except for the botulism, the factors affecting the Bear River waterfowl had been operating even more relentlessly elsewhere. There were still a lot of ducks by 1900—perhaps 150,000,000—we don't know; we had no bookkeeping system then. But the ever-increasing human population soon exceeded that of the declining waterfowl. More land, of necessity, was put to the plow, and between eighty and a hundred million acres of marshland were drained, although much of it proved worthless to agriculture. Superimposed on this, a dry cycle gripped the prairies in the twenties. The dust bowl made headlines and the very river bottoms blew away with the wind. During 1929, when it was estimated that 300,000 ducks died of botulism on the Bear River, the hunting pressure continued unabated, and two million ducks were brought to bag in the State of Minnesota alone. The fortunes both of ducks and of men were riding for a crash. The course of the waterfowl depression paralleled that of our own economic depression, and by 1935 the ducks reached an all-time low, 27,000,000 according to the estimates of the Fish and Wildlife Service. But forces were already at work that would aid their recovery. In 1929, a Migratory Bird Conservation Act had been passed, authorizing an expenditure of nearly ten million dollars during the following ten years for the establishment of waterfowl sanctuaries, but because of the depression this appropriation was cut. Not until the mid-thirties when the ducks were at their lowest point did the program really get underway. Unemployment relief and the retirement of submarginal land made it possible to secure labor and land cheaply. Millions of dollars in CCC and WPA money went into a mighty chain of refuges along all the important flyways. The Migratory Bird Hunting Stamp Act was passed, requiring each waterfowl hunter over sixteen years of age to buy a "duck stamp" at one dollar, to help finance the program.

At the mouth of the Bear River steam shovels and bulldozers had already transformed 58,000 acres into the first of the federal government's "super-refuges" for ducks and geese, and the wildlife engineers were benefiting by many of the lessons they had already learned there. Twenty miles of dikes had been thrown up to cut off the marshes from the salty waters of the lake. After a slow process of de-salting, the large bays were planted with choice duck foods; nesting islands and "loafing grounds" were created. A duck hospital was set up and by means of fresh water and an antitoxin that had been developed, thousands of ducks from nearby areas of Great Salt Lake were cured of botulism each year and sent to join their fellows on the flyways. One pintail, released after it had been treated for botulism at the refuge, was retaken at Palmyra Island, 3000 miles out in the Pacific Ocean.

Bear River is now only one of many refuges where biologists, by experimenting with food plants, and by managing the marshes, have made it possible for five ducks to live where there had been but one before. Each refuge has its special problems. P. J. Van Huzen, manager of the Sacramento reserve, in California, told me that most of his work was that of a dirt farmer—planting fields of rice and millet to hold the ducks and geese on government land while planes herded foraging flocks out of the nearby acres owned by irate commercial rice planters whose crops would otherwise be destroyed. In a world that is already suffering from an excess human population the problems of human survival will come into increasing conflict with wildlife.

To gain some idea of the immensity of the effort that has been devoted to the restoration program, look at the figures. There are now 218 refuges specifically created for waterfowl, and they cover more than 3,500,000 acres. More than 700 miles of dams and dikes have been built, 1000 miles of roads and trails, 1500 miles of fencing, 500 miles of ditches, nearly 1000 water control gates and more than 200 bridges.

When the funds are put up for a new refuge, all marsh birds increase, not only the waterfowl. At Sand Lake, in South Dakota, 6000 Franklin's gulls nested in the newly flooded marsh the first year. Within five years there were 60,000. On the Lower Souris, in North Dakota, 65,000 of these black-hooded gulls now breed, and additional tens of thousands reside in many other federal sanctuaries. Now when the great hordes of these "prairie doves" journey south through the plains to their winter home in the cold waters off the coasts of Peru and Chile, they fill the air for miles. At Sand Lake, one migrating flock, ten miles long and a mile wide, was estimated at 1,000,000 birds. Mrs. Jack Hagar has seen migrants over her cottage at Rockport, Texas, in flights that look like confetti in the sky.

The insignia of the flying goose marks the Fish and Wildlife Service refuges. These sanctuaries are usually the best places for wildlife for miles around, and bird watchers who live within striking distance of one often make it their headquarters on weekend trips. A trip across the northern tier of states, with a day or two at each of the federal refuges, makes an ideal vacation.

Today as we drive out along the broad dikes which impound the water at the mouth of the Bear River it is again possible, as it was in Jim Bridger's day, to see a million birds. Even in the summer months the marsh is teeming with life. A few steps off the road along any ditch will flush a gadwall or some other duck from its hatful of eggs. On all sides little male ruddy ducks slap their cobalt-blue bills on their chests for the benefit of the females. Scores of family convoys of Canada geese swim on the bays, and young western grebes ride on the backs of their graceful, serpent-necked parents, like children on the swan boats in the Boston Public Gardens.

Sable-plumaged glossy ibises and immaculate snowy egrets—hundreds of black wings and hundreds of white wings against a backdrop of snow-capped mountains—lend a curious southern note to this western marsh.

Every refuge is different. Seney, in northern Michigan, is a marsh in the pine forest, with sandhill cranes bugling in the beaver bogs. Bombay Hook, in Delaware, has nesting shovellers and gadwalls, induced by marsh management to nest near Atlantic tidewater for the first time in ornithological history. Aransas, a 55,000 acre super-refuge on the coast of Texas, boasts the last whooping cranes, and such Mexican creatures as armadillos and caracaras. Mattamuskeet, in North Carolina, is a gathering place for thousands of whistling swans while Sacramento, in California, is the winter home of Ross's goose, the little white goose that numbers not more than several thousand in this world.

Although even rails, marsh wrens, swallows and blackbirds benefit in these waterfowl nurseries, they are primarily "duck factories." Banding is done on a large scale for it is important to know where ducks go, what paths they take, and what the survival ratios are. The records at headquarters show that many hundreds of thousands of mallards and pintails have been ringed with numbered aluminum bracelets.

By using the banding records as a basis, the continent has been divided into four broad belts, each containing a waterfowl breeding area and a wintering area, connected by a system of migration routes. These swaths, which run north and south on the map, are called "flyways." The eastern seaboard states are in the *Atlantic Flyway;* those bordering the big river lie in the *Mississippi Flyway;* the Great Plains are designated the *Central Flyway;* and the Great Basin and the Pacific States are in the province of the *Pacific Flyway.* Although the travels of a few waterfowl are quite complicated, and cross more than one flyway, this system has proved a convenient tool in administering waterfowl problems.

The U.S. Fish and Wildlife Service takes a yearly inventory of the waterfowl so that the federal government can adjust the hunting regulations and keep the kill below the crop of new ducks produced. It is handled like any other intelligent farming or business practice. Frederick C. Lincoln, who organized the inventory system, emphasized that the census figures are not as precise as one might suppose; they are merely "informed estimates." It is tricky indeed to appraise large flocks of waterfowl when they swarm over the water or fill the sky. I no longer trust my own "guesstimates." Once, near Point Pelee, Ontario, I saw a long raft of whistling swans, looming big and white on the water. I supposed them to number 2000, but when I counted them, beak by beak, there proved to be only 700. But whereas I tend to overestimate large white birds, I have found that I consistently underestimate by a third, flocks of small black birds, like starlings and redwings.

One winter, during a bitter freeze, great rafts of scaup ducks were forced into the East River on the outskirts of New York City. A party of Connecticut sportsmen who flew over the concentration said there were half a million birds. Two members of the Linnaean Society who carefully counted sample sections of the flocks from the shore, calculated there were only 65,000. To find out for myself, I made arrangements with the coast guard to fly out over the river in one of their patrol planes. My own private opinion was there were nearly 100,000 birds.

So you can see that a considerable margin of error must exist in such an elaborate undertaking as the annual winter duck inventory in which many dedicated observers take part. The country is divided into five regions, with headquarters at Boston, Massachusetts; Atlanta, Georgia; Minneapolis, Minnesota; Albuquerque, New Mexico; and Portland, Oregon. Each regional director supervises the work of a number of Game Management agents, who in turn are helped by biologists, bird watchers, game wardens, forest service and park service men. Even Navy blimps, Army planes, and Coast Guard craft are pressed into use.

But the most thorough check is made by several flyway biologists who literally live with the ducks throughout the year and follow them on their travels. Bob Smith, the Mississippi Flyway biologist, commented, when we flew over the clouds of blue geese on the Louisiana marshes, that they must know his plane well by now, and undoubtedly swear at him in goose language each time he appears on the horizon. He flew over the same flocks on their feeding grounds in James Bay in the fall, in Louisiana in the winter and in Minnesota in the spring.

Experts like Smith are so practiced in evaluating numbers that they often do not differ from each other by more than five per cent in their figures. In estimating the number of birds in large rafts of waterfowl, they often use Mr. Lincoln's favorite formula "one duck or goose per square yard." The length of the flock is multiplied by the depth, but as rafts are very irregular in shape, not neatly square or rectangular, one-third is deducted from the total. Although Lincoln stated that this method is an oversimplification of things (lesser scaups, for example, do not bunch as tightly as greater scaups), it is nevertheless as practical as any yet devised, as actual counts from blown-up aerial photographs have proven.

Year by year the inventory showed that the refuge program was working. More ducks could be seen beating over the bays and settling into the marshes. At the same time bag limits were pegged so as to further augment the seed stock, and hunting practices were revised. Baiting and live decoys became illegal.

Herculean though its task was, the U.S. Fish and Wildlife Service did not accomplish the entire restoration program single-handed. Many states and provinces maintained refuges of their own, and the Canadian Government, through the Prairie Farms Rehabilitation Administration, built thousands of dams and reservoirs, and in all completed more than 20,000 water restoration projects—all of which meant more ducks. Ducks Unlimited, a membership organization, also did fine work in putting water on great tracts of submarginal land in Canada.

In 1937, when both ducks and men started their slow progress out of the deep pits of their respective depressions, 600,000 duck stamps were sold. When war came, the sale of stamps dropped somewhat, but the ducks, with the hunting pressure eased, continued their steady climb. In 1944, there were 125,000,000. But it was "boom and bust," for as soon as the war ended the waterfowl went into a tailspin. Gasoline and shells were once more available and men by the millions, released from the services, took to the outdoors. The wildlife administrators, not foreseeing how immediate the increased pressure would be, did not take countermeasures in time. The ducks dropped to 80,000,000 in 1946; then to 54,000,000 in 1947, while at the same time the sale of duck stamps rose to 2,000,-000, three times that of a decade before.

In the summer of 1947, Albert Hochbaum, whose book *The Canvasback on a Prairie Marsh* won the coveted Brewster Award, was alarmed by what he saw on the nesting grounds in the Lake Manitoba basin. Addressing the readers of *Audubon Magazine* he wrote:

"The wandering eye seldom catches the darts of courting parties over the marsh, for they are few and far between. . . . Where the roadside pond held fourteen breeding pairs last year, there are only three now. The pothole by the crossing that had three pairs last year, has none. The ditch along the marsh trail, so crowded with ducks other years, has only a scattered few this May. The channel by the village store, always with its many families, has only a lone pair of gadwall. The big bay, where canvasbacks were always found in numbers of at least a dozen pairs, is empty. The country doctors who travel the same roads year after year speak of the shortage. The trappers and farmers and woodsmen speak of the scarcity of breeding ducks."

Although a few sports writers tried to cover up the facts, the forboding signs were plainly visible and everyone asked: "Where are the ducks?"

The wildlife experts, badly jolted by this setback, started on the second round of their long fight to build back the waterfowl population to the maximum carrying capacity of the continent only to lose all their gains in the great drought of the early 60's.

There can never be the old-time bag limits. Simple logic indicates that if the duck population is to remain constant, the bag limit will have to be cut in half each time the hunting pressure doubles. It is questionable that there can ever be bags of more than four or six birds per man, and proportionately less as the number of gunners increases. Like most conservation problems, it is fundamentally a problem of human populations. When our country reaches 300,000,000 we can no longer expect the high standard of living that was possible when there were 150,000,000. The good things of the earth just won't go around.

However, there will always be ducks, if only to look at. Some state game departments, recognizing this, are beginning to think of recreational values in terms of non game species and the binocular.

West of the 100th Meridian

TO SOME New Yorkers, the West begins at Jersey City.

Ornithologically, the West starts 1500 miles from Manhattan. Even the banks of the Mississippi are populated by eastern birds, much the same species that live on Long Island and along the Hudson. It is not until the hundredth degree of longitude is reached, far out on the high plains, that one eastern bird after another drops out and the avifauna takes on a western flavor. But the line of transition is not clear-cut. There is a broad belt through the western parts of the plains states (Oklahoma, Kansas, Nebraska and the Dakotas) where a bird watcher must carry two *Field Guides*, one in each pocket—the eastern one for use along the creek bottoms, and the western guide in the more arid outcroppings.

It is as difficult to describe the west as it is to paint it. An artist can succeed when he makes a composition of a single gnarled tree at timber line in the Sierras, or a lone Monterey cypress perched on the rocks at Point Lobos, but no matter how faithfully he records the Grand Canyon or the panoramic sweep of the Rockies, his efforts look, at best, like picture postcard landscapes. Recognizing this handicap, I am not going to attempt a complete or detailed picture. Rather, I shall draw a few comparisons and vignettes; those of an eastern bird watcher who snatches his trips west whenever he can.

It is no accident that so many of our best field biologists come from the West, for there the story of ecology is printed on the mountains and in the valleys in clear legible type for all to read. One can see the relation of the birds and other animals to the plants; he can see why they are where they are—because of the climate, soil and terrain. The contrasts are vivid. In

MALLARDS JUMPING. The world's most hunted wild duck is also the ancestor of most of our domestic ducks. In China alone their eggs feed millions.

SIX DIVING DUCKS are known by their field marks. At the upper left is a ruddy duck; at the upper right, a bufflehead; left center, a canvasback; right center, a scaup; lower left, a ring-necked duck; at lower right, a common goldeneye.

the east the book is harder to decipher, and the illustrations are often blurred.

On the other hand, the east is a better proving ground for students of migration, for, as I have pointed out earlier, the small songbirds arrive there like waves breaking upon the beach. In the western states they come and go without fanfare over a longer period of weeks. They drift seasonally from the mountains into the valleys and back again. There is none of the bombshell effect of a good migration wave in New England or on the shores of the Great Lakes. Spring, therefore, does not mean so much to a bird watcher who lives near Portland, Oregon, as it does to one who has been snowed in all winter near Portland, Maine.

But the great flights of waterfowl that throng the Pacific flyway make up for the undramatic passage of the passerines. There seem to be twice as many ducks and geese as there are on the Atlantic side, and in cities all down the coast—Victoria, Seattle, Portland, San Francisco, Oakland, Santa Barbara, Los Angeles and San Diego—ducks of a dozen species become so tame in the parks that they scramble for corn with the domestic mallards. Lake Merritt, in Oakland, is no longer the only place where pintails and canvasbacks will take bread from your fingers. But along the Atlantic seaboard one is doing well if he approaches a canvasback within a hundred yards—or, in some places, a quarter of a mile.

And this difference in temperament extends to many other birds. The mottled young gulls that beg for a handout around the docks of San Francisco or Seattle may be somewhat more confusing to identify than gulls are in New York or Boston, but they are so much tamer—almost like chickens—that they can be examined as critically as though they were museum specimens.

Although tradition calls them "sea gulls" they are far less pelagic than certain of the other water birds. In fact, surprisingly few North American gulls have been recorded in Hawaii. The *Larinae* not only hug the coast, but some penetrate far inland. Everyone knows of the miracle of the gulls that came like delivering angels when a great irruption of crickets threatened to destroy the Mormons' crops. The California gull, the savior of the Mormons, did not, as legend would have it, come all the way from the Pacific to meet the emergency. Eighty thousand of them breed on Gunnison, Bird, Egg and White Rock Islands out in Great Salt Lake.

On one of these islands, Gunnison, 10,000 white pelicans have nested for years in one great colony. The island is so far offshore that no one disturbs it. The pelicans pay for this security by going long distances for food; some fly all the way to Utah Lake, seventy-five miles distant, for there is nothing for them to eat in Great Salt Lake. It is almost an aquatic desert. Only three creatures live in its water—a brine shrimp and the larvae of two species of brine flies.

From the air there is hardly a more impressive vista anywhere in America than this inland sea, whether you come from the west across the Nevada desert, or from the east over the rugged Wasatch hump, where even the most blasé sky commuters peer through the small observation windows at the wild snow-capped peaks that tower nearly to the level of their air-borne cabin. Far below on the plain spreads the lake, blue and shimmering. It seems endless, like the ocean, its horizon obliterated by heat haze and alkali dust. More than twenty per cent salt, it is six times as saline as the ocean. Gulls standing on the shore are caked with salty crystals. Bathing there is a strange sensation; you cannot touch bottom in deep water but bob around like a cork. An eyeful of this solution is like a dash of acid.

Twenty-five or fifty thousand years ago, not long as geologists reckon time, huge Lake Bonneville lay here. Fed by melting glaciers, it was the size of Lake Superior, but with the change in climate it slowly dried up. The successive drops in the water level can be seen etched in stone on the lower slopes of the hills around Salt Lake City. Today only a few puddles remain. The largest puddle is Great Salt Lake—a dead sea without an outlet.

To the west, the white flats of the old lake bed, blistering hot and hard on the eyes, are a boneyard of early pioneers. This great alkali desert, barren as a skating rink, is probably more birdless than any other area its size in the United States. It is with amazement that we hear of large "fossil" nests in the midst of this desolate waste. I have seen snapshots of some of these ancient nests, resting on pinnacles of sand and salt, photographed by explorers who were retracing the historic trail of the ill-fated Donner party. What made these nests—herons? Or ospreys? Or did they belong to birds that no longer exist? They were probably built on low bars or islands in the old lake, covered over and semi-petrified by the shifting of water and sand, and exposed again by wind action and erosion, centuries later, after the lake had dried up. No ornithologist has investigated these unusual nests, to my knowledge.

Not all of the Great Basin is barren. Three per cent of Utah has been brought under irrigation. The low flat country between the lake and the high wall of the Wasatch is verdant, and on the northeast arm of the lake, where the Bear River brings its fresh water down from the mountains, exists the immense "duck factory" described in an earlier chapter. Although its function is to produce waterfowl for the sportsman it is also one of the best shorebird nurseries on the continent. Avocets with cinnamon necks wade in the puddles, swinging their upturned bills like scythes through the silt. Black-necked stilts dance on red bean-pole legs and yip disapprovingly. Even more exciting are the long-billed curlews, the chicken-sized waders with the incredibly long sickle-like bills.

It has always seemed to me as if the Creator had put the shorebirds in a huge sieve and sifted the small fry over the eastern seaboard and dumped the larger birds out in the West. At Newburyport Harbor, in New England, I have seen 10,000 "peep"—the small sparrow-sized sandpipers— sprinkled over the flats with nothing larger than yellowlegs in sight. But in San Francisco Bay I have estimated an equal number of marbled godwits, big as ducks, probing the mud with their long recurved bills. The eastern bird watcher is lucky to see one or two in a season. Because there are many more of the large birds such as the godwits, curlews, avocets and willets in the West, and relatively few good spots for them to gather, the general impression is that shore birding is a lot better there. Doctor Harold Axtell, making the rounds of San Francisco Bay one day, estimated over 2,000,-000 shore birds, and he was told that the migration was not yet at its peak.

There appear to be more hawks, too. Much of the west is gopher country, with a multitude of mice and ground squirrels for *Raptores* to wax fat upon. And, besides this, the human pressures upon these persecuted birds are not so great as they are east of the plains.

The same might be said for the owls. However, some species like the spotted owl, a large brown earless owl whose dog-like barking is sometimes heard in the mountain groves, are hard birds to find. When Bert Harwell was park naturalist at Yosemite he took me one night to a tall grove of firs and sugar pines where he thought we might locate one. Instead we were entertained by a tiny saw-whet owl which repeated its bell-like whistle in monotonous succession. Timing the tireless little singer, which was invisible in the immense sugar pine which towered over our heads, we found that it repeated its mechanical *too, too, too, too, too,* etc., as much as 130 times per minute, and never less than a hundred. One night Harwell spent six hours keeping tabs on this bird, and, except for a short period at midnight when it probably sallied forth to catch a mouse, it tooted incessantly.

"Northern" owls like the saw-whet and the long-ear, rare south of Pennsylvania in the Appalachians, nest almost to the Mexican border in the Pacific states. Both are found in the Yosemite; and high over the floor of the valley where the road winds to Glacier Point, even great gray owls have been seen, and it is believed they have nested there. This big earless owl is several inches longer than a great horned owl, but only about half its weight. It is all fluff and feathers; the most bird with the least substance of any I know. I had never expected to see this inhabitant of cold Canadian bogs in the United States. Yet one June day the Craighead twins, who were then working on their theses on predation, showed me a pair in Wyoming at the foot of the Grand Tetons, the southernmost breeding station in the Rocky Mountain states. The bench of lodgepole pines where the birds lived stretched for miles, and they could have been anywhere in it, but just as we were about to begin our search we discovered the first owl, perched on a post in the open, spotlighted by the last rays of the setting sun. Typical of so many birds of the far north, it allowed us to approach within twenty feet before it flew. Later it dropped with a noiseless swoop into the long grass only twelve feet from where I stood. Blinking its small yellow eyes, it looked at its feet and looked at me. When it rose a meadow mouse dangled from its claws.

To me this big nocturnal predator represented two things—the night and the North, yet in this same meadow I saw broad-tailed hummingbirds, symbolic of the sun and the tropics. Such are the contrasts to be found in the mountains. The broad-tail, the typical hummer of the Rockies, looks so much like a ruby-throat that it often goes by that name. But the ruby-throat is eastern, the only one of the three hundred twenty species of this incredible family adventurous enough to cross the Gulf of Mexico. The west has fifteen hummingbirds. Of these, ten can be found in southern Arizona, and there is always a chance that some unrecorded Mexican form will cross the border. California is nearly as fortunate, with six kinds, one of which, the Anna's hummingbird, not only spends the winter there, but is already nesting by January or February.

Mr. B. F. Tucker, whose home in Modjeska Canyon, south of Los Angeles, has become a showplace, erected a hummingbird cafeteria, a long rack of quart bottles filled with sugar water. Each jar, cleverly constructed so as to discourage ants and bees, could accommodate four hummingbirds simultaneously. Dozens of hummers buzzed about the flasks that lined the full length of the porch, and Tucker told me that several hundred made their headquarters in the canyon. To fully savor the jewel-like beauty of the feathered mites that hovered an arm's length away as he sat in his easy chair, Tucker rigged up a fluorescent spotlight. A flip of a switch brought out the full iridescence—emerald, ruby, flame and amethyst—of each species as it came to sip the nectar.

One of the western hummers, the rufous hummingbird, is an even greater traveler than the ruby-throat, reaching the sixtieth parallel in Alaska. To equal this, the ruby-throat would have to fly to southern Greenland. In spring rufous hummers often swarm in the orange orchards in the valleys of southern California, but in late summer they return to Mexico a different way, by the mountain route, where they disport themselves in the high meadows with other *trochilidae*.

The smallest of the American hummingbirds is the calliope, a tiny bee of a bird, identified by the red rays on its throat. In the Sierras it probes the snow flowers, the big red saprophytes that thrust their fleshy fists from the mat of needles beneath the pines. Like all hummers it is attracted to anything red. Once one investigated the flaming red shirt my companion was wearing.

Even though there are so many new species, the easterner, traveling for the first time over the Rockies, or along the Pacific Coast, is surprised to find that half the birds he sees are birds he already knows. Of the 530 species covered in his western *Field Guide,* nearly 300 are included in his eastern book. The redwings, song sparrows, horned larks and mourning doves look like those along the Atlantic seaboard, even though they are different subspecies. The meadowlarks and flickers appear much the same, too, but are called specifically distinct from their eastern counterparts. In the Northwest, in particular, the bird life resembles that back home. The contrast is much greater in the Southwest, in the dry country and the deserts.

It does not take long to learn the new birds, although their voices are puzzling at first. But soon they fall into place and even in the movies, California made, they intrude themselves upon one's consciousness, and can often be detected in the sound track. House finches, Gambel's sparrows and wren-tits must be especially numerous around Hollywood, for I have distinctly heard them in a score of pictures. In fact, the known geographical range of the wren-tit has been greatly extended by the motion picture industry. Although it is almost exclusively a native son of California, scarcely crossing into Oregon and Baja California, I have heard its unmistakable staccato song in *Wyoming,* around Lake Champlain (in *Northwest Passage*), in the bluegrass country of Kentucky (I have forgotten the name of the picture), and even as far distant as the Vienna woods (in the *Waltz King*).

California leads all other states except Texas in the variety of its birds, and little wonder. It boasts the lowest and hottest spot in the United States, Death Valley, slinking like a desert reptile, 280 feet below the level of the sea, and the highest, Mt. Whitney, whose bald summit climbs nearly three vertical miles—and the valley and the peak are within sight of each other! Hollywood directors claim they can duplicate the Alps, the African veldt, the Sahara, and the shores of the South Seas or the Mediterranean without leaving the state.

As we cross the hot, dry San Joaquin Valley and ascend the Sierras, the rooftree of California, we see what is meant by "vertical birding." We see why Clinton Hart Merriam coined the term *life zones* when he and his colleagues climbed San Francisco Peak, in Arizona, over a half century ago. They found that the bird and other animal life changed as they climbed. When they left the low desert many birds dropped behind. New ones replaced them among the piñon pines, and others not seen before, appeared when they reached the cool fir forests. The birds and mammals seemed to be tied up in some way with the plants, an obvious fact that many naturalists had noticed before. Striving for some sort of order or system by which he could describe the distribution of these plants and animals, Merriam devised the zonal terminology that bird students know so well. To a small degree you can see some of this "zoning" in the Appalachians, where most of the ridges are under 4000 feet and only a handful of peaks exceed 6000, ancient worn-down mountains, mere "hills" in the language of the westerner. In the young vigorous ranges of the western cordillera between Canada and Mexico, no less than 1500 peaks thrust themselves 10,000 feet or more above the level of the sea.

There is a lure in the mountains, and as we head the car their way, the landscape changes, the birds change, and so do we. There is a lift to the spirit in the sudden transition, heightened with each switchback up the stony flanks of the mountain mass. There are places in the Southwest where we can go through five or six life zones in half a day, from desert lowlands similar to those of the hot, dry province of Sonora in Mexico, to the wind-swept spruce of the Hudsonian Zone, or even to draughty alpine meadows dotted with flowers that look just like those that carpet the sub-arctic tundra. To accomplish such a change of scene in the East, we should have to journey two thousand miles, from Florida to the Gaspé or New-foundland.

The undulating seas of grass and grain that stretch for miles in the golden-brown valleys of California, lie in the *Lower Sonoran Zone*. Horned larks fly from the fence posts as the car speeds by. Meadowlarks rise from the longer grass, and there are occasional sparrow hawks and shrikes hunting grasshoppers. In the narrow strip of trees that follow the river there is more variety. Western kingbirds bicker with each other and Bullock's orioles flash like flaming torches among the tall cottonwoods. Goldfinches, yellow warblers, and yellow-throats are like those widespread species else-where—subspecifically different perhaps, but essentially the same birds that occur the length and breadth of America. Least Bell's vireos sing their husky phrases as if through clenched teeth; *cheedle cheedle chee?—chee-dle cheedle chew!* Blue grosbeaks, so dark as to look like cowbirds at a distance, warble from the willow scrub. They are seldom found outside the Lower Sonoran belt. But many other species do not conform to a single life zone, especially if the plants they depend on are not thus re-stricted. Horned larks nest from the hot valleys of Mexico to 14,000 feet in the Rockies and even to the shore of the Arctic Sea. They like sweeping expanses of short grass with bald spots. It does not matter in what life zones they find them. Because there are so many examples like this I believe that the vegetational form or environmental niche is more useful than Merriam's system in describing a bird's distribution.

The zones are an oversimplification of things, perhaps, but they are convenient pigeonholes; and as we climb the mountains they present a forceful sermon in ecology, the relation of living things to their environment.

As we gain elevation in the low foothills, the live oaks, blue oaks and digger pines indicate that we are in the *Upper Sonoran Zone*. Troops of noisy California jays swarm through the oaks calling *kwesh kwesh kwesh kwesh*. Several other species have carved themselves a niche here: Hutton's vireo, monotonously repeating its insistent *zu-weep* on the hot brushy hillsides; Nuttall's woodpecker, like a downy with a barred back; the big tan California thrasher, hoeing the dry debris under the bushes with its long curved beak; and its ecological competitor, the brown towhee, just a plain brown bird, ignored by nature when good looks were distributed among the *Passeriformes*.

The trend in the mountains is from oaks and chaparral below to evergreens higher up. The belt where they meet and mix is called, appropriately, the *Transition Zone*. We are plainly in this region when our altimeter registers 3000 feet and yellow pines begin to dominate. The crestless California jay, the bird of the sunny oak groves, drops out, for this is the shady realm of the big dark jay with the crest, Steller's jay. Western tanagers, yellow with red faces and black wings, brighten the somber pines. Cassin's blue-headed vireos sing their short musical phrases, and we can detect no noticeable difference between them and the blue-headed vireos back East. The same is true of the warbling vireos in the aspens. In fact, a good percentage of the birds in the transition zone are merely western races of birds which the eastern traveler already knows. Let him not be fooled by subspecific prefixes (now seldom used) into thinking he is dealing with something fundamentally different. They are still robins, winter wrens, purple finches, brown creepers and song sparrows. Not long ago many names were entirely different, and it was very confusing to find that the Calaveras warbler was merely the western race of the Nashville warbler, and the russet-backed thrush was the same as the Swainson's thrush.

Three thousand feet higher hermit thrushes sing their incomparable flute-like phrases and olive-sided flycatchers cry *hip-three-cheers!* from their high perches on the dead lodgepoles. This is *Canadian Zone* timber. There are many unfamiliar sounds in these high forests. Some turn out to be small mammals. Sooty grouse intone their muffled hoots from the

HANGING IN THE BREEZE as if by an invisible wire, a glaucous-winged gull maneuvers for a landing on a davit. Scores of his fellows followed in the wake of our ferry across Puget Sound, waiting for a handout from the galley.

LIKE A RUSTY HINGE. But it is song to a yellow-headed blackbird. Yellow-heads share the marshes with the redwings in the western half of the United States.

IN THE HIGH MOUNTAINS of the west, Clarke's nutcracker caws its crow-like *khaaa*. This audacious fellow stole my sandwich while I was busy changing film.

NINE FOOT WINGSPREAD has the white pelican, above.
The brown pelican, below, attains six and one half feet. Both
are master gliders, for they are not as heavy as they look.

shadows, an octave lower than those of a horned owl; and slaty-looking fox sparrows and green-tailed towhees with rusty caps sing from the manzanita scrub. A sharp *chick-ik-ik* announces the white-headed woodpecker, the unique bird of the Sierras. You will not find it in the Rockies to the east, nor in the humid coast ranges to the west.

In the mountains that tower against the sky like a frozen sea of tossing white-caps there are still two life zones to go. The belt of hemlocks, lodgepoles and white-bark pines just below timber line where the last of the stunted trees are sculptured by the wind, between 8000 and 9000 feet, marks the *Hudsonian Zone*. In this cold boreal forest we find the Arctic three-toed woodpecker, with a yellow cap, chipping the bark from the dead conifers. The pine grosbeak, the largest of the winter finches, is here, too, along with its smaller counterpart, Cassin's finch. We have had one form or another of these rosy sparrow-sized finches ever since we left the valley. First the house finch, then the purple finch, and now Cassin's with its sharply defined red cap. The three look enough alike to confound the beginner, but they overlap very little and divide the Sierras altitudinally among themselves.

Aside from a few white-crowned sparrows that venture from the Hudsonian belt into the thickets of dwarf willows that crouch in sheltered pockets in the *Arctic-alpine Zone*, the whole of the windswept roof of the Sierras is the undisputed domain of one bird, the leucosticte. On peaks like Clark, Florence and Dana, which rise from 11,000 to 13,000 feet, these dusky, rosy-rumped finches nest, hiding their treasures in crevices on the talus slopes. They are the "refrigerator birds" that feed at the edges of the melting drifts, and pick up the insects that drop chilled upon the snow fields.

Further north, the leucostictes have more company on their lonely mountaintops. On Rainier, whose extinct volcanic cone rises 14,408 feet, horned larks live close to the glaciers. Pipits, which seem so drab and uninteresting when they flock to the flats in winter, develop a dynamic personality here. The skylark may be a more gifted musician, but when a pipit soars over the slopes decked with avalanche lilies and chants its repetitious *chwee chwee chwee chwee chwee chwee chwee* to the rhythmic beat of its wings, the effect is just as dramatic.

Once, as we came down the cloud-shrouded slopes of Rainier where we had been looking for white-tailed ptarmigan, the little arctic chickens that live among its bleak boulder fields, a sudden storm swept in from the low peaks to the west. There was no shelter where we were, so we hurried the last few hundred yards to a ranger's cabin at timber line. As we waited on the porch for the black clouds to break, a chorus of varied thrushes, the robins of the rain forest, made cathedral music with their eery harmonic whistles in the dark firs below. When the first big drops fell one thrush hopped from its shelter in the shadows, and as the downpour increased in tempo, flew from branch to branch until it perched on the tip of the tallest tree. There it sang, as I have seldom heard a bird sing, while the rain pelted down. Never have I seen a bird express such oneness with the elements, nor in such a setting, for to face the fresh breeze on Rainier is to blow the cobwebs from one's soul.

Rain Shadows of the Mexican Border

THE southeastern corner of Arizona has a greater variety of nesting land birds than any comparable area in the United States. Box Elder county, in Utah, may exceed it in the number of all breeding birds, but only because it has both the land birds, with their vertical distribution from the plains to the high mountains, and the waterfowl of the Bear River marshes.

If I were to pick a place in the Southwest to live, a place that is paintable, where every landscape composes and has color, where I could always have my fill of birds and of plants, mammals, reptiles, insects and all the things that make an artist-naturalist happy I should choose Tucson. From there I could have most anything within a day's reach—the low desert and the high mountains, too.

As our horses come to halt on the crest of one of the desert ranges, the insatiate eye commands a great domain. It encompasses thousands of square miles at a glance, for in the desert country there are no curtains of haze to obstruct, and a lone tree miles from us stands out sharp and clear. Range upon range of mountains fall away into the blue distance. Their summits are dark with evergreens, while lower down, the sparse brown oaks straggle to the desert's edge. Purple-blue shadows on the steep slopes mark the gorges where the water from bursting clouds plunges down during the rainy season, taking much of the mountain along, to be piled in a fan of boulders and gravel at the canyon's mouth.

Even though broken masses of clouds scud overhead and close in, shutting out the sun, the desert far below remains hot and shimmering, a study in pastel colors, scorched and burnished except for the thin green ribbon of cottonwoods and willows that traces the course of a distant river. Under the noonday sun the low country is a furnace unendurable, but where we are, at 9000 feet, it is cool enough for a jacket. Sudden claps and rumbles of thunder sound as if the gods were at a game of tenpins, sheets of rain obscure the peaks across the valley, but still the desert below may not see a drop of moisture for weeks. The desert, it has been said, is the answer to a mountain. The mountains pull the clouds to their peaks, wring from them their moisture, and send them on, while the broad flatlands lying between the ranges go dry and thirsty.

Of all the rugged outcrops in the land which became ours through the Gadsden Purchase, none are more puzzling than the Huachucas, a three-hundred-square-mile fortress on the border, south and east of Tucson. There lives the Willard's rattlesnake, confined almost to a single canyon—and to one spot in the canyon, around the diggings of an abandoned mine. Local herpetologists tell of a pygmy rattlesnake, substantiated by a single specimen found dead one morning on the Parade Ground at Fort Huachuca. There are also reports of a "two-legged lizard."

These transected slopes are the best place I know for those big Mexican hummingbirds—the Rivoli, the dark one with the green throat, which dashes about the open pine parks on the peaks, and the blue-throated hummingbird that rifles the monkey-flowers and the large pale yellow columbines that grow about the little mossy waterfalls in the canyons. And there is no telling when some very rare hummer may turn up. One July day, many years ago, two Heloise's hummingbirds were found, the only record for this species north of the Mexican border.

What mountains these are! Where else can one follow a coppery-tailed trogon as it intones its deep *cowm cowm cowm cowm* among the oaks and sycamores of a hot canyon, and an hour or two later see evening grosbeaks in the firs at a higher altitude? The trogon, colored with the same tropical reds and greens of its Central American relative, the quetzal, watched the Aztec empire spread over Mexico. Later it saw the coming of the conquistadors and the Franciscan friars, but whether or not it lived on our side of the border in those days we do not know. But today, the "Mexican Bird of Paradise" can be found in any one of half a dozen canyons in the Huachucas. The State of Arizona excludes it from all collecting permits and not even in the name of science can one take an egg or touch a feather of a trogon.

The grosbeak, on the other hand, is the same plump yellow bird with the big pale bill that one sees in the fir forests of Canada or on New England feeding trays in winter, a different race, perhaps—they call it the Mexican evening grosbeak—but to all appearances the same bird. There must be a point in the canyon, I suppose, where the oaks give way to the pines and where it is possible for a grosbeak to look upon a trogon.

Insects new to science have been described from their isolated realm on these peaks and more than one plant bears the name *huachucensis*. Little wonder museum men from coast to coast have camped here for two generations. To one biologist the lure was so strong that when he was retired from the United States Biological Survey, he returned to spend his last years in the spot on this earth he loved the best. Today Biedermann's grave, marked with a simple headstone, can be seen beside a path in Carr Canyon. His white cottage is still there, and some day I should like to rent it for a few months from Major Healey who runs the dude ranch down the canyon. Perhaps then the Huachucas would take me into confidence and share some of their secrets. Today the canyon is drier than it was when Biedermann was alive. There are probably more trogons now and little troops of coati-mundis often pass up and down the defile. The coatis or "chulas," raccoon-like animals with the pointed snouts and long banded tails, wandered across the flats from Sonora a few years ago, and now these tropical carnivores have spread all through the range. One day we glimpsed seven of them, traveling in a tight little band, their long tapering tails erect. I jumped from the car to see them better, but they clambered over the rocks and disappeared among the grass and yucca further up the slope.

When I first visited southern Arizona, they told me that I would return. Its magnetic pull cannot be denied, and I found myself going back to the same valleys, the same canyons and the same mountains. But one can never seem to know these desert ranges. Other western mountains appear to have a plan; they make sense; but not so the wild peaks of the Mexican border. They leave one puzzled and a little disturbed.

I suppose if one stayed in these mountains long enough they would tell their story. I won't even attempt an interpretation. I will leave that to

Herbert Brandt whose book *Arizona Bird Life* describes the things he saw during eight seasons in the land of the Apaches. He tells us in his word pictures about these magic mountains; the Santa Ritas and the big blue Chiricahuas, the historic stronghold of Cochise and his Apaches; where we watched the Merriam's turkeys as they came down from their roost in the tall Chihuahua pines on the ridge to strut and gobble in the iris-carpeted glades; and where he showed me my first Mexican chickadees. It is not often now that I can add a new bird to my life list within the limits of the United States.

I had hoped, as I had on a previous trip to the Chiricahuas, that we might run into the thick-billed parrots that twice have been known to invade this range from their pine-clad mountains in Mexico. I talked with a man who saw them in 1917, the last time they crossed the border. He said the big green parrots with the red faces and huge bills appeared suddenly in August. They came by the hundreds and the hurtling flocks made the canyons echo with their noise. He told me he shot fifty-seven of them. They stayed until January when snow blanketed the Apache mountains and covered the juniper berries lying on the ground. Once he saw two or three hundred of them swarming over the branches of a single tall pine like living ornaments in a gigantic Christmas tree. "Old Lil," who hung around the café in the little mining town of Paradise, kept one of the parrots in a cage for four or five years. It never learned to talk.

In the Chiricahuas at 9000 feet, pine siskins fly wild and free, and sometimes there are crossbills, for all the world as in a Canadian forest. There, over the high country, ravens play on the up-drafts and violet-green swallows weave a pattern through the blue. White-throated swifts slit the rarefied air with their scimitar-like wings and hurtle past the crags with a speed probably matched by no other small North American bird. At the climax of a reckless chase two of these diminutive black and white torpedoes lock in copulatory embrace and fall a thousand feet, their wings flailing the air like a pin-wheel.

At times there is a stillness over the high mountain forest, but audibility is great in the clean air and little voices can be heard far down the slope. So let's go down; down through the yellow pines where the red-faced western tanager sings its husky phrases, the big Steller's jay cries *shook shook shook* and pygmy nuthatches swarm over the rough branches; down into the steep-banked canyon where those two unbelievable warblers live—the painted redstart and the red-faced warbler—the only warblers north of the Mexican border that are decorated with intense rosy red; down still further where the oaks take over and a new jay, one without a crest, the Arizona jay, dominates the scene, and where lives the bridled titmouse with a harlequin pattern upon its face, and the little olivaceous flycatcher, the saddest voice in the Arizona woods; down past all of these to where the big sycamores shade the widening streambed, where big sulphur-bellied flycatchers creak like unoiled wheelbarrows in excited duet; and on down through the rocky gap at the canyon's mouth where the last few sycamores trail out across the flats. We will then be on the desert.

The high desert of the upper Sonoran Zone, which shelves off slowly for miles and miles is characterized in southern Arizona by grass and yucca. Most of the long native grass has been chewed so short by half-starved cattle that the trampled earth will never again be the same. The little scaled quail, the one with the tuft of cotton for a top-knot, is no longer common, nor is the Arizona meadowlark, for the grass is too short for their liking. One bird, however, and only one, finds an ally in the bovine herds. It is the horned lark, which builds its nest in the shade of a dried cow chip and is attracted to partially bald grasslands throughout the northern hemisphere, from the dry plains of Mexico, where they take on the scorched look of the desert, to the tundra close by the Arctic Sea. In parts of the rolling grasslands of Arizona it is the only bird one sees in summer except for an occasional white-necked raven.

Here in the high desert, grow lilies, or at least members of the *Liliaceae,* for the yuccas, believe it or not, are lilies. But, as befits plants that would survive in the desert, they are arsenals of defiance; they bristle with daggers and bayonets. One bird, the Scott's oriole, a lemon-yellow oriole with a black head, which sings much like a western meadowlark, is completely dependent upon the yucca, tucking its nest under the thatch of dead daggers that lie like shaggy brown shingles along the stalk. I have never seen a Scott's oriole without finding at least one or two yuccas nearby.

The transition from the high desert to the low, or, to put it in the faunalist's terms, from the Upper Sonoran Zone to the Lower Sonoran, is a subtle one, accomplished gradually. Here is much for the traveler to see —a strange bird beside the road, huge boulders of grotesquely eroded rhyolite, a hillside decorated with the scraggly witch wands of the ocotillo, their scarlet blossoms held high like flaming torches, and jagged "cardboard" mountains, as unreal in the distance as stage sets. Suddenly one realizes that the character of the desert has changed. No longer is it predominately grass and yucca; great gardens of cactus stretch for miles.

To a stranger, the desert seems harsh, indeed brutal. I have seen a woman reduced to tears after a few hours on the roads that aimlessly wander among the weirdly gesturing Joshua trees of the Mohave. On the other hand, I have talked to a poet (who terms himself a "desert rat") who spends months camping alone in the desert and feels more secure there than anywhere else. He knows the desert's secrets and can live off the land. He admitted he would be lost and would probably starve in an eastern wood-land. However that might be, the desert has the look of hunger upon it and everything suggests a slender margin of survival and a fierce defense of the right to live. From the windows of a passenger plane the pattern of the plant life below is that of dark specks, clusters and polka dots on the bare desert pavement. Each plant keeps its distance, drawing the precious mois-ture from whatever radius it can command.

Nearly everything that grows in the desert is armed to the teeth with spines, hooks and needles, threatening and defying. Unseen cholla knuckles, lying on the ground, jump at the slightest touch of a shoe and sink their painful barbs into the ankle. But even such armor does not always repel the invader. During times of drought I have seen the flat bristly pads of the prickly pear half chewed away by pack rats, desperate for want of moisture.

I should like to see the desert in one of its happier moods, like the spring of 1941, when abundant rain and full streams turned the Arizona desert into a flamboyant carpet of blossoms. The parched soil, rich in nutriment, requires only a good drenching to bring to life seeds that have lain dormant for years. These ephemeral plants waste little on stems and stalks but spend everything on showy blossoms. Soon they wither and die, their brief but gaudy show over, but in that short span the cycle is completed and new seeds have been produced, to lie waiting in the naked sands while the sun burns down. It is a story of resurrection; and they say that when it hap-pens, the spectacle is unbelievable. The plants of the xeric world, where water is scarce, fall into two sorts then; these fairy-like flowers of the flash

TINIEST of all its tribe, the elf owl lives in the most gigantic of the desert plants, the saguaro cactus. This wide-eyed gnome which we removed from a woodpecker hole in a saguaro is under restraint while posing for its portrait.

SNAKE KILLER. Weirdest of the desert's birds is the roadrunner, described as "a cuckoo compounded of a chicken and a magpie." Mexicans affectionately call it *paisano* which means "compatriot," or more freely translated, "little friend."

existence often "born to blush unseen," and the long-lived growths of the devil's garden, grotesque plants that store up moisture against the dry spells and defend it with their armature.

To me, the desert seems drier each time I see it, and last time even the little streams high in the mountains were reduced to a trickle. The water table they said was the lowest in seventy years. Still local Chambers of Commerce were talking of attracting new industries and building bigger cities. How can they supply water to larger cities and have enough left to irrigate an agricultural region, too? The bitter struggle for water is one that will soon limit man's ambitions here, for though, in his conceit, he insists that he "subdues" nature, or "conquers" nature, he does not. To survive in the desert he must meet the same harsh terms set by nature for the plants and the animals.

To the easterner the giant cactus or saguaro is the real symbol of the desert, and in travel advertisements and on decorative maps, designed by commercial artists who have never set foot west of the Mississippi, the candelabra-like figures are spotted everywhere from Texas to California. But as you drive west or glide along on the silver rails of the *Southern Pacific,* do not expect to see these monolithic showpieces of the Southwest until you reach Tucson. North of town you will find them, stark and tall, rank on rank, by the scores and the hundreds, marching with arms upraised in a gesture of hosanna, from the cholla gardens up the rocky slopes to the buttressed base of the Santa Catalinas.

It takes a century for a Saguaro to attain its full fifty feet, and the big ones are almost certain to have at least one woodpecker hole in them some-where, or as many as a score, for the Gila woodpecker and the gilded flicker, the two master artisans of the desert, never use the same hole for two families. Hard scar tissue forms about the cavity, sealing in the moisture, otherwise the Saguaro would literally bleed to death by evaporation. The hard-walled cavity then becomes a serviceable bird house, preserved for years, perhaps for a century or more, a home which may be leased successively by purple martins, Arizona crested flycatchers, sparrow hawks, screech owls and elf owls, until the skyscraper apartment house collapses, perhaps at the age of 200. Even after the carcass of the fallen giant lies prostrate and its flesh rots away, leaving the bleached ribs exposed like a bundle of laths, the gourd-like woodpecker holes, encased by the indestructible scar tissue remain intact. Pimas and Apaches once used them for drinking flasks.

As I wandered among the saguaro groves I often noticed great chucks broken out around some of the holes, twenty or thirty feet up, as if decay had done its work, followed by healing. I now realize that these marks were left by collectors, perhaps some of the pioneer ornithologists of Arizona, who chopped out the holes to get at the white eggs of the elf owl, once so prized by oologists. These little owls, the tiniest of all the owls, live in the largest of all the cacti, like Lilliputian ghosts in a cemetery of Brobdingnagian tombstones. There must be many of them, but there are so many Saguaros and so many woodpecker holes that it is a job to find them. But at night, as you spread your sleeping bag near the mouth of any of the canyons, you can hear their rapid high-pitched notes, not like an owl's at all: *chew-chew-chew-chew-check-chewk-chewk,* rising almost to an excited chatter. Sometimes you can pick one up in the beam of the spotlight, a little "earless" gnome, no longer than a sparrow, with wide yellow eyes staring from under bushy white brows.

Flesh eaters and insect eaters like the elf owl have an advantage; for their water problem is solved for them through the prey they eat. Doves, quail and other seed eaters, on the other hand, are forced to make long daily pilgrimages to slake their thirst.

In the soft sand of a shallow wash we see strange footprints shaped like a Maltese Cross, obviously not the imprints of a quail. These are made by the road-runner. With apologies to Byron, it has been said that:

"Nature formed but one such bird and broke the die in molding him."

If we are lucky we may see this unlikely looking bird streaking after a lizard. It is a desperate race; and when the whisking reptile is pinned to earth, it surrenders its tail which wriggles and twists upon the sand. The "paisano," not to be fooled by this device, takes a firmer grip on the body of the lizard and picks up the squirming tail, too. The shaggy-headed clown shows real satisfaction with its success as it slowly raises and lowers its expressive crest. A young visitor from Holland once asked me where he could see this "American cuckoo that runs on the ground." For a moment I was puzzled; it is easy to forget that a road-runner is a cuckoo.

The low desert is a very birdy place. You would not think so at mid-day when the sun climbs toward the zenith, throwing a black pattern of shadow on the glaring sand below the sprawling paloverde and cacti and making of each saguaro a gigantic sundial, marking the hours. It seems deserted then, but the birds, like all prudent residents of the Lower Sonoran Zone, are taking their long mid-day siesta within their barbed fortress. But go out at daybreak and see the difference. In the crystal blue morning, life is everywhere. Gambel's quail, like small plump chickens with nodding topknots, run across the open stretches; from the tops of bristly teddy bear chollas, Palmer thrashers, big tan birds with sickle-like bills, call *whit-wheet!* sounding for all the world like some one whistling for attention. House finches, those adaptable birds with the look of a purple finch and the habits of a house sparrow, are everywhere, and seem just as much at home on the sandy windswept desert as they are in the comfortable Spanish-style patios in town. We find their nests in the cholla, defended from our probing fingers by a million murderous needles, and near them the oval nests of the cactus wren. These wrens, so big they look like small thrashers, are numerous, chanting their unbirdlike *chug-chug-chug-chug-chug-chug-chug.* Most of their nests are empty, for like all wrens the energetic males build "extra" nests and even the young are said to build their own roosting nests within a few weeks. In fact, nests seem to be everywhere among the cactus and the mesquite, partly because birds are fairly numerous, partly because each plant stands alone and can be easily examined, and also because in the arid air, old nests last longer before they disintegrate. The little football-like fortresses of the verdin are built so solidly and withstand the assault of wind and sand so well that one gets the impression there must be many more of these little yellow-headed titmice than there are.

Only in the great stretches of creosote bush, shunned by nearly all birds, does the desert seem lifeless.

But go down to the river, its winding course traced by the light green of willows, cottonwoods and mesquite thickets, and you will find the opposite extreme. Even though the stream in the month of May is so dry you could "fall in and come out dusty," the birds are there—blue grosbeaks and yellow-throats, just like yellow-throats elsewhere, and chats, song sparrows, yellow warblers and summer tanagers. It might very well be an eastern river, the bird association is so similar. But behind the thin line of willow scrub and cottonwoods at the edge of the streambed, in the mesquite thickets, the desert begins to take on its true character. White-winged doves coo harshly like crowing cockerels; male vermilion flycatchers, the little "Mexican fireheads," dance their sky dance. Twiggy nests with spotless robin-blue eggs tell us that Crissal thrashers are about, even though these shy skulkers, darker than the other desert thrashers, keep from our sight. Here, too, are silky black phainopeplas with pointed top-knots and big white wing patches, black-chinned hummingbirds, green-backed goldfinches, and little gray Lucy's warblers.

In our grandfather's day bird watching along these desert creeks was a he-man's game. During the era of the Apache wars, when so many stages and wagon trains were ambushed on their way in and out of Tucson, the only safe way to pursue the hobby of bird study was to have the protection of the United States Army. It is no accident that most of the early ornithological work in Arizona was done by surgeons attached to the Army Medical Corps.

Major Bendire, who started a monumental work on the birds of North America, once discovered a zone-tailed hawk's nest in a big cottonwood on the banks of the Rillito, near Tucson. Climbing to the nest, he found an egg which he coveted for his collection. Out of the corner of his eye he glimpsed something else—several Apache Indians crouching on the side of a little canyon which opened into the creek bed nearby. They were watching him, no doubt with lethal designs, but Bendire pretended not to notice them. Putting the prized egg into his mouth (and an uncomfortably big mouthful it was), he calmly descended until within reach of his horse. Quickly leaping to his mount, he was off on the wings of the wind, his scalp and his egg intact.

Ornithology certainly has changed in Arizona!

Wanderers of the Waves

OR every square mile of land in our world there are two and a half square miles of sea. Five-sevenths of the surface of the globe is a heaving, shifting expanse of water, unknown to few men save those hard-bitten mariners with salt in their beards who spend their lives plying the trade routes. Even they deviate little from the traditional sea lanes across these saline wastes, as one would follow familiar paths in a little-known wilderness. Great sections of the ocean are like a void, unvisited by any navigator for months or even years.

The countless emergent rocks, coral atolls, volcanic islands and buttressed headlands that defy the incessant surf are the breeding homes of sea birds by the billions. Some of the world's most abundant birds are oceanic. Darwin said he believed that the fulmar (a stubby gull-like bird) was the commonest bird in the world. Disagreeing, the famed British ornithologist, James Fisher, writes: "In Iceland, and the Faeroes, Jan Mayen, Bear Island and Spitzbergen there are millions of fulmars. There may even be tens of millions, but I doubt whether there are hundreds of millions. Darwin may have got his idea from the abundance of fulmars at sea in the north Atlantic. All the same, the most abundant bird in the world is certainly a sea bird, and probably Wilson's petrel." One man's guess is as good as another's. The Wilson's petrel, the little black bird with the white rump that flits in the wake of ships, might be the world's number one bird, but there are many others that would offer stiff competition. Some of the shearwaters are enormously abundant. Flinders computed a flock of slender-billed shearwaters or "mutton birds" off Bass Strait, Australia, to number more than 150,000,000 birds.

As is well known, the cooler current areas are far more prolific in oceanic life than the warmer waters. In the chilly Humboldt current that laves the west coast of South America the numbers of sea birds are staggering. Between 4,000,000 and 5,000,000 guanay cormorants have been calculated to inhabit a single barren island in the Chincha group off the coast of Peru. Similar assemblages of cormorants and of penguins are described from the cape region in Africa. Further to the south, in the Antarctic Sea, 5,000,000 Adelie penguins have been estimated about one small group of islands.

Parts of the Arctic are almost as prolific in pelagians as the Antarctic. Who knows how many dovekies or "little auks" throng the inaccessible cliffs of Greenland, Iceland and Spitzbergen? On the other side of the Arctic ice cap, in the fog-bound Aleutians which chain the eastern world to the west, their relatives, the penguin-like murres and auklets, crowd the slippery rocks by millions, competing for space like bathers on the beach at Coney Island on a summer Sunday.

The sea is a bountiful larder with a far greater abundance of life in its shadowy blue depths than exists on the land. This life is not distributed evenly throughout the seven seas like sugar stirred into a teacup. It runs in streaks and veins like the mixture in a marbled cake. Just as most people mistakenly conceive of the Arctic as one great ecological block, without marked subdivisions, so they view the sea. Sea birds do not wander willy-nilly over any part of the endless oceanic wastes they choose. They are as much creatures of habit as land birds, nesting on ancestral rocks and bars, feeding in certain watery pastures, following definite oceanic currents, avoiding others. Their peregrinations are ordained by the movements of the small sea animals on which they feed, and by the lush plankton-filled currents, upwellings, and "tongues" that nourish these small creatures. Where the "soup" is thick, there shall we find the birds.

The wanderings of sea birds seem even more mystifying than those of land birds. They are not guided by coastlines, chains of mountains or broad river valleys. There are no sea marks for them to follow. Yet the fabulously acute ability of oceanic birds has been proved scores of times. A Manx shearwater, taken from its burrow on the island of Skokholm off the British coast and set free near Venice at the head of the Adriatic Sea, came back to its burrow in fourteen days. If it returned by sea, it covered 3700 miles, virtually traveling three sides of a square as you will see if you study a map. If the bird took the shortest route, like a taut rubber band that has been snapped, it would have crossed Europe by way of the high Swiss Alps, but this does not seem likely.

The greater shearwater nests only in one spot in all the wide world— Tristan da Cunha—a remote dot of land in the middle of nowhere, like a flyspeck on the map of the South Atlantic. How, after eight long months of cruising on the high seas, as far as Greenland and Iceland, does it find its way back again? The smallest error with compass and sextant would cause a ship to miss the island by a wide margin.

Off the coast of Australia there is a dark member of the family called the short-tailed or slender-billed shearwater. It wanders over millions of square miles of the Pacific from Japan to California and north to the Aleutians Any navy man knows how great these spaces are. A handful of birds, a few dozen, arrive on their nesting island three or four days before the others, but the main breeding population, *millions of birds,* returns to their tiny dot of land *within the space of an hour.* Some insist they arrive not only en masse but also on the very same date each year (regardless of leap year), like the swallows of Capistrano, whose well-publicized punctuality has caused many an ornithologist to raise his eyebrows.

Mr. Davies in his *Tasmanian Journal* writes: "It is not in my power to describe the scene that presents itself on the night of the 24th of November. A few minutes before sunset, flocks are seen making for the island from every quarter, and that with a rapidity hardly conceivable; when they congregate together, so dense is the cloud, that night is ushered in full ten minutes before the usual time."

Of all the birds that forage on the bosom of the sea, the most pelagic, the ones that shun land most, are the tube-nosed swimmers of the order *Procellariiformes.* These—the albatrosses, shearwaters, fulmars and petrels—are the greatest mariners of all, living their entire lives far at sea, coming ashore only to nest. Unlike mythical *Halcyon,* the kingfisher, they have not found how to perform this important duty away from land.

The official check list of the American Ornithologists' Union lists thirty-seven species of tube-noses from American waters. Eighteen or nineteen of these are strictly accidental and are listed as American birds by grace of one, two or half a dozen records—strays borne far from their usual sea lanes in the teeth of gales. Most of the others are more normal; you can find them every year off American shores at the right time, if you have a stout boat and a strong stomach. Even so, they are less known than any other group of American birds. Bird students spend hours squinting through telescopes from Atlantic beaches, hoping to pick up the stiff-winged form of a shearwater, scaling against the mirage-distorted horizon. Along the Pacific coast these birds range closer inshore and sometimes great milling rafts of sooty shearwaters come close enough to the jutting headlands for observers to pick out the scarcer white-bellied species. Only once have I seen shearwaters like this on the Atlantic side—one October day, from the weathered bluffs at Montauk light, I saw 1000 Cory's shearwaters, gliding and weaving beyond the surf. Their presence so close inshore was explained by great masses of a small red planktonic creature that had drifted in from the ocean. Hordes of small fish were attracted to the feast and their ranks in turn were counter-attacked by a curtain of dive-bombing gannets—hundreds of them—plunging like gleaming white rockets into the intricate pattern woven by the shearwaters.

When I was first learning about birds in the hills around Jamestown, New York, I came across a book by Herbert K. Job. Written more than forty years ago, and chock-full of photographs, its title was *Wild Wings*. My favorite chapter in this exciting book, which I borrowed often from our small public library, was "Off Chatham Bars," a story of sea birds and adventure in a small open boat on the fishing banks of Cape Cod. As I read that book I planned some day to do what Job had done; to encounter some of these feathered mariners in their own element. My first chance came when I was scheduled to give a bird talk to a garden club on the outer Cape. After the ordeal was over, I made arrangements to go out to the fishing grounds the next morning with a Captain Nickerson.

Crossing Chatham Bars, the choppy dangerous rips that guarded the entrance to our mooring in Pleasant Bay, we headed southeastward until the poplar-studded bluffs of Chatham dropped below the horizon behind us. Fifteen or twenty miles out, we cast anchor. We had seen no birds save one lone sooty shearwater, or "black hag" as Nickerson called it. He said that a week before the fishing grounds had been swarming with "hags," especially the white-bellied ones.

There were no birds, so we fished. In an hour or two we filled the bin with cod, haddock and hake. How many of these goggle-eyed fish I caught I do not know. I was too green and queasy from the oily sidling of our small craft to care. Catching cod is like pulling up old boots full of water from the floor of the ocean. They do not fight much, but fifty yards of slippery cord hauled rapidly hand over hand soon takes the skin off the fingers. The only bit of excitement came when a huge banded shark that, to my startled eyes, looked almost half the length of our boat, snapped off a cod I was pulling in and carried it away, hook, sinker and all.

We saw no more shearwaters—not even a petrel. The only birds of interest were—of all things—four red-breasted nuthatches! These came aboard one at a time, and crept mouselike over the ropes and woodwork. One even allowed me to stroke its back. These little waifs, at home only in the spruces and firs of the northwoods, were on one of their mysterious lemming-like journeys to destruction. They had probably flown on their stubby little wings all the way from Maine or Nova Scotia. When they left the boat, they headed due south over the endless water—not landward toward the low line of dunes dimly visible on Monomoy to the west. They seemed so pitifully small as they stoutly started out for nowhere over the waves.

Several years later, I made another journey to Chatham, hoping to get offshore. Overnight, an easterly blow sprang up and none of the catboats dared cross the dreaded bar which was whipped into a cauldron of foam and spray. These shoals, which one must cross to reach the fishing grounds, are a graveyard of many small craft that have been tossed about and sent to the bottom.

Again I tried. Ludlow Griscom had promised the Joseph Hickeys and me that if we drove up from New York he would arrange for the boat. Navigating across the shoals, calm for once, we left the gulls and terns behind us (compared to the quarry we were after, these birds are landlubbers). The gentle rise and fall of the ground swell as we passed the Stone Horse lightship told us we were really at sea.

To insure our success, we had taken along almost every lure we knew of for "chumming" the birds to our boat. At Fulton Fish Market, in downtown New York, I paid out a dollar and a half for a large can of halibut livers. Green and mouldy, they had been earmarked for sale to a manufacturer of haliver oil capsules. They were frozen into a solid icy cake when I bought them, but the heat in the trunk compartment of the Studebaker soon thawed them into a liquid stinking mess. In another fish stall I had picked up two gallons of "mossbunker" oil—extracted from the crushed bodies of the little fish known as menhaden. We also had several pounds of suet, diced fine through a meat grinder. The idea was to lay down a slick with the livers and oil, and drop just enough suet into it to keep the birds interested. Someone told us that puffed rice worked just as well as suet, so we added a couple of boxes of this well-known breakfast food to our pelagic smörgasbord.

A light fog coming in from the east cut down visibility and our chances of success. The theory on which we worked was that the first shearwater or petrel that discovered our slick would attract others by its actions, as a circling vulture signals its comrades to a corpse. If we were lucky we would soon have a swarm of birds skimming the floating tidbits in our wake. While we doled out the oil and the suet, the captain and the children fished. We soon found that fresh livers ripped from the bellies of the cod and chopped into small pieces made a much better slick than the lure we had brought along. My precious halibut livers were so dessicated that they sank almost immediately.

Chatham must be my jinx, for Griscom said he had never had a poorer day offshore in twelve years. Again, one lone sooty, scaling by on stiff wings, was the only shearwater we saw all day. It didn't seem at all interested in our bait, which extended in glistening patches behind our boat.

A flock of small whitish birds dashed past in close formation. Twisting and turning in military fashion, they looked like sanderlings until they abruptly settled on the water. There were about forty of them; we could see them plainly, as the pulsing heartbeat of the ocean lifted the whole flock from a trough high onto the crest of a comber. These little swimming sandpipers were northern phalaropes, the famous noncomformists of the bird world, southbound from their tundra nesting grounds in Greenland and Labrador, to their winter *Shangri-la* in the South Atlantic.

As the fog started to burn off in the hot noonday sun, the wind rose and the water became rougher. A Wilson's petrel skimmed across our stern, discovered the slick and paused a moment. Soon another followed. These little black birds, the size of martins, with white rump patches, are the "Mother Carey's chickens" or "Kerry chickens" of the sailors. Some sailors say they are the souls of lost seamen. They were a long way from home, for their nesting grounds are at the other end of the world from those of the phalaropes—at the edge of the Antarctic. This August day was summer to us, but it was winter in Antarctica.

I tried photographing the petrels with my unwieldy 4 x 5 Graflex, but they were too fast. They would skip across our bow, swing astern, and pause with rigid wings for a moment over the silvery slick. Before I could get a crisp focus, they would give a kick with both feet and dance on. A dozen birds came in and departed. We should have stayed to watch them longer had not one of the boys sunk the barb of a heavy cod hook deep into the palm of his hand. He needed a doctor to cauterize the jagged wound, so starting the engine, we left the petrels to their bleak and turbulent wilderness.

It seemed as though I should have to live on the Cape if I were to see a good day offshore during the summer. On winter cruises, in pursuit of sea ducks and the auk clan, I have always had good luck. My series of bad breaks with the tube-nosed tribe was finally broken on one of my trips to California while gathering material for my *Field Guide to Western Birds*.

Guy Emerson was in San Francisco on one of his business trips at the time. A year before he had taken a boatload of Californians a few miles off Monterey and shown them their own albatrosses. When he returned to New York, I listened with rapt interest to his story, and he promised that he would take me out to see the albatrosses, too, if I would bring along my cameras. *Life* magazine, hearing of our plans, wired Peter Stackpole, one of their photographers, to run up from Los Angeles to join us.

So it was that the early morning of May 23, 1940, found five of us gathered together in a diner near the water front in Monterey, eager to start out. Around us, at the counters, sat young all-night revelers, boisterous and bleary-eyed, eating their scrambled eggs before going home.

At dawn, in this picturesque fishing village, we boarded our boat, the *Pleasure II,* with Captain Arcoleo at the helm. We had brought along three large cans of oil, twenty pounds of chopped suet and two buckets of squids. The best way, Emerson said, was to start the slick while we were still in the harbor, so that we would have a following of gulls. The gulls would attract the albatrosses when we were out far enough.

We had hardly reached the harbor mouth when we ran into great milling rafts of sooty shearwaters, spreading like a dark carpet over acres of water and feeding on some sort of swimming crustacean that swarmed on the surface. Many of the shearwaters, resting gull-like, were so stuffed they could hardly get under way as the prow of our boat bore down upon them. Some flopped aside, others dived in panic. Shearwaters find it difficult to rise in a calm and spatter along like coots, but once underway they are masters of the air, gliding stiff-winged and banking against the subtle wind currents generated upwards by the long gentle swell. We estimated between 15,000 and 20,000 sooties, an unbelievable contrast to the scattered individuals that we see on the Atlantic. Masters of navigation, they had come a long way from their breeding grounds "down under" in the neighborhood of Cape Horn, the Chilean Andes or New Zealand. Yet each would return next winter to precisely the same burrow, thousands of miles away, to lay its single egg.

Black and white pigeon guillemots buzzed by, their bright orange feet straddling the air. A score of black brant, the first I had ever seen, hugged a barnacle-encrusted rock. Parties of cormorants, like small black geese, passed continually. A flock of 200 Pacific loons, all in breeding plumage, with pearly gray crowns, flew in a northerly direction, close to the water, in a long straggling skein.

We had become so wrapped up in this great show that we had forgotten the gulls and the suet. Circling back we started our slick. A few gulls investigated it, but they did not follow far. Like the shearwaters they seemed as stuffed as a small boy after Thanksgiving dinner. Again we tried, but they would not follow for more than half a mile. We decided to go out to sea, gulls or no gulls.

The long, smooth swell was beginning to have its effect on Stackpole who had never had an assignment like this before. His specialty was photographing glamour girls and movie stars in Hollywood; he hadn't the remotest idea what an albatross looked like. His tinge of green disappeared when two large whales rose to starboard and snorted forth their plumes of spray. He suggested we chase whales instead of albatrosses. A whale at close range would be a scoop—something that by Hollywood standards would be super-colossal. Voted down by the rest of us, he slumped dejectedly back into his deck chair.

A flock of twenty rare Sabine's gulls, a life bird for me, flew out of the fog at close range. They were migrants in exquisite breeding plumage, with gray hoods and forked tails, northbound from the coast of Peru to their summer home on the Arctic Ocean.

A petrel flitted across our bow and soon we were seeing dozens of them. They were dark all over, without the white rump patches of our eastern species. Soon we became conscious that there were two sizes of them, one with an easy wing motion, and a smaller one with a more fluttering flight. The larger species was the black petrel, the other the ashy.

Emerson, his reputation at stake, was standing up forward, like the mariner of old, straining his eyes, when the bird of Coleridge finally appeared:

> At length did cross an Albatross,
> Thorough the fog it came;
> As if it had been a Christian soul,
> We hail'd it in God's name.

Everyone was up on his feet. We poured the oil and threw out handfuls of greasy suet. Stackpole, who had not quite believed we should ever see an albatross, stumbled across the deck and made his battery of cameras ready. The bird, its long rigid wings cutting the air like a saber, banked, came about, lit on the water a hundred yards aft and gobbled up our offering.

> It ate the food it ne'er had eat,
> And round and round it flew.

Soon there was a second albatross; like the first, it seemed to appear from nowhere. Another and yet another came, until we could count fifteen around the boat. The Captain said that in twenty-five years of fishing in these waters he had never before seen more than one or two at a time.

By putting the motor at its lowest speed we could drift down on little parties of four or five birds until we were but several feet away. We even tossed squid to them, which they caught in their great horny hooked bills, just as we would throw bread to the tame ducks in a city park. The year before Guy Emerson tried to feed an albatross from his hand and almost succeeded. It came within six inches of his fingertips but did not quite dare nibble the suet. One ornithologist, taking advantage of the trusting nature of albatrosses that came up to his boat to eat bacon grease and puffed rice, spattered them with white, green and red paint and was able to recognize them days afterwards at points miles away.

As if the gods conspired, the wispy fog drifted away and let through the sun. Conditions for photography were perfect. I took a hundred pictures and Stackpole snapped twice that many.

These big friendly birds, towering above the handful of California gulls like giants among the dwarfs, were the birds we had read about in a dozen novels of the sea. These were the fowl that for days, could follow ships effortlessly in the strongest gales, yet which became as violently seasick as any landsman when captured and placed on the deck. There was a gentle dignified look about them as they watched us with seeming curiosity. Like the shearwaters, they found it difficult to rise into the air on this calm morning without taxiing a bit. On the wing, the great dark birds had a span of about seven feet.

Coleridge, a master of the imagination, never saw an albatross in his life any more than Poe had seen a raven when he wrote his poem. The albatross he wrote about was probably not this golden-brown bird—the black-footed albatross—swimming near us on the water. It was more likely the wandering albatross, the great white sea bird that is credited with a greater wingspread than any other bird in the world—including the condor—a spread of eleven and one-half feet.

Albatross is a corruption of "alcatraz," the Spanish word for pelican. Actually albatrosses and pelicans are not related. There are thirteen kinds of albatrosses in the world, most of them in the southern seas. Tars divide them roughly into "gooneys," the more northern species, and "molly-mawks," those that ride the roaring forties below the equator.

A generation or more ago two kinds of "gooneys" reached California. In addition to the black-footed albatross there was a white one, the short-tailed albatross which came every year all the way from its breeding station in the Bonin Islands, 500 miles southeast of Japan. At one time it was the commoner albatross of the two, but none of the present generation of bird watchers in California has ever seen one. For a few years it was believed that the bird was extinct.

The men of the Rising Sun "had done a hellish thing." On one of the Bonins, "the Seven Islands of Izu," killing albatrosses for their feathers and for fertilizer became a big business. They even set up a railway to the top of the island and a cableway to the bay. Every man on the island killed 100 to 200 birds a day, until, over a period of years, at least 5,000,000 albatrosses had been slaughtered. Then, in 1903, while the remnant of the birds was away at sea, Olympian justice interceded. The lid blew off the volcano on the island and every last one of the three hundred inhabitants lost his life in the eruption.

> He prayeth best, who loveth best
> All things both great and small.

In 1907, the Japanese government put the short-tailed albatross on the protected list, but the islands were so remote that they could not enforce the edict. New settlers came in and resumed the killing. By 1932 there were only a few hundred birds left, and in December of that year the inhabitants held one last massacre. They never referred to the incident, but said that a storm killed the last birds. Actually they had heard that the island was to be made into a bird sanctuary. The next year, the island became a Japanese National Monument, but it was almost too late. As a final divine gesture, the volcano again blew its top in 1939 but somewhere at sea there were still a dozen birds. These are the hope of the future.

The black-footed albatross, fortunately did not have all its eggs in one basket. Nesting on a number of very scattered islands in the Pacific, it survived the marauding Nipponese who once even made a bird raid on United States-owned Laysan to the west of Hawaii. The early travelers said there were millions of albatrosses on the portulaca flats of remote Laysan; actually there were hundreds of thousands—Laysan albatrosses in the inner basin; black-foots on the sandy beaches.

In 1909, during the presidency of conservation-minded Theodore Roosevelt, Laysan and other islands of the Leeward Chain were set aside as the Hawaiian Bird Reservation, for it had been rumored that the Japanese were planning to land on the rookeries to destroy the birds for their use.

The executive order did not stop the Japanese. Before the ink was dry, twenty-three Japanese poachers, under the direction of a German in Hawaii, landed on little-visited Laysan and started the systematic destruction of the birds. When news of this reached Honolulu, in January, 1910, the U.S. Revenue Cutter *Thetis* sped westward. The surprised looters were stopped none too soon. One lot of plumes had already been shipped off to

Japan, while in the old buildings were stacked the feathers of a quarter of a million birds. Read the graphic report published in 1912 by the United States Biological Survey:

"An old cistern back of one of the buildings tells a story of cruelty that surpasses anything else done by these heartless, sanguinary pirates, not excepting the practice of cutting the wings from living birds and leaving them to die of hemorrhage. In this dry cistern the living birds were kept by hundreds to slowly starve to death. In this way the fatty tissue lying next to the skin was used up, and the skin was left quite free from grease, so that it required little or no cleaning during preparation.

"This wholesale killing has had an appalling effect on the colony. No one can estimate the thousands, perhaps hundreds of thousands, of birds that have been willfully sacrificed on Laysan. It is conservative to say that fully one-half the number of birds of both species of albatross that were so abundant everywhere in 1903 have been killed."

The black-footed albatross still lays its single egg on Laysan, Midway and a number of other islands in the mid-Pacific, thousands of miles from California. There the courting couples dance their famous "gooney cake walk," strutting, bowing and waving their beaks in the air. The reluctant eggs, laid in November, do not hatch until February, and the fuzzy, pot-bellied young must be fed for six months more. Only September and October are left to the hard-working parents for a brief gooney vacation. That is why so many of the albatrosses seen off California seem to be immature birds.

On that warm May morning as we doled out our offering, all seemed well with the world. As our suet gave out, the gooneys scaled off, one by one, to be lost in the long gentle swell of the Pacific. We did not dream that the drolleries of these amiable birds would soon win the affection of legions of American men stationed on their nesting islands to the west. We did not know that their watery domain was soon to become a great theater of war.

"SEA GULLS" are really landlubbers in comparison with some of the other water birds. Very few of the gulls that populate the beaches of the West Coast venture across the broad Pacific to the Hawaiian Islands.

AT LENGTH DID CROSS AN ALBATROSS. Yearly, the black-footed albatross, shown above, visits Californian waters. Below, Guy Emerson (right) and the
author take time out to add Sabine's gull, ashy petrel and black petrel to their list.

VOYAGEURS from the West Indies rest on the buoys that mark the channels near the Dry Tortugas. Neither the white-bellied booby, above, nor the man-o'-war, below, are known to breed within the continental United States.

TROPICAL SEAS are the home of the sooty tern, above, but hurricanes have carried strays as far north as Maine and Nova Scotia. Below is the 'noddy,' another West Indian tern. It does not seem so subject to the winds.

Hurricane's Waifs

WHEN West Indian storms sweep up the Atlantic coast, leveling all before them, rational folk tremble and question God's wisdom. The birdomaniac, awed by such celestial violence, but oblivious to its wantonness, scarcely thinks of the destruction of property or the loss of life; keyed up, he wonders what rare sea birds the winds will bring. Nothing can keep him from hurrying to the shore—before the vortex has passed, if he can.

Most of the records of tropical sea birds in the northern United States can be tied up with hurricanes. A storm in September, 1876, struck the West Indies with all its fury. On many of the islands people were washed into the sea or were buried beneath the houses where they lived. Forty-five ships were battered to kindling in Puerto Rico and the American steamer *Liberty* was lost somewhere between Havana and New York. This storm which caused so much human misery left in its wake sooty terns in New England, a tropic bird in New York and a man-o'-war bird in Nova Scotia. All these had been picked up somewhere in the Caribbean, and carried along for 2000 miles or more before they were set down in an unfamiliar landscape.

In August, 1893, a storm passed over mountainous Haiti and Dominica, wiping out fields of bananas and sugar cane, laying low the coconut palms and scattering like chaff the boats that rode at anchor. During its passage it picked from the sea a number of black-capped petrels, a species so rare that for a while it was thought to be extinct, and dropped them exhausted or dying in Virginia, New York, Massachusetts and Vermont. Five years later, after an October hurricane that swept inland to the Mississippi, two more of these petrels, which suggest greater shearwaters, were captured in Kentucky and Ohio.

The sooty tern, the "sea swallow" with the black back and white breast, seems to be the most frequent of these oceanic waifs. The natives of some of the Lesser Antilles call them "hurricane birds" because swarms of them often appear out of a seemingly birdless sea just before a blow. Ober tells of this in his *Camps in the Caribees,* written in 1880:

"Immediately preceding the hurricanes there arrive off the Caribbean coast (of Dominica) vast numbers of birds called from their cries Twa-oo. They are said to be the harbingers of hurricanes, and they appear only during the calms immediately before a storm. They cover the water in large flocks and come in from the desolate sandy beaches where they breed. They are the sooty tern (*Sterna fuliginosa*). When I arrived in Dominica the sea was black with them, but on the morning after the storm they had disappeared to a bird, as completely as though blown into another sphere."

In the third week of September in 1933, the north Atlantic shores were peppered with sooties just after a wild storm had ravaged the coast. Two days later I picked up a beautiful specimen lying dead among the drift on the marsh grass on Staten Island, New York. The nearest place of origin of this bird would be the Bahamas or the Dry Tortugas off Key West. The following January, while searching for winter sea birds along the bluffs at Montauk Point on the eastern tip of Long Island, I spied a bleached skeleton, half buried in the sand. Pulling it out, I saw by its long black bill it belonged to a sooty tern, undoubtedly another casualty of this same storm.

During September of 1945, when I was stationed at the air base at Orlando, Florida, the storm warnings went up. All planes were sent scurrying to safer airfields to the north. We battened down the barracks, ate K rations and waited indoors. For hours the driving drizzle sounded on the roof while the howling wind slowly increased its tempo. When the storm reached the peak of its fury, limbs of pine trees, roofing paper, shingles and boards hurtled through the air, but the buildings held fast. The following day we drove to Cape Canaveral on the east coast and there, on the lighthouse keeper's well-kept lawn we picked up two dead birds. One was a sooty tern and the other, slightly smaller and paler, with a light nape was a bridled tern, the fifth record for Florida. The keeper of the light said that there had been several others on the lawn in the morning before the cats got them. During the night, he told us, when the gales were still raging, clouds of sooties, or "wide-awakes," fluttered before the huge lenses. It must have been an eery sight. Once the storm is spent the birds seem to disappear into the void, as if they were the souls of lost sailors; and although we stood on the dunes and searched the disturbed sea till our eyes smarted, we did not see a sooty or a noddy, or anything out of the usual run.

According to my encyclopedia, the word hurricane comes from *hurakan* of the Arawak speaking Indians of the West Indies. It is used by mariners to denote a wind force of more than seventy-five miles per hour, which Admiral Francis Beaufort described as "that which no canvas could withstand."

The majority of hurricanes in the Atlantic originate in late August, September or early October, between ten and twenty degrees north of the equator, out toward the Cape Verdes, far to the east of the Caribbean. As if the gods conspired to stir the oppressively hot and humid doldrums into action, winds and squalls start converging on the overheated patch of ocean until a revolving tropical storm is born. Moving westward and gaining force, it skirts that fabulous waste of drifting seaweed, the Sargasso Sea, which is an *anti-cyclone* (high pressure) area. To avoid this region of opposing air currents the cyclonic storms must pass through the West Indies before swinging violently northward and then northeastward to final dissipation. Anywhere from two hurricanes to a dozen or more are reported each year. Not all of them reach the United States; but when they do, they usually skirt the coast. A few even pass inland before turning out to sea.

The system of one of these storms is like a whirlpool, sucking the winds into its vortex in a counter-clockwise direction. These winds come from a long distance and attain a speed sometimes exceeding 100 miles per hour. On the bosom of these violent gales, which pour into the storm center from all points of the compass, birds are borne like swimmers in a strong current. It is not unusual then, after a hurricane, to find birds not only of southern origin, but also from the Northeast or the West. After one such September storm had passed over Long Island, I saw on the same mud flat, many scores of skimmers and Forster's terns from the South; golden plovers that normally by-pass Long Island to the east, out at sea; and, most remarkable of all, an avocet from the West.

At the center of a cyclonic storm is a dead spot, from five to twenty-five miles across, where the winds are lulled. This calm area, or "eye," travels along at a relatively slow pace at first, perhaps not more than fifteen miles per hour, but as it moves northward it gains speed, traveling as much as thirty miles per hour or more. As the whirlpool grows wider, it loses its destructive potency. Robert Cushman Murphy, the famous student of oceanic bird life, believes that many birds actually travel within this "eye." Once caught *inside* the swirl of the storm, he says, "they might be carried along without becoming panicky, without experiencing any sense of difficulty, feeding normally, and tending always to turn inward toward the calm of the slow-moving center when they had flown far enough in one direction to come into heavily wind-whipped waters. Only when the vortex comes into close proximity with the land, as I conceive the situation, would birds thus held in unconscious durance begin to fight the gales, perhaps to be carried into the higher altitudes of the atmosphere and to be buffeted as helpless waifs for long distances overland before being cast out centrifugally, subsequently to fall exhausted. It is only through some such process as this that I can comprehend the transportation of black-capped petrels from points east of the Caribbean to the Mississippi Valley, or of Madeira and South Trinidad petrels from the central or eastern north equatorial Atlantic to Ottawa and Ithaca, respectively."

There are actual records of the presence of birds in the center of hurricanes. Ships entering the windless eye have found the air filled with the fluttering wings of sea-fowl, and the decks and rigging were sought by hundreds of small land birds.

One of the most destructive hurricanes on record (in the United States, at least) struck New England on September 21, 1938. It started as any other ordinary hurricane, but before it reached Florida where everyone awaited it, tense and expectant, it veered and raced to the north. Instead of growing weaker as it went along, its winds became more violent. The storm found itself hemmed in by two high pressure areas, one to the west on land, and another to the east at sea. Between lay a passageway across New England, a low pressure corridor of light air. Forced into this path of least resistance, the hurricane hit the eastern end of Long Island with a huge wave that swept great stone mansions off the dunes. Water rose fifteen or twenty feet and many people drifted for hours on rafts that had been the roofs of their homes.

Spinning overland, it tore across Long Island, sending the century-old elms in East Hampton and Bridgehampton crashing across the highways. Seven hundred summer homes at Watch Hill, Rhode Island, were washed away. In Providence, the crest of the tidal wave swept into the downtown business section and drowned a man in front of the City Hall. Fantastic as it sounds, passengers were reported drowned in a train stalled on the tracks between Boston and New York.

The sea storm became a land storm, a sort of super-cyclone. Church steeples were snapped off in little towns in the Connecticut Valley, and forests of white pine were laid down like matchsticks on New England hillsides. Even the anemometers by which men measure the wind blew away, but the one on Mount Washington held fast. It recorded a velocity of 183 miles per hour! On the next day, the 22nd of September, the equatorial storm roared into Canada, weakened and slowly passed away.

Although there had been very little official warning, there was no doubt, as it approached, that this was not an ordinary storm. Our barometer at the Audubon office in New York went into a nose dive. I had never seen a barometer show such a sharp drop. Then came a frantic phone call from Mrs. Robert Allen out on Long Island. "The water," she told her husband, "is up to the top of the steps, and if you are coming home tonight you will have to swim."

It was hard to keep my mind on my work the next morning. What birds would there be on Long Island? If rare birds had been brought by lesser storms, what would this one bring? A friend dropped by to tell me he had gone out on the marshes at sunset, when the gales from the south were still blowing strong into the retreating storm center. Clapper rails, flooded out of the salt meadows, were crushed by cars on the highway. On a mud flat he had seen several suspicious-looking terns. From his description they sounded like sooties. That settled it. Perhaps there might even be tropic birds and boobies around, I thought. Grabbing my coat and binoculars, I quit the office for the day.

We cruised beach after beach within thirty miles of New York, but saw even fewer birds than usual. Only a few gulls were around, and the small shorebirds were completely dispersed by the storm. We did catch sight of a small dark sea bird that scaled by beyond the surf, but it was lost among the waves before we could determine what it was. The brief glimpse suggested an Audubon's shearwater, a resident of the Bahamas. Aside from that one unsatisfactory observation we saw nothing exciting. Where were the fancy birds we should have seen? Other members of the Linnaean Society scoured Long Island and asked the same question.

Not until a week or two later did we know the answer. Yellow-billed tropic birds, the "long-tails" which nest in the coral caves of the Bermudas, were borne across Long Island, up the Connecticut Valley, through western Massachusetts and were dropped like spent meteors at three places in Vermont. How many of these streamlined wanderers came to earth but were never found, no one will know. Cory's shearwaters and greater shearwaters, gull-like travelers of the ocean spaces, which never of their own volition leave salt water, were found inland in Massachusetts and in Vermont, hundreds of miles from their element. Leach's petrel, the dark swallow-like storm petrel with the white rump patch and the notched tail, was scattered through the heart of New England, and its small square-tailed cousin, the Wilson's petrel, the one that follows boats at sea, was recorded on Lake Ontario, Lake Champlain and on the St. Lawrence River.

The birds had, if we accept Dr. Murphy's explanation, followed the tranquil eye of the storm until it reached Long Island. As land approached, they struggled offshore to keep over the water, the element on which they were most at home. Encountering the revolving winds again, they fought to leeward until they were carried up and up into the mad swirl. Once trapped there was no escape until they were thrown out, exhausted or dying, hundreds of miles from their familiar environment.

What do these storms do to the lives of birds? Some of the sea birds die, we know, particularly when the hurricane elects to travel overland. But in most storms that dissipate themselves over the ocean the birds ride out the tempest and make for home waters posthaste. No birds have a keener homing ability than the pelagic birds; the unleashed winds are a routine part of their lives.

But the myriads of small migrating land birds that are trapped within the windless eye probably never see land again if the storm dies far out over the Atlantic. I have wondered what the effect would be on the few Kirtland's warblers of this world if they were intercepted by an October hurricane while making the flight to their winter home in the Bahamas.

We do know that the dwindling population of the great white heron was cut way down by the Labor Day hurricane, in 1935. During this storm which took so many lives, fifteen feet of water swept across the Matecumbe Keys. One of the Audubon wardens told me two years later that in a day's cruise he could show me a score of human skeletons lodged among the mangroves. A month after the storm, when Alexander Sprunt flew over nine-tenths of the range of this largest of all American herons, he saw only 146 birds, and in the center of the swath cut by the wind and waves, where everything looked as though flattened by a steam roller, not a bird could be found.

George Sutton had the presence of mind, during a violent October hurricane in Florida, to watch the small birds in order to see how they fared. The battering winds reached seventy-eight miles per hour, with gusts up to 108 miles per hour. The blue jays seemed to enjoy it all, but a mockingbird squatted behind one of the solid supports of a low porch. A shrike, dispossessed from a clump of Spanish moss in an oak tree when the trunk snapped, scrambled to the lee of an outhouse. Palm warblers hid under porches, under ventilators and among the grasses. A flicker hurtled out of a falling pine, bounced on the ground, and dazedly flew to the trunk of a sturdier tree. All the birds seemed to survive, for in the afternoon, with the storm's passing, the cardinals, ground doves, red-bellied woodpeckers and the rest came forth from their hiding places unharmed.

The real effect of a hurricane on land birds is an indirect one, one that might not be felt until the following year or even several years later. When the hurricane of October 17-18, 1944, blasted the west coast of Florida, it blew down eighteen of Broley's eagle trees, threw many nests to the ground and damaged all the others. Although the birds rebuilt all but one, they laid no eggs that season in twenty-four of them. In twenty-one others the eggs did not hatch, for some unknown reason. Thus, forty-five nests out of 115 were failures in 1945, because of that one storm, which Broley believed set up a chain of reactions that upset the eagle's pattern of life.

It would be trite to moralize about "an ill wind," but the great New England hurricane of 1938, which brought death to so many sea birds, made survival easier for the small birds that live on land, as the next several years proved. The ravaged woodlands were opened up; there were more clearings on New England mountainsides for olive-sided flycatchers and white-throated sparrows; more piles of brush for winter wrens to hide in; more decaying timber for woodpeckers to forage among. Wendell Smith, an outstanding bird-watcher who lived in Vermont, had made a breeding census of a fifty-acre tract of pine-hemlock forest near his home. In 1936 he found seventy-five pairs of birds representing thirty-two species. That was before the great storm tore through and littered the ground with the fallen conifers. The summer after the blowdown there were not fewer birds but more, and each year for nine years the number kept climbing until in 1947 there were 187 pairs of birds, representing forty-six species—an increase in density of nearly 150 per cent!

THE MAINE COAST is symbolized by two gulls, a cormorant and a sail. The headlands and innumerable rocky islets are the home of hundreds of thousands of seabirds. There are far more birds along the coast today than there were in 1900.

FOURTEEN THOUSAND gannets crowd the ledges of Bonaventure. Half
of the gannets that live on this side of the Atlantic make these cliffs their home.

ROCK COAST ROOKERY. The sea bird colonies are closer to the mainland on the West Coast than they are in New England. This oceanic tenement, crowded with murres and Brandt's cormorants, is off the tip of Point Reyes, north of San Francisco.

KYOWK-KYOWK-KYOWK! screams this tough, noisy herring gull just
beaten in a brawl. The clouds of gulls that nest on sea-washed New England
rocks find their living around the docks and dumps of the big cities in winter.

The Rock Coast

*O*OWN East" in New England the continent sinks into the sea. The fretted coast, sculptured by glacial ice sheets, is defined by drowned valleys where the salt water flowed in among the hills as the land slowly submerged. The State of Maine, within the 250 air miles from Kittery to Eastport, has a water line 1300 to 2400 miles long, depending on how you measure the countless coves, harbors and inlets. Hundreds of islands, remnants of mainland hills, now isolated by the encircling sea, stand offshore, their rocks bared to the erosive action of the surf and the tides.

Some of these islands, particularly the ones close under the lee of the mainland, are a mile or even several miles across, supporting sprawling towns and tight little farms. Others are scarcely more than ledges, almost immersed at high tide. The most seaward of these marooned hilltops, bereft of trees and barely clearing the waves, are the homes of thousands of birds of the littoral who find in these oceanic tenements their key to survival.

They say that the State of Maine is a state of mind. If that be so, I achieved it early. The spired spruces, the bright summer sky and the little white towns like Wiscasset and Damariscotta are part of it; but when I think of Maine I think first of the rock coast, the islands and the sea. My first visit to the Egg Rocks off the mouth of Muscongus Bay could not have been more exciting had these emergent boulders been the fabulous bird islands of Peru. That was long before the Audubon Nature Camp moved into the old ship chandlery on Hog Island, near the head of Muscongus Bay. Now hundreds of campers each year enjoy the same experiences I had in the black-hulled Friendship sloop that we sailed out of Wiscasset.

Hog Island is a good place to start from if you wish to see the birds of the Rock Coast. Midway down the coast of Maine and snuggled close inshore, it is within half a day's sail of almost every species of sea bird that nests in New England. It is not always possible to go offshore when the whim strikes, for Maine weather is capricious. Heavy seas running into the bay and opaque blankets of fog drenching the spruce forests and shutting the nearest islands from view make navigation dangerous. I once thought the lobster fishermen were a timid lot when they refused to take us out in such weather. But they know what they are doing. It is not adventure to them to run needless risks, to act the role of the bold mariner; boating is their livelihood. When the wind swings into the east and the fog rolls in, we must be resigned to three days ashore, three clammy gray days, perhaps more. The west wind, born of the mainland, brings the blue skies back. Then, if our captain deigns, we may go to the islands.

As we skirt the shore, with its crowded spruce trees festooned with clumps of witches' broom and hung with usnea, like tangled green-gray witches' hair, we hear the flutings of thrushes from the shadows. The olive-backed thrushes have nests in the small evergreens, like the one we found one Yuletide in the Christmas tree in our living room. This is a landscape full of Christmas trees, the tag end of the great coniferous biome that stretches diagonally across Canada to Alaska, and the birds are those of the Canadian wilderness. Here the birds of the north woods meet the birds of the sea.

Ospreys lift on heavily beating wings from their bulky nests, and protest our passing with an annoyed *chewk, chewk, chewk, chewk.* Since the early 1900's, these white-bellied fish hawks seem to have increased here like all the other fish-eating birds, but are now again in a decline.

A great blue heron flies over the boat, its rubbery neck in a loop and its collapsible legs trailing like loose baggage. It is headed for Otter Island, far off to larboard, where a heronry of hundreds of great blues and a few night herons is hidden deep behind the wall of straight dark spruce. If we were closer we could hear the young ticking, but we won't stop there today. Nor will we stop at the bare ledge known whimsically as Jones' Garden where the gulls and the cormorants maintain a bachelors' club.

We will make Eastern Egg Rock our first port of call; Eastern Egg with its huge wooden tripod, ten miles as the tern flies from the boathouse. Western Egg lies off to the right, but it isn't as good as it was in the old days. It once had guillemots and petrels, and, best of all, the only colony of laughing gulls on the Maine Coast. The local Audubon Society bought the island, they say, to protect the laughing gulls, but the very next year, the gulls moved to Little Green.

Cormorants, somber as Poe's raven, perch gaunt and upright atop the tilting spar-buoys, holding their wings "spread eagle" to the breeze, like satanic laundry hung out to dry. Launching forth with an awkward shove, they drop almost to the water before gaining enough momentum for the take-off. Our boatman tells us that the "shag" must always wet its tail before it can fly.

As we approach Eastern Egg, the light slip-slap of the waves gives way to a choppier movement, for we are at the threshold of the open sea. Far off to starboard, guarding one portal of the bay, stands Pemaquid light, a sleepless eye that watches while the world slumbers. I think I should like to own a lighthouse such as this if one were ever put up for sale. Aside from its symbolism of universal brotherhood, a lighthouse can be made into a good studio. I have always envied the lighthouse studio that my friend Peter Scott, the bird artist, once owned on the east coast of England.

Monhegan's foghorn, lowing mightily like Paul Bunyan's blue ox "Babe," moans to the south. The fog must still hang heavy out there, but the ascending sun will burn it off. Our small boat climbs each charging comber, up and down, up and down, the dory skipping aft like an empty pea pod. Little parties of black guillemots buzz across the bow, their white wing patches flashing and scarlet feet spraddling the air as they veer off in a half circle. They nest somewhere in the jumble of rocks on the perimeter of the island. As we round the point a black-backed gull, perched like a sentinel at the tip of the great tripod, takes off, and as if this were the signal, a thousand wings are in the air. This is it! This is what we have come to see. Swinging to the lee of the island, we drop anchor and haul rope on the dory.

Landing from a dory in a dancing sea is only for the surefooted and the agile. The surf rides up and down the kelp-covered ledges. You must choose your moment. Jump from the bow to the barnacle-encrusted rocks

—they will give a gritty foothold. Avoid the rockweed with its little bladders that go pop when you step on them. The *fucus* and *laminaria* that drape the boulders in green-gold masses are as slippery as grease.

The sky is a snowstorm of birds, wheeling, complaining. The wailing cries of the gulls, and the boisterous *yowk-yowk-yowk-yowk,* give way to notes of anxiety, a dry *gah-gah-gah,* a note we hear from a thousand throats whenever we invade a colony. But we won't disturb them more than we can help. While we watch from the sidelines, the more distant birds settle like doves among their nests in the grass; others, nervously watching, swim offshore, "high-floating like a sloop unladen."

There were scarcely more gulls than this nesting on the whole New England coast in 1900, when the first Audubon wardens were put on the job. Protection came just in time, for the professional feather hunters had laid plans to raid the last gulleries. This is but one colony, in hundreds of colonies on the rock coast of New England and the Maritime Provinces, a few thousand birds in hundreds of thousands.

Above the mark of the storm tides, where the gales have thrown the sea-wrack, we find the first nests, hollows shaped by the bodies of the birds and lined with grass and seaweed. There are eggs in many of them, almost always three, brownish or olive-drab, with dark blotches. Buffy-gray babies with long silky down crouch in some of the nests, but the larger youngsters squat under the grass. A gull's nesting territory, only a few square feet, or several square yards at most, has three elements, three things that are essential to the sea-gull standard of living: the "standing place," a rock or piece of driftwood where the adults can stand and berate their neighbors; the nest; and a hiding place, a tuft of grass or a few weeds for the young to hide beneath.

I had not realized how important this hiding place was until I saw a young gull wander into the territory of a neighboring family. It toddled up to the owner, begging for food, but it got instead, a sharp rap on the back of the head, and another and another. Finally, the gull picked the little thing up and shook it until it was quite dead. I have seen dead young in every gull colony I have ever visited. One shocked ornithologist, witnessing this for the first time, called it the "massacre of the innocents." We, of course, have a tendency to judge wild things by our own moral codes, forgetting that anthropomorphism is a false thing, and that the behavior patterns of birds are instinctive. That gulls should kill their neighbor's children who wander from their hiding place perhaps serves a Spartan function in a colony, where there would be chaos if all wandered willy-nilly. The hiding place is an important thing then, a place where a gull can expect to find its own young when it returns. That the gull should kill strange chicks coldly and deliberately is an unfair assumption. The individual has no clear realization of self. An action from one bird calls forth a specific response from its neighbor; the pattern can almost always be predicted. One watcher saw a downy young gull run up to the wrong parent. The bird jabbed at the unwanted foundling, but missed, and the youngster nuzzled its breast. Immediately the reaction switched from infanticide to brooding.

Never stay too long at a bird colony; not unless you are in a blind. So let us cast off for Old Hump Ledge, two miles to the east. Its double hump, whitewashed with a dazzling coat of guano, suggesting a miniature snow-capped mountain, is clustered with double-crested cormorants, sitting about like ebon-hued gargoyles. They build their twiggy nests on the highest exposed rocks. There are herring gulls, too, nesting on the slopes under the rank clumps of ragweed.

As we walk about among the excrement-befouled cormorant nests, we see chalky eggs, babies just hatched, looking as if they were made of dark rubber, and we see others that are a little older and a little more presentable, their nakedness covered with coal black fuzz. They gape wide at us; they dart their sinuous necks back and forth like besieged snakes; they shake their orange throat pouches and whine nervously. As if this were not enough, some lay a mess of half-digested fish at our feet. A cormorant colony is no place for the squeamish.

The larger young huddle in a gang and crowd to the water's edge. Some of the oldest dive through the breakers where we can see them cleave the green depths like veterans. They bob up beyond the surf to join the flotilla of cormorants riding at anchor offshore.

Old Hump is a study in black and white; and a study in smells, especially on the leeward side. Except for the pools of penetrating ammonia lying in the hollows, I do not mind too much the odor of a seabird colony. Perhaps a bird watcher is willing to overlook anything. William Vogt, who was sent by the Peruvian Guano Commission to the islands in the

Humboldt Current to see what could be done to "augment the increment of the excrement," lived for three years with *millions* of cormorants. He said the smell was not bad, once you got used to it.

The main reason we cannot harvest the guano on our own rocks is because ours is a humid coast, and the white deposits are washed away each year by the fog, the rain and the winter gales. The west coast of South America is dry as a bone and the nitrogenous powder, packed almost as hard as rock, was 180 feet deep in places, deep enough to mine, when the first foreign ships came for the precious substance over a century ago.

Neither do we have enough birds. Rather than a natural asset our "shags," as the fishermen call them, have been regarded as competitors, to be done away with, destroyed. So complete was their annihilation that the last two lonely pairs nested on Black Horse Ledge in Jericho Bay, in 1896. For a quarter of a century the old black shags were gone. But by 1923 a few stopped short of the Canadian line in migration and again nested on the coast of Maine. When Robert Allen cruised eastward down the coast, in 1931, he found four nests on Old Hump. In 1934, when I passed close by the rock in a sloop, I could count at least thirty-five through my binoculars. When we landed, in 1936, there were 135 nests, and three new colonies had been started nearby. By 1941 there were 367 nests on Old Hump and 1600 in the bay. Today, along the New England coast, there are several thousand nesting pairs, and all this from a starting point of zero!

Conservation is not just an ideal that we read about; it works. I know of no more vivid demonstration than the astounding return of the seabirds along the New England coast. I thought for awhile that man's change of attitude and his helping hand might be only a part of the story, that much of it might be explained on biological grounds. Perhaps the pasturage of the ocean had undergone a change—the minute floating plants and animals of the sea, had become more numerous. On black nights our boat churns up a luminous wake, and at each stroke our oars sparkle, for many of these minute forms are phosphorescent. The colder the water, the more plankton, and a drop of a few degrees in the temperature of the water multiplies it a hundredfold. It is the food base for all other sea life. The little fish thrive on this planktonic fare and, in turn, the bigger fish and the birds prey on them.

A shift in ocean currents could conceivably have cataclysmic effects on the birds. Off the coast of Peru, a cyclic countercurrent, *El Nino,* comes down every few years, warming the cold Humboldt Current by ten degrees or more. First the plankton succumbs, then the fish die and finally sickness and death come to the myriads of birds which drift upon the shore in windrows. But there is no evidence that any such thing had happened on the Maine Coast. Man had been the agent that nearly wiped out the birds. The comeback was slow at first, but, once the rhythm of the colonies gained impetus, their numbers shot skyward.

One day in late summer, I passed a dome-like rock off Penobscot Bay and on its crest was a bird blind. Intrigued, I bent my back to the oars and landed the dory on the cobble. Feeling somewhat like Stanley meeting Livingstone, I introduced myself to the young Crusoe I found there. His name was Howard Mendall. It was his last day on the rock, and the last young cormorant of the colony stood disconsolately at the edge of a cliff with two ratty-looking young herring gulls. Mendall had just completed his study of the food habits of the cormorant. He found that these maligned birds do not destroy many food fish but eat instead the competitors and predators of food fish—things liks sculpins and cunners. Local lobstermen, noting that the improved lobster trapping in recent years coincided with the increase in cormorants, believe it is because these birds feed on the "rock eels" and cunners that destroy the newborn lobsters. Yet there is pressure again to "control" cormorants. If only they would leave them alone!

No comeback is more spectacular than that of the cormorant, unless it be that of the black-backed gull. Perhaps "comeback" is the wrong word to apply to the black-back, because it never had been known to breed within the limits of the United States prior to 1928, when three pairs were found nesting on one of the Duck Islands. Now there are thousands; seven hundred pairs in Muscongus Bay alone. The black-back, the largest of our common gulls is a predator, devouring some of the eggs and chicks of neighboring species, and prospering when the colonies from which it exacts tribute prosper.

From Old Hump, past the Seal Ledges and through Davis Strait to Little Green Island, is a run of seventeen miles, almost due east. We sail among endless islets, wishing we owned one of them—what fun we would have with it! We pass Port Clyde, the Brothers and Gunning Rock. Here where the increased pitch and roll test our sea legs as we straddle the unstable deck, we once sighted two killer whales, smartly-marked black and white cetaceans, leaping like porpoises off our bow, their long dorsal fins projecting like spar buoys. We often see the huge fin-back whales, but only once have we seen killers.

The open stretches are never dull. There is always the chance of spotting a shearwater, a jaeger, or a flock of phalaropes. So as the boat spanks along we peer ahead, like an admiral on his quarter deck, with glasses hanging ready.

Little Green is a lonesome island; not a soul lives upon it except the lobsterman, whose gaudily painted buoys we have been seeing bouncing on the waves. We round the moaning bar where the white water breaks, and land our dory by his shanty, a little weather-beaten shack piled high with lobster pots.

Every island is different, each seems to have a personality all its own and an ecology of its own. The rocks on one island are gaudily decorated with golden lichen, and little black-winged day-flying moths are everywhere; on the next islet, seaside mertensia dangles its heavenly blue bells. One island is a headquarters for common terns, the next for guillemots. Little Green is distinguished by the numbers of black swallow-tailed butterflies, and formerly had the lushest growth of grass I have seen anywhere. This rank grass, longer than marsh hay, was the nesting ground of a screaming cloud of laughing gulls that hovered above us when we landed. It was the only colony on the Maine coast.

One year they put sheep on the island, and while the grass was being transformed into lamb chops the gullery dropped from 300 pairs to zero. The buoyant little gulls with their black hoods and hysterical cries went elsewhere, as you would expect them to, but another bird—the Leach's petrel—prospered, for petrels like open ground around the burrows where they live. Man, the great disturber, unwittingly benefits a species by one move and destroys it by another. The sheep on Little Green made the island a better place for petrels, but on Big Green, several miles away, where a fur farmer turned some foxes loose, the whole petrel colony was wiped out in a year.

The petrels nest under the very floor of the lobsterman's tiny shack, and all around outside. To locate them, we just kneel to the ground and smell. If a strong musky odor hangs heavy about a hole, there is a petrel inside. I saw my first Leach's petrel, not at sea where you would expect to find

YELPING like a small lost dog, the black skimmer sweeps buoyantly over the phragmites. Except in the Florida peninsula, nothing short of a hurricane would compel this bizarre bird to leave the salt water.

WORLD WIDE, the graceful terns cruise the seven seas. Above, a Forster's tern broods its eggs on the marsh drift at Cobb's Island, Virginia. The roseate terns, below, have nested for years on an island off the Connecticut shore.

LOTS OF KNOTS, weary from their arctic hop, crowd a Long Island sand spit exposed by the receding tide, while a yellowlegs, below, snatches a killifish.

ROYAL TERNS crowd their sandy nesting beach at Cape Romaine, South Carolina. Like most other colonial birds they find security in numbers.

such a pelagic bird, but under a rotten piece of ship's timber which I lifted from a suspicious-looking hole. The little dove-like bird, dusky brown with a white rump patch and a notched tail, blinked in the unaccustomed light and crept into the shadow, partly exposing its one white egg.

Once the egg is hatched into the sooty puff that looks so much like the linty sweepings from a vacuum cleaner, the parents are rarely seen. And that is where the mystery lies. Except for a party of a hundred or more I once saw dancing at the edge of the surf on the outer arm of Cape Cod during an autumn hurricane, I have never seen one during the daytime. Where do they go? Time and again, off the Maine Coast, I have seen Wilson's petrels from the other end of the world, but never Leach's.

Yet at night, out of the mist and blackness, home they come. Bat-like they flit through the long beams of the beacons. They sing a little song, a rhythmic eight-syllabled chant, elfin cries that one awed listener attributed to "singing rabbits." The eerie calls seem to come from all around, from the air, the ground, even under our feet, like the voices of brownies—or if you are more imaginative, like the tortured demons and lost souls on Bald Mountain, for with the first light of dawn they fade like a dream.

On the far horizon, at the limit of our vision rises Matinicus Rock. Its tall beacon, visible fifteen miles away, is the light farthest to seaward on the Maine coast. The rock has taken some mighty thrashings from the cold angry sea, and many times Old Neptune has threatened to wipe everything off it. Once, after crossing the long open stretch with great combers rolling our rails under, we had to lie off the rock, while the boat rolled, eyes rolled and stomachs rolled, only to find it was too rough to land. But today the lighthouse attendants launched a broad lifeboat down the skids with a splash.

Matinicus Rock has one of the largest colonies of Arctic terns on the Maine coast—three thousand pairs or more. There are a few common terns with them, but we have always found on these Maine islands that the two separate out pretty well, the common terns nesting in the bays, and the Arctics on islands in colder water offshore. The Arctic, with its grayer look and blood-red bill, *red to the tip*, is easy enough to tell when you see it well; you don't have to split hairs the way some bird watchers do. In accomplishing its migration, the longest flight of any bird on land or sea, this tern crosses the North Atlantic to the European side before turning south to the underside of the globe. It sees more hours of daylight in a year than any other bird in the world.

Terns are constantly in motion for the very love of flight. As we walk among the nests, some with three dappled eggs, some with fluffy young, round as silken balls, we are conscious of the unity of the flock that controls so many sea bird colonies, but the tempo here is faster, more hair-trigger. There are few gulls on Matinicus Rock. They flee in panic before the furious attack of the mob. And so might we. Twice a dive-bombing tern scored a direct hit upon me and drew blood.

The star of the show at Matinicus Rock is the puffin. On these beetling crags, where the wind heaps up the forbidding surf, live fifty or more of these serio-comic gnomes. Sitting erect on the rocks before us, with black coats and white vests, they remind us of penguins. In fact, the auk clan, the puffins, guillemots and murres are the closest thing we have to penguins in this part of the world. There must be millions of *alcidae* on the rocks that fringe the cold coasts, rivaling the multitudes of their flightless counterparts in the Antarctic. Matinicus Rock is the southernmost puffin outpost in the New World.

The pudgy young birds squat like inert balls of dusky fluff under the very boulders on which we sit. We could locate several of them if we had the inclination to peer into every cranny, or if we watched where the adults disappear. But neither the puffins nor we seem to care about the vital statistics at the moment. We are too interested in each other. A dozen puffins hobble about on their favorite boulder, stretch to see better, and then settle down in silent contemplation of us. A newcomer arrives from the sea, splays its big red feet and lands *ker-plunk* among the others. In its bill are six small slim fish, all facing the same direction, heads on one side of the big triangular red beak, tails on the other. Here is a riddle—how can it hold onto five slippery fish while adding a sixth to its collection.

While we are trying to figure that one, a glint of white flashes on the horizon. Our glass picks up a gannet. It is way off-season, for at this date it should be in the Gulf of St. Lawrence. As it vanishes over the waves on stiff black-tipped wings, much longer than those of any gull, we half wish we could launch from our ledge and follow it—down east past the Bay of Fundy and around the peninsula of Nova Scotia to the tip of the Gaspé and fabled Bonaventure Island where 14,000 of its kind nest on the vertical cliffs. But that would be a flight of nearly a thousand miles.

Sand and Tide

GREW up in the hills of western New York. When I thought of the ocean I envisioned it as a large lake, with woodlands and farms coming down to the shore like the lake at home. The largest sand beach on our lake was at an amusement park, a beach that had been dumped there by sand trucks, a strip a few feet wide for bathers to lie on. There were no marshes, except for the few acres of cattails where Goose Creek emptied its sluggish water.

So when I took the train out of New York's Pennsylvania Station for the south shore of Long Island, nearly forty years ago, a new world opened to me. The broad sand beaches stretched ahead for miles, as firm to walk on as a country road. Above the high tide mark there were dunes where storm winds off the ocean had piled the sand high, to be anchored by the beach grass. Behind lay the marshes we had crossed on the train, flat miles of salt hay bending in the breeze like fields of grain, with little creeks interlacing. There were new birds, too. I added thirteen species to my life list that day.

Since then, I have lost count of all the strands I have tramped, or the bars and islands I have beached my boat upon. The hills are the place to be in June when song is at its peak; but for summer birding, from July on, the coast pays better dividends.

On the Atlantic rim of our continent, the flexed arm of Cape Cod separates the Rock Coast from the Sand Coast. To the north lie the battered rocks and the gulleries; to the south, the long smooth beaches. For three thousand miles, from the Cape to Key West, and along the deep curve of the Gulf, to Texas and Mexico, are strung these barrier islands, built up of shell and sand, brought from the bottom of the sea by the waves. These strands are the meeting places of the land and the sea; and the birds that live along the point of contact of these opposing spheres, the terns and the shorebirds, are the greatest travelers on earth.

The humans that visit the ocean in summer are sedentary by comparison. Most of them are tired workers from the cities, recharging their batteries. The closer to a metropolis, the more crowded the sands. At Coney Island, a subway ride from the world's largest city, hundreds of thousands of bathers swarm on a hot week end. But at Assateague Island, in Maryland, miles of white beach cut off from all ordinary travel, the only people I saw one hot Saturday in July were two parties who landed in small planes. They had the whole place to themselves.

The birds have been crowded off the more accessible beaches but there are still bars and islands isolated enough for the terns to raise their families in peace, even in populous Long Island or New Jersey.

The "sea-swallows," as much a part of the seascape as the glint on the waves, are too often taken for granted. On streamlined sails they skim effortlessly along the surf or poise in one spot on rapidly beating wings. With bills pointed mosquito-wise, they hesitate a moment, cleave the water headfirst, and rise with a silvery minnow.

When we beach our skiff on the gritty sand at any one of the colonies of common terns along the south shore of Long Island, we are besieged by a snowstorm of silvery wings. We pick our way carefully, for every few feet a scrape holds three drab mottled eggs, so closely matching the drift and shell that we could easily step on them. We know who the owner is when a screaming tern peels off from the whirling formation and plunges headlong, like a dive bomber. The bird zooms up sharply just short of our ears, but we instinctively duck.

These excitable birds with their black caps and forked tails are the same species we should find nesting along the coasts of Europe, whether it be Spain, Ireland, Norway or the White Sea in Russia. We should also find them in the West Indies, in coastal Venezuela, the Azores, North Africa and even in western Asia—on five of the six continents. No birds are more cosmopolitan than the terns.

But though the terns roam the world, survival depends on colonization at scattered places. We should know what is meant by the "rhythm of the colony" if we could put up a blind and watch their posturing, the symbolic

"scrape-making" by which a bird shows its desire to nest by making a
little hollow in the sand, or the "fish presentation" by which one tern tests
the sex and willingness of the other, or the strutting and the cake-walking
and all the other stimulatory actions that tend to synchronize onlooking
birds. In colonies, mood is infectious. There is value in this unity, for
when egg-laying is telescoped into a short span more young survive.
Dragged out over a longer period, predators take more of them. The larger
the colony the greater the social advantages; an alarm by a single bird will
instantly bring the whole mob to the attack.

But colonization can also make them vulnerable. I have heard of boys
"playing ball" with the eggs in one ternery. That sort of thing happens
even when birds are protected by law. But in our grandfathers' time
there was no protection. Milady had to have feathers for her silly-looking
hats, so the terns were shot. Two men out of Freeport, Long Island, killed
600 in one day. Their gun barrels became so hot they thrust them in the
water to cool. With this sort of thing going on, by 1884, the last colony
of common terns on the south shore of Long Island was gone.

And that happened all up and down the coast. The least tern, hardly
larger than a sparrow, was small enough so the whole bird could go on a
hat. By 1882 it disappeared from Long Island and very few were left in
New Jersey. At Cobb's Island, in Virginia, the captain of the station told
Dr. Frank M. Chapman that two men killed 2,800 least terns in three
days. In a single year, 100,000 terns were shipped from the Virginia
Islands to New York, where they brought ten cents apiece. When Dr.
T. Gilbert Pearson visited Cobb's Island in 1892, he saw only one least
tern. He wrote: "It perceived me apparently at the same time and with a
startled cry was off like a bullet upon the wings of the wind." That was
the last record for many years. In South Carolina, the story was the same.
Arthur Wayne, who dedicated his life to the birds of the Carolina low country, said that hunters came from the North, and in one season alone, all of
the least terns on Bull's Island were killed.

Every bird of the sand coast was fair game. They were shot and they
were egged. Laughing gulls and royal terns were robbed of their eggs so
continuously that their ovaries became depleted. Negroes hawked skimmer
eggs in the streets of Charleston, chanting "Loon aigs . . . loon aigs!"

Glue manufacturers started a traffic in eggs in Louisiana and 50,000 were collected in a season by a single boat.

The turn of the tide came with the turn of the century, when birds that numbered in the millions had been reduced to a few thousands. At that time, just as the Audubon movement was hitting its stride, a naturalist-president, Theodore Roosevelt, came to the White House. During his term of office, which meant so much to the wild creatures, his pen created thirty-eight federal refuges. Ten years later, when he visited one of these along the coast of Louisiana, he remarked, as a cloud of royal terns rose from their eggs, that this sight alone was worth all the effort.

The comeback was rapid. Aging Arthur Wayne was gratified to see the least terns return to Bull's Island before he died. At Cobb's Island the birds came back—all except the royal terns. There were a thousand of these gull-sized terns on Cobb's in 1880. A few have nested in the region some years, pioneers from the Carolinas where there are thousands of birds —each laying its single egg so close that the whole colony takes up only an acre or two.

In 1927, on the new fill of sand and shell that was pumped onto the marsh at Long Beach, I found two least tern's nests, the first to be seen by mortal eyes in New York State for forty-five years. There are now several hundred pairs in scattered colonies along the south shore of Long Island each summer and a number of colonies of common terns.

The laughing gulls, whose hysterical cries had not been heard in New York harbor for thirty years, returned, too. When I crossed the lower Hudson on the Erie ferry in the mid-twenties and gazed open-mouthed at the fabulous skyscrapers of Manhattan for the first time, I became suddenly aware that the gulls that passed back and forth were not all herring gulls— heavens, no! They were small and dark-winged. Were they kittiwakes? They had lost their black hoods of early summer, and it was with some difficulty that I decided they were laughing gulls (I did not own a copy of my *Field Guide* then). They outnumbered the other gulls two to one. The members of the Linnaean Society whom I met at the American Museum were still talking about this recent eruption of *Larus atricilla* from its populous marsh cities to the south.

But laughing gulls do not build their straw nests anywhere in the marshes along Long Island's south shore today. These marshes have changed since 1888 when the last colony bred. Now they are transected by long straight mosquito ditches which drain off the water, and baccharis and phragmites grow where once spartina flourished.

The laughing gull colonies in New Jersey and Virginia are now as big as they were in the old days. Eggers sometimes sneak in and fill a gunny sack, but the only real catastrophes are the occasional storm tides. Several years ago I visited one of the large colonies back of Cobb's; it was either on Gull Marsh or one of the Eastward Islands. The gulls filled the sky when we beached the dinghy and armies of fiddler crabs retreated through the sedge. We started to count nests but had to be satisfied with an estimate. Here and there on the drift were the three eggs of the Forster's tern—the marsh-loving tern that looks so much like the common tern but has such a different way of nesting. Parting the tall grass where it arched suspiciously we found the basketful of eggs of the clapper rail, the big gray hen of the marshes whose clattering we heard on all sides. There were between 2000 and 3000 nests of the laughing gull, thirty of the terns and a dozen of the clapper. That night a storm blew out of the east and the waves from the ocean rode rampant into the bay, making an island of our lodge on the mainland. During the terrible hours of darkness the whole colony was drowned out. By morning every nest was gone.

Gulls can take to their wings and make another start in a week or two, but the clappers are hard hit by storms such as this. Once as I drove across the causeway to Atlantic City, during a storm of hurricane intensity, I saw clapper rails flattened on the pavement by passing cars when they sought the protection of the last bit of high ground. Here might be a clue to the extraordinary geographic variation in this bird and its sedentary neighbor, the dingy little seaside sparrow. Few eastern birds have been split into as many local races by systematists. It is probable that great storms of the past were responsible for complete isolation of groups by wiping out whole segments of the population, until in time they developed recognizable distinctions.

In summer, boats by the hundred crowd the inland waterway, the maze of channels and bays guarded by the string of barrier beaches that line the Sand Coast. Speedboats, launches and rowboats with outboards augment the weathered craft of the baymen, particularly near the yacht basins of the large cities. Families on vacation, dressed in shorts, bathing suits and sun glasses, sprawl on the deck while the skipper at the tiller spreads the Geodetic Survey charts before him and carefully tacks past the numbered channel markers. It is a sleepy world of sparkle, glare and sunburn, with sails silhouetted dark against the silver water of the bay. It is also a world of flat green marshes stretching off to the hazy blue line of the mainland, with white herons on their post-breeding flight, going north, monarch butterflies going south, and terns and summer people going nowhere in particular.

The notes of passing shore-birds—the *phee-er-eee* of black-bellies, the short soft whistles of curlew or the *dear-dear-dear!* of yellow-legs—plaintive sounds, voicing the mood of the marsh, drift across the water. It is fragmentary music—impressionistic as the symphonic sketches of Debussy, an accompaniment to the lazy days of deep summer. The birds, too, are negotiating this inside passage by which small craft can sail from Long Island to Florida, scarcely touching the sea. A small boat takes two or three weeks to make the trip, a plover probably not more than two or three days. In fact, the southbound migrants seem to arrive in Florida almost as soon as they are reported in New England. Hudson, hardly believing his eyes, saw pectoral sandpipers near Buenos Aires in August, among them some so young that they still had threads of yellow down adhering to the feathers of the head, and so weak in appearance that he marvelled that they could have made the 8000-mile flight from the shore of the Arctic Sea.

Of all birds, the shore-birds seem most closely attuned to the heartbeat of the world. Watch the sanderlings, pale as beach fleas, as they chase the receding waves like clockwork toys, only to retreat on twinkling legs as the next wave breaks. Back and forth, back and forth, as if timed with Neptune's throbbing pulse. So, also, do the flights of sandpipers and plovers synchronize with the ebb and flow of the daily tides. The feeding flocks scatter over the exposed mud at low tide and disappear when the rising water covers the flats. Some of the waders are resting about the pools back in the marsh where the rose mallow blooms, but others use the hours between the tides for travel, moving with military precision in smoky clouds so high they escape our notice.

Then there is the yearly ebb and flow of migration, spectacular in its sweep. The warblers and thrushes travel by night, unseen; but the migration of shore-birds is a visual thing. We can see flock after flock appear over the marsh and rush by. In spring, the crest of their flood comes late, after the warblers in late May, concluding the spring migration. Some of the birds have come all the way from Patagonia, and they are headed for the fringes of the polar basin. They travel fast; they must get in and get out during the few short weeks when the surface of the tundra is melted. It is an incredibly busy time in the arctic—plants quickly spreading their showy inflorescence like scatter rugs, invertebrate life teeming in the shallow puddles—shore-birds courting, laying eggs, winding up their family affairs.

As early as the Fourth of July, when most of us have not yet gone on vacation, the first of the shore-birds, least sandpipers and a few others are back. Perhaps these first returning travelers are the unsuccessful birds that could not fit into the crowded pattern of the tundra, or birds that lost their brood. It takes only six weeks to hatch out eggs and bring young to the flying stage, but there is not time enough in the brief arctic summer to recoup a failure.

And that explains, in part, why we nearly lost our shore-birds two generations past. Although most of them make hardly more than a mouthful, they were legitimate game, but they melted before the barrage like snowflakes in summer. They are not satisfactory gamebirds, like ducks or grouse, which lay a dozen eggs or more; most species lay but four. They travel in narrow lanes. Along the Atlantic coast this path is only a few hundred yards wide in places, easily commanded by a few strategically placed blinds. The flocks bunch so tightly a gunner just can't miss as they come to the decoys.

I once accompanied two museum men who were planning a habitat group depicting the outer beaches. A large flock of knots and dowitchers flew by and one of the men singled out the last bird in the flock. He wanted just one bird, only one, the end bird. It was a knot in high plumage with a bright rusty breast. He carefully centered that bird in his sights and fired. Thirteen birds dropped. We sat up half the night making skins, so that they would not go to waste.

It is easy to see why the shore-birds came close to the ragged edge. The killing had been going on for a long time. Audubon said that twenty or thirty dowitchers were often shot at once. He added, "I have been present when 127 were killed by discharging three barrels."

Bent, in his *"Life Histories,"* quotes George MacKay, that prior to 1850 it was impossible to estimate the numbers of knots that were collected on outer Cape Cod. MacKay wrote, "It was at this time that the vicious practice of 'fire-lighting' prevailed, and a very great number of them were thus killed on the flats at night in the vicinity of Billingsgate (near Wellfleet). The mode of procedure was for two men to start out after dark at half tide, one of them to carry a lighted lantern, the other to reach and seize the birds, bite their necks and put them in a bag slung over the shoulder. When near a flock they would approach them on their hands and knees. I have it directly from an excellent authority that he has seen in the spring, six barrels of these birds at one time, on the deck of the Cape Cod packet for Boston. He has also seen barrels of them which spoiled during the voyage, thrown overboard in Boston Harbor on the arrival of the packet."

The record is full of such statements as this: "Ninety-six red-backs tumbled at one discharge," etc. No shore-bird was immune—pectorals, black-bellies, turnstones, curlew or even the tiny "peep." As someone remarked, "There just weren't enough birds to go around." The Eskimo curlew, once the most abundant of the three curlews, was shot out before the shore-birds were taken off the game list, and until recently it was believed to have become extinct. Dense flocks which reminded Audubon of swarms of passenger pigeons were assaulted all along the line. One man saw 2000 birds hanging in the store at a Hudson Bay post in Labrador, the result of one day's shooting. They ran the gauntlet on the New England coast where A. C. Bent's father saw a wagonload of "dough-birds" shot on the Cohasset "plains" in a day. After the long trip to their wintering ground in the Argentine, they were shot on the Pampas. The final bombardment took place in spring on the plains of Nebraska when the birds returned along the inland route. It is said that hunters out of Omaha would slaughter them by the wagonload; and if the flight was still heavy, would dump the loads on the prairie to rot while they refilled their wagons, until ammunition gave out.

Protection came belatedly for the Eskimo curlew, but saved the others. Most species can be seen in large flocks again, but several have made only a moderate comeback. These are birds that go to the Pampas where they are still shot—the upland plover, whose eerie windlike whistle once came from every midwestern field; the Hudsonian godwit, one of the most sought-for shore-birds, and the golden plover which Hudson saw in southern Argentina in such numbers that they blackened the ground for acres and sounded like the roar of a cataract. Of another shore-bird, the buff-breasted sandpiper, now so rare that few of my friends have seen it, he wrote: "I sat each day for hours on my horse, watching them pass, each flock first appearing as a faint buff-colored blur or cloud just above the southern horizon, rapidly approaching, then passing me, about on a level with my horse's head, to fade out of sight in a couple of minutes in the north; soon to be succeeded by another and yet other flocks in endless succession, each appearing at the same point as the one before, following the same line, as if a line invisible to all eyes except their own had been traced across the green world for their guidance."

Along the three thousand miles of sand coast in the east, all of which looks good, there are long stretches with few birds. True, the sanderlings that whisk along the foam and gobble up the sand fleas seem to line the outer beach. I have seen squadron after squadron rise and wheel out over the surf as our car bore down the hard-packed beach, until in a few miles we had counted 1500 or more. But there was little else with them. The great unbroken stretches are not suitable for most shore-birds. For variety, head for the inlets. There will we find the birds; at the tips of the barrier strips where the sea breaks through and forms flats to the leeward; points such as Nauset on outer Cape Cod, the tip of Monomoy, Fire Island Inlet on the south shore of Long Island and Beach Haven at the lower end of the Barnegat strip in New Jersey. The terns and the shore-birds rest there by the thousands, all facing the breeze.

If the nearest inlet is too far away, look for a brackish pond. A pool with a muddy margin, untouched by the rise and fall of the tide, is always good. Sandpipers that scatter thinly over miles of mud flats crowd into these standing puddles when the tide forces them to take wing. Jones Beach Pond on Long Island, so close to New York that the tops of the Empire State and the Chrysler Building can be seen on the horizon on crystal clear days, is one of the best shore-bird resorts I know. There, in a walk along its mile-long margin, next door to one of the finest bathing beaches in the world, I have seen twenty species of sandpipers and plovers. Yellow-legs, slim and wary, give the alarm as they flash their dark wings and white rumps. Dowitchers, hunch-backed, like busy snipe, probe with their long bills. Among them are a few stilt sandpipers, wading up to their bellies, stitching the mud with the same rapid up-and-down sewing machine motion. They are easy birds to overlook among the dowitchers and lesser yellow-legs, with a little of the character of both. We can understand why the Long Island baymen thought them hybrids and called them "bastard yellow-legs."

The several species of little streaked sandpipers that we call "peep" patter about by the hundreds, until their footprints make a lacy pattern on the soft mud. The beginner is so puzzled by them that he feels like throwing away the book. Lucky that there are birds so easy to tell as the turnstone that hunches along on its bright orange legs, or the little ring-neck with its single black collar.

The bigger shore-birds haul sail on the pond now and then; and early in the morning, before anyone else has made the rounds, there might be a willet, so puzzling and nondescript at rest, so unmistakable when it flashes its black and white wings. There might even be a flock of curlew, but these big brown birds with the sickle bills usually pass over without stopping. Rarities like golden plovers, which can be picked out from the black-bellies by their lack of wing and tail pattern, and Hudsonian godwits, like willets, with long upturned bills, drop in once in a while; but their normal path from Nova Scotia to South America is far offshore. A prolonged northeast gale, whipping across the North Atlantic, will bring them in. The shore-bird watcher, like the hawk gazer, always studies the weather maps.

Just why some of the wading fraternity should be so wild that they take off in a panic as soon as we lift a glass, and others should allow us to kick sand over them, I do not know. I have dug old wooden decoys from under the paint cans and tools in a Long Islander's cellar and have pegged them out on the mud, hoping to lure passing birds within range of my Graflex. I crouched behind burlap for hours while the wind threatened to blow my blind over, without making a single exposure. I have teamed up with a friend who "walked" the birds toward my hideout with only fair results. Yet a greater yellow-legs, one of the shyest of them all, allowed me to walk within a few feet and snap a whole pack of close-ups. It had traveled a long way and was more hungry than scared, I suspect. Once, when a school of tiny killifishes swarmed from under my feet, it ran straight toward me.

At a Long Island inlet I have come upon a hundred knots so tired from their long hop that they ignored me as I crept among them, hunched over my Graflex like a clumsy turtle. Bulky though it is, I now never leave my camera behind when I labor across the flats to some bird-covered spit, even though the mud sucks at my boots like an osculating cow. If I add a single species to my gallery one time in ten, I shall some day have them all.

My own birding which started more than forty years ago saw many of the birds along the coast make their greatest comeback. It has been thrilling to watch. It is good to know when I start for the coastal beaches that I will see terns by the hundreds, where once all had been shot out; egrets again wandering northward in the marshes; and not just "one little sandpiper," but thousands.

The Oldest Bird Colony

FAR out on the blue-green waters of the Gulf of Mexico lie the Dry Tortugas. Seventy miles west of Key West, and 125 miles from the Florida mainland, they are more removed than any other spot in that tropic state. These six low coral bars on the fringe of the continental shelf were known to mariners as early as 1513, twenty-one years after Columbus reached the New World. Ponce de Leon, searching for the fountain of youth, first chanced upon them. There, on a June night, he captured 160 huge sea turtles as they crawled from the ocean to lay their round eggs in the coarse shelly sand. Ever since, for more than 400 years, these islets have been called the Tortugas—the Spanish name for tortoises. To American bird students, Tortugas suggests terns, the sooty and the noddy—birds that range widely through the pan-tropical oceans, nesting by millions on countless sand bars and coral atolls, from the Caribbean to the shores of Asia and the Indian Ocean. Probably the most abundant terns in all the world, they reach the United States only here and in the Hawaiian Islands.

I believe the sooty tern colony of Bush Key to be one of the top ornithological spectacles of the continent. The gannet ledges of Bonaventure cause one to gasp; the white ibis rookeries of the Everglades are impressive, too, and so are the murres of Three Arch Rocks in Oregon and of the Aleutians; but from what I have seen, only the bird cities of the Pribilofs surpass the spectacle of the ternery of the Tortugas.

For many years the Florida Audubon Society has sponsored annual trips to these historic keys to band the terns and study their habits. In early June of 1941, I joined one of these excursions. Boarding the United States Park Service tug, the *F. W. Meade,* we left Key West with its Bahaman frame houses and flaming royal poincianna trees about mid-way. The unbelievable jade-green waters close to the palm-fringed shores gave way to the bluer and deeper seas as we spanked westward on our six-hour journey. The violent throbbing of the engine made impossible the use of binoculars, but there were not many birds to see.

We passed the Marquesas, a cluster of small, mangrove-covered keys, lonely islands where no one lives. Three or four white specks against the dark green mangroves were probably great white herons—solitary waders —whose numbers in this world can be counted only in the hundreds. The Captain pointed to the murky plume of a waterspout joining sky to horizon. Glistening flying fish skipped from our bow, and once a school of streamlined porpoises paced us for a short distance.

Late in the day we chugged up to the dock at Garden Key and famous old Fort Jefferson, the ominous pile of masonry that dominates the Tortugas group. Bush Key, on which the terns nested, was separated from the fort by a channel and we could see the birds boiling up from the shrubbery in clouds, augmented by a steady stream pouring in from the sea. We wanted to hurry over there—but decided to wait until morning.

Crossing a medieval-looking drawbridge spanning a wide moat, we entered the old fort. It covers eight acres of Garden Key and encloses a hexagonal court or parade ground studded with graceful coconut palms and Jamaica dogwoods with big scarlet blossoms. The caretaker assigned us rooms off one of the upper corridors. As we trudged up the stone spiral staircase, a scorpion, looking like a dead thing, sprang to life when prodded and ran across the rubble with its venomous tail held high. We noticed small stalactites forming from the ceilings where seeping moisture had carried the dissolving lime through chinks in the masonry. A gloomy place, we thought; a good place for a murder.

Fort Jefferson, we found, has quite a history. It was erected in 1846, a century ago, to guard the sea approaches to the Gulf of Mexico. The old fortress never fired a shot at any enemy and has gone into ruin. Built over a period of years by great gangs of slaves, it is said to have cost a dollar for each one of its millions of bricks. During the Civil War it was used as a penal colony for political prisoners. Legend has it that sharks were kept in the moat to discourage these unhappy men from attempting their escape.

Fort Jefferson's most famous prisoner was tragic Samuel Mudd. It was he who bound the broken leg of John Wilkes Booth when he stumbled into his house after the murder of Abraham Lincoln. Any other doctor would have done the same. But Mudd was convicted by a hysterical public for conspiracy in the assassination and sentenced to imprisonment in this Bastille of the Caribbean.

Two years later, yellow fever broke out among the soldiers, spreading like wildfire, until the Army doctors themselves succumbed. They buried the corpses beneath the coral sands of Bird Key, where the terns nested. In this time of terror, the officers turned to Dr. Mudd as the only one left who could help. He ordered walls torn open and the apertures of the gun emplacements enlarged, for he had noticed that those men fared better whose quarters were swept by a breeze. (The yellow fever mosquito was not known then.) Ministering to the sick and the dying, Dr. Mudd stayed the ravages of the disease; when the epidemic subsided, he returned to his dark cell and his chains. Later, when the story became known, President Johnson gave him his pardon.

This titanic fortress with its gloomy battlements, could tell many a story of suffering and death among its builders and prisoners. It has seen many sorts of men, from the turtlers and wreckers of the old days to a former caretaker who, not so many years ago, dynamited some of the buildings to the amount of a million dollars' damage because he had not received his back pay.

Whereas the history of the fort spans a century, no one knows how far back the bird colony goes—certainly it saw the first Spanish galleons sail treasure-laden out of the great Mexican sea; perhaps the birds were there many centuries before that, when the coral reefs at the edge of the continental shelf first broke surface above the rippling waves.

After dinner that first evening, the Captain, a lean taciturn fellow, more like a New England sea captain than a Key West "Conch," asked if we would like to look for turtles. We said we would. There was a small key several miles to the east where they ought to be crawling that night. Furthermore, on our way in we had passed a loggerhead turtle, its head bobbing along the surface like a piece of drift.

We set out just as the sky burst aflame in refulgent glory—the sunsets in the Tortugas are among the most brilliant in the world. The clamor of terns settling down for the night on Bush Key was deafening. Our dory, with its one-lung outboard, soon left them far behind; and when we struck the beach of the small sandy key where we had hoped to see turtles, it was quite dark, the huge pale disc of the moon giving the only illumination. Slowly we shuffled through the loose sand around the perimeter of the island, searching for the tracks where some chelonian leviathan had dragged its plastron, wide as a tub, across the strip of beach and into the low dunes to lay its eggs.

But this evening we saw no turtles, for a great change has taken place since earlier days. Turtlers who made their living by capturing the huge armor-plated reptiles and digging up their eggs have nearly wiped them out. A half century ago sea turtles were still common, and it is said that as many as forty came ashore to lay their eggs in a single night. Today, as few as four or five come ashore in a whole season. They are protected now, but protection has probably come too late.

I think back with guilt to the time thirty years ago when I helped dig up a batch of sea turtle eggs on a bar off the Carolina Capes. Following the tracks into a hollow in the dunes, my bayman guide probed the loose sand with a sharp stick until yellow yolk appeared on its point. With our hands we unearthed a hatful of eggs the size of pingpong balls. That evening we scrambled them. They will not fry, as their whites do not coagulate. They were good, but I did not know then that the big turtles were getting very scarce.

It would have been fun to see the turtles, but our trip to the Tortugas was for noddies and sooties. Twice I had picked up dead sooties in New York State after tropical hurricanes, but I had never seen one alive. I could now appreciate the mariners' nickname "wide-a-wake." All night long the hubbub across the channel never ceased, and whenever a lone bird flew close above the fort, it took no imagination to make *wide-a-wake, wide-a-wake* out of its nasal cry.

In the early morning, the clamor of the colony, greeting the swollen red orb of the rising sun, reached a crescendo that banished sleep. After tapping our sneakers against the wall to dislodge hiding scorpions, we quickly dressed. We circumvented several abortive stalagmites rising in round humps from the floor, shuffled downstairs to the fort's mess hall, had a bite to eat, and hurried out. This was the adventure we had read about. Here were Florida's own South Sea islands complete with birds, shells and brightly colored fish. As our rowboat spanned the channel and scraped onto the beach, the black and white sooty terns rose in a smoky cloud, like bees swarming from a hive. Their cries were deafening as they milled and protested. The whole island seemed to take wing, yet only the birds nearest us left their nests. Back among the Bermuda grass and bay cedars we could see windrows of birds, black against the glaring sand, each standing over a single mottled egg. They kept their neighbors at the distance they could strike with their bills. The territory which each defended was confined to a circle not over two feet in diameter. Squabbles flared up whenever an outsider stepped over the invisible line. The scrappers would crowd the sacred domain of a third bird and so on until a dozen sooties were in the brawl, fluttering, screaming and tugging.

The nests of the sooties were just little scrapes in the loose sand, so close together that it would have been like a game of hopscotch to pick a way through the heart of the colony without crushing eggs. Rather than disrupt the great bird metropolis too much, we walked around its outskirts which crowded the last bit of vegetation to the very edge of the beach-shelf. Many of the birds refused to fly, rushing at us on their diminutive sea legs, bluffing with half spread wings and striking our fingers with their bills. Some ran rat-like into the shrubbery; others stood their ground, allowing themselves to be picked up. They were about sixteen inches long from the tip of their sharp black bills to the end of their forked tails. Their snowy underparts contrasted strikingly with the black cap and mantle. On the legs of many birds we could see the shiny aluminum bands that had been put there in other years by parties of Florida Audubonites.

The nests of the noddies were placed in the bushes, substantial platforms of twigs and seaweed. No other tern in Florida nests off the ground. The noddies were no less aggressive than the sooties. The main difference between them was their method of attack. Like most other terns, the sooties swooped down like dive bombers with sharp screams that made us duck. The noddies came in at eye-level like torpedo planes. They were far more intimidating.

Wherever we went there was a fresh eruption of black and white birds, billowing skyward and sweeping down upon us like a tornado. As we walked on, these phalanxes receded and in a few minutes, a swirl of birds dropped back to the nests they had abandoned on our approach. We wondered how each bird could recognize its own egg among thousands of similar eggs, but apparently they react to its position. An egg removed a few feet presents a puzzling problem to its owner. One bird brooded a flash bulb which a photographer substituted for its egg.

Birds returning to their mates went through their traditional "walk-around." Cocking their heads and perking their tails, they moved with dainty steps around each other. Some terns, alighting several feet away from their tiny territory, were forced to run a gauntlet of vicious pecks from sharp beaks before reaching the security of their inner sanctum. Tiny young, innocently toddling away from home, are mauled in the same way. More than once we saw a pale ghost crab hauling away a young bird, stiff with rigor mortis, a victim of the intolerance of its neighbors.

How far back does the history of the colony go? Audubon, visiting the Tortugas in 1832, reported "that the birds have been known to collect there for the purpose of breeding since the oldest wreckers on that coast can remember." Going back more than two centuries before that, to Elizabethan times, we learn that Captain John Hawkins, the slave trader, cast anchor in 1565 off these coral reefs while his men laid in a supply of turtles and loaded his pinnace with the myriads of sea birds that nested there. Ponce de Leon himself, according to his historian, Herrera, "killed many pelicans and other birds that amounted to five thousands." The "other birds" were most likely noddies and sooties.

However, ornithology was an unknown science in those rugged times, and Audubon was the first to write about the birds of the Tortugas:

"As the chain grated the ear, I saw a cloud-like mass arise over the 'Bird Key,' from which we were only a few hundred yards distant. On landing, I felt for a moment as if the birds would raise me from the ground, so thick were they all around, and so quick the motion of their wings . . . We ran across the naked beach, and as we entered the thick cover before us and spread in different directions, we might at every step have caught a sitting bird, or one scrambling through the bushes to escape from us. Some of the sailors who had more than once been here before, had provided themselves with sticks, with which they knocked down the birds as they flew thick around and over them. In less than half an hour, more than a hundred terns lay dead in a heap, and a number of baskets were filled to the brim with eggs."

Robbing the colony of its eggs and killing the birds for food was the normal procedure in those days. No one but an Audubon would have thought of spending time in a tern colony for any other purpose. Even commercial eggers looted the Tortugas. Audubon wrote: "At Bird Key we found a party of Spanish eggers from Havana. They had already laid in a cargo of about eight tons of the eggs of the tern and the noddy."

Stop a moment and figure that out. A sooty's egg weighs about thirty grams, or about fifteen eggs to a pound. Eight tons would come to about 240,000 eggs. As sooties and noddies normally lay but one egg this seems to indicate that the concentration was far larger than it is now. But we cannot believe Audubon's extravagant statement that "both species were on their respective breeding grounds by millions."

The Cuban eggers disposed of their harvest at seventy-five cents per gallon. Some eggers who came from Key West sold their eggs at twelve-and-one-half cents a dozen. It is a wonder the great colony was not wiped out. We have only to look at the records to see what happened.

In 1903, Herbert K. Job estimated a total of only 4000 birds—3600 sooties and 400 noddies—a tiny fraction of the numbers Audubon found. Even at this low point, sooty tern eggs could be bought at Key West for fifteen cents per dozen. In 1907, after several seasons of warden protection, the sooties were estimated at 18,000. It was not until the 1930's that the sooties made their real comeback. At that time the islands were turned over to the National Park Service. Fishing parties and Key Westers pleaded for permission to take eggs, "even if only a hundred dozen." The answer was a firm *no*. The next several seasons the sooties skyrocketed: there were 30,000 in 1935; 40,000 in 1936; 64,000 in 1938; 70,000 in 1939; 100,000 in 1940. On our visit in 1941 we hardly dared estimate the number exactly, but it may well have been way over the 100,000 mark.

The gentle noddy has made no such comeback, drifting back and forth between 400 and 4000.

Bird Key was the spot where Audubon found the sooties, but today Bird Key no longer exists. It started to sink in 1928 and disappeared entirely during the great hurricane of 1933. Since then the terns have used Bush Key, closer to the fort and closer to the eyes of the watchful wardens.

On our visit fully two-thirds of Bush Key was taken over by sooties, the other third by hermit crabs. These bowlegged gnomes were everywhere, running by droves through the grasses and even climbing the bay cedars. They were not the hermit crabs of New England—puny things carrying periwinkles on their backs. These were lusty creatures, some hauling sea shells the size of my fist. This was the reason we had seen so few shells along the beach. The crabs had appropriated them all. It was a curious experience, picking pink-lipped Murexes, fragile tulip shells and small conches from the bushes. Back at the fort they showed us a similar crab so large that it used the shell of a great conch (*Strombus gigas*) nearly a foot long for its home.

On the back side of the island, half-hidden among the bay cedars, lies a small pond where the man-o'-war-birds roost. It always sends a kind of chill through me to see those great "marine vultures" at close quarters as they flap on loose wings of black satin from the bare snags of their roosts. Their slim bodies, all head and shoulders and their fantastically long wings —a foot longer than those of an eagle but less than half as wide—give them a prehistoric look, subconsciously reminding one of pterodactyls and other creatures that flew over the ancient seas long before man was man. Louis Halle puts it very well when he says "If Satan should ever choose to reincarnate himself as a bird, he would find the man-o'-war cut to his measure."

There are always a few man-o'-wars cruising over the tern colony, their long bony beaks swinging from side to side as they survey the ground below. I never saw one take a young tern but was told that they frequently do, washing down the fuzzy morsel with a drink of water after they have swallowed it. Well, maybe so. They have a sinister look, as they hawk back and forth over the colony, but I am inclined to believe that most of the time they are engaged in pilfering minnows from the terns, not bent on infanticide. Mr. C. R. Vinten found a man-o'-war on Bird Key in a starved condition as a result of a broken wing. It was roosting in a place where the ground was covered with hundreds of eggs and young chicks, yet it starved to death while surrounded by an abundance of food within easy reach.

Disturbed from their favorite snags, the somber birds flap off slowly, gain altitude, and pass from thermal to thermal across the channel until they poise over the long east wall of the fort. There they often ride the updraft for an hour or more, hanging motionless or slowly, slowly, wheeling, their long thin wings crooked at the elbow, their forked tails folded like closed shears. These are the "frigate birds," the birds with the greatest wing length for their body weight of any bird in the world, birds that can weather a hurricane so long as they keep flying, but which become water-logged in a moment if they alight on the sea. These are the birds the Polynesians have used for carrying messages from island to island—the same birds Columbus saw plundering boobies. These are the *Rabihorcados,* which, according to Latin-American legend, commit suicide in a fit of frenzy by hanging in the crotch of a tree. These marvelous flying ma-chines, so typical of the Florida Keys, are known to breed nowhere in the United States outside of Hawaii. If, some day, someone finds them nesting in Florida my guess is that it will be in the Marquesas group.

From the bastions of the fort, after our mid-day siesta, we could see three or four great black patches on the glaring white beach of Bush Key across the channel. Each of these patches was made up of thousands of terns standing so close together that the sand was obscured. Joe, a refugee from the saloons of Key West, working out his salvation on the "dry" Tor-tugas, told us that the terns always acted that way on hot days. He thought the solid blanket of birds acted as a cooler on the sands on which they rested.

It was at this time of day that we noticed a very curious illusion. Many of the birds coming in from the sea had *bright green* breasts! Could these be sooties? Our binoculars brought out the green even more vividly. I was reminded of a hat I once saw in a milliner's window on Fifth Avenue in New York city. On this hat was an entire sooty tern, its white under parts dyed green, the more to tempt the vain female. But these birds skimming past were not really green; it was the reflection of the jade waters over which they flew. As an artist, I have always been conscious of reflected color, but this was truly startling. The reflection was almost as brilliant as the water itself.

On the rusty girders of the old abandoned coaling station near the Fort scores of noddies came to loaf. The long rows of gentle birds sitting on the hurricane-twisted wreckage had picture possibilities, I thought. To reach them I waded waist deep under the dock, picking my way cautiously among the strange corals, huge bristly sea urchins and bizarre starfish. Formations of gray snappers sped through the limpid water; I saw a yellow-tail and several green and rose-colored parrot fish. An exquisitely wrought angel fish hugged one of the piles. Twenty feet away where the water shelved off into the deep channel darted schools of slender needlefish—and then, a giant dispersed these pallid pygmies. It was a barracuda, long and wolfish, with the diagnostic black spots on its sides. Taking no chances, I pulled myself up onto the girders and waited until this most feared of all fishes idled off into the deep water.

So tame were the noddies that I could reach up and touch them. Only by waving my hands and shooing them off could I get the action shots I wanted. At times, in the afternoon, several hundred of the dove-like birds, brown with white caps, lined the girders—some coming over from the colony, others from the fishing grounds out in the Gulf beyond Logger-head Key.

On Loggerhead Key, the westernmost of the Tortugas, a tall lighthouse has stabbed the Gulf of Mexico with its beams nightly for many years. The head lightkeeper, Tony Candaleo, invited us to be his guests for a day. He feelingly described his island as "paradise" quite in contrast to Fort Jefferson, "the melancholy island." It was on the way to Tony's paradise that we spotted what we had hoped so much to see, a brown booby. Atop a channel marker sat a strange wooden-looking bird, shaped like a small gannet, but white only on the belly. Tony told us he always saw three or four boobies there—usually two old ones and two young ones. This gawky bird sitting before us was one of the young ones, he said. Inquiring how he told the old ones, he replied, "They are white." White, indeed! He was talking about blue-faced boobies. Until today I had never seen either kind of booby. Where were the white ones? Tony didn't know, but they usually were on these buoys whenever he passed on his way to the Fort.

Tony, who lived with his son and two assistants, was proud of his housekeeping, the spic-and-span buildings, and the carefully raked lawns. After solemnly saying grace over an ambrosial fish chowder, he turned to the three ladies in our group and tactlessly observed, "We get along pretty well without women, don't we?"

While the ladies were examining the collection of porcelain-like shells that Tony had gathered, I scoured the island from end to end, but Loggerhead Key was devoid of birds with the exception of one stray barn swallow. Two months earlier, on the right day, I might have seen swarms of small migrants using this key as a stepping stone from the West Indies. It was on my way back along the beach that I spotted two white dots on top of one of the large can buoys back toward the Fort. They must certainly be the white boobies—Tony's birds, returned from their morning's fishing, their craws full of flying fish and mullet.

We scrambled down the wooden ladder into the boat, stowed the cameras and shoved off. As we approached the distant buoy we could see the black wing tips and dark faces of two bona fide blue-faced boobies. Cutting off the motor, we drifted within thirty feet of them, while I took shot after shot with the Graflex. They were exceeded in tameness only by a brown booby that we found later in the day close to the Fort. This latter bird was less than fifteen feet away before it grudgingly abandoned its perch.

These birds had probably come from colonies in the Bahamas or the West Indies, as none are known to nest in the Dry Tortugas today. However, when Audubon made his visit, in 1832, he found great numbers of brown boobies nesting with the noddies on one of the Tortugas. No one has ever found boobies nesting there since.

The Tortugas, remote as they are, can boast a more remarkable ornithological history than almost any other spot in North America. They possess the oldest known bird colony in the United States—dating back to the time of the conquistadors—and the most spectacular concentration of birds. As previously mentioned, they were visited by Audubon, and later by Agassiz, Chapman, Bartsch and a long stream of others who came to see and marvel. But their brightest chapter was written when John B. Watson, the behavior student, undertook the first "modern" study of bird psychology and behavior, using the terns as his subjects. Between 1907 and 1913 he conducted the first important experiments that had ever been made on the homing or orientation of wild birds. The results captured the imagination of the scientific world. Three noddies and three sooties, marked with paint, were put in a cage and sent by ship to Cape Hatteras, a point far out of the normal range of these birds. Hatteras is 1000 miles from Bird Key by water and 850 miles in a straight line. Eight days later

GLOOMY BASTIONS of old Fort Jefferson stand guard over the colony of sooty terns in the Dry Tortugas. One hundred thousand terns nest in America's oldest known bird colony whose record dates back to the days of Ponce de Leon.

DOVELIKE, two noddies perch on the corroded steel fragments of the old coal dock at Fort Jefferson. While I photographed these gentle tropical terns, schools of brightly-colored fish sped past in the knee-deep water.

SAILS TO THE BREEZE. Probably the most numerous terns in the world, the sooty terns reach the United States only in the Tortugas and around Hawaii. Away from their metropolis they seem swallowed up by the immensity of the sea.

COURTSHIP? A student of bird behavior could probably explain the droll behavior of these two blue-faced boobies perched on a buoy in the Gulf of Mexico. They are far from their home in the West Indies.

Watson excitedly discovered two of the sooties back at their nests. One of the noddies returned later.

Another batch, two sooties and two noddies, were painted up and sent to Havana. They covered the ninety-odd miles in short order and were all back the next day.

Encouraged, Watson continued his experiments with the help of K. S. Lashley, a former president of the American Psychological Association. They transported noddies and sooties for hundreds of miles in all directions. Many failed to return; others made their way back at the rate of 100 to 150 miles per day. The ability to "home" is especially important to these long-winged birds of the ocean, whose nesting colonies are but tiny dots in vast expanses of ever-shifting water where there are no landmarks. Although sooty terns probably have a cruising range of as much as 200 miles from their colony in their daily wanderings, there are, as Dr. Robert Cushman Murphy points out, "extraordinarily few published notes on birds seen in any abundance at a distance from their breeding grounds." Although they nest "on the sands of countless islands in numbers that beggar description . . . it is almost incomprehensible that *millions* of conspicuous black and white terns which do not perch, which are incapable of swimming without becoming sodden, which are constantly flying, perhaps for days on end, should be almost unreported, swallowed up in the immensity of the Atlantic."

One of the most bizarre invasions of World War II was the "Battle of Ascension," a campaign waged by the United States Army against the sooty terns of Ascension Island. The terns had made this island below the equator their headquarters for as long as anyone could remember. There were hundreds of thousands of them; some estimated there were millions. One valley where they were thickest was known as "Wideawake Fair." This dot on the map, midway between South America and Africa, suddenly became important when huge transports were shuttled between Brazil and Egypt and India. An airstrip was built right across Wideawake Fair, whereupon the terns laid their eggs all over the end of the runway, and planes taking off were confronted by a dense cloud of birds hanging in front of the whirling propellers.

Every device was used to discourage the terns—smoke candles, fifty-caliber machine guns, even airplane cannons. Strings of half-pound packages of nitro-starch were exploded every two hours. This kept the birds away from the strip for ten minutes at first, but after a month of this they were back in five minutes. Finally the Army began to remove the forty thousand eggs that covered the end of the runway. This worked, according to Doctor James Chapin who was there at the time. Each time they laid, the eggs were removed, until the dispossessed birds joined colonies elsewhere on the eight-mile long island.

Although the Army won this engagement, the "Battle of Ascension" will probably be won by the birds in the long run. Eventually, sand will drift across the black runways and Wideawake Fair will be reclaimed by the screaming horde of terns.

Most of us cannot go to Ascension Island to see the sooties, or to the remote atolls of the Pacific, where there are millions more, but on a two-week vacation trip we can go to the Tortugas—a spot as intriguing, as different, and as foreign as any spot on the American continent.

Photographic Postscript

The one hundred photographs in this book are selected from more than ten thousand negatives which I exposed during a period of twenty years. They are still among my best, even though I have added a number of new cameras and lenses to my arsenal.

Photography is not as grim a proposition to me as my painting, hence I enjoy it more—more, in fact than anything else that I do with birds. My quota each year is ten new species photographed. This "life collection" has now passed 400 species.

I started with a 4x5 plate camera (a Primo No. 9), but soon graduated to a 4x5 revolving-back Auto-Graflex equipped with a ten-inch Protar VII lens with an old-fashioned "compound" shutter. This between-the-lens shutter was synchronized with a Mendelson flash gun. Although some of my friends teased me about the size of my Graflex, insisting that it was large enough to use as a dark room in which to develop my films, I found it an excellent all-around camera for wildlife work. Most of the pictures in this book were taken with it. Exceptions are the wild turkeys, the young eagles and the Clark's nutcracker, all of which were taken with a 4x5 Speed Graphic; and the brown pelican and reddish egrets which were secured with a Leica and a 135 mm. lens. However, except for color transparencies, where a miniature camera is more practical, I prefer to work with a larger film surface. (I have recently compromised by using a 2¼x2¼ Bronica, the Japanese version of the Hasselblad.)

The use of synchronised flash or strobe is the most satisfactory technique for photographing small songbirds. It allows high speeds at small apertures, with the resultant depth of definition, so desirable when working at close range. Most of the following pictures were taken in this way with the Mendelson flash gun: songbirds at the nest (brown thrasher, house wren, crested flycatcher, white-eyed vireo, phoebe, European goldfinch, prairie warbler, oven-bird, hooded warbler); birds attracted with food (evening grosbeak, song sparrow, tree sparrow, downy woodpecker,

nuthatch, chickadee); birds at water (wood thrush, blue-winged warbler).
Synchronised flash was also used in the pictures of the barn owls and as a
supplement to normal daylight in the portrait of the turkey gobbler. The
turkeys, by the way, were baited with corn for two or three weeks until
they became used to the burlap blind.

For most water birds and other large species I used a 17-inch Dallmeyer
lens on the Graflex and depended on normal daylight. As standard practice
I used a fast film with a speed of 100 Weston, usually Super XX or Super-
pan Press. Birds at rest were usually so photographed at a speed of less
than 1/100th of a second with the diaphragm closed down to about F.16.
Birds in flight were shot with the lens fairly wide open at a speed of not
less than 1/400th of a second for leisurely flyers like gulls to 1/1000th of a
second for ducks.

Every photograph brings back memories. The whooping cranes, photographed at 225 feet, had been baited with corn and although I entered
the blind shortly after daybreak, I did not get my pictures until fifteen
minutes before sundown. The Kirtland's warbler would have been photographed with flash instead of daylight had not my front shutter refused
to operate—after I had traveled a thousand miles for the opportunity! The
picture of the turkey vulture roost took three days of planning. In contrast
to these difficult subjects, the birds in the Dry Tortugas or at Lake Merritt
in Oakland might as well be barnyard fowl. Yet, they are under no restraint and are therefore quite legitimate subjects.

As in painting, there is more than one way to create a picture. A bird
photographer can either take highly definitive portraits with the light at
his back and full on the subject, or he can shoot against the light or across
it, with the resultant third-dimensional feeling and atmosphere that back-
lighting always gives. Bird photographs can be as totally different in
approach as the bird paintings of Fuertes and Benson. The important
thing to me is not simply to record a bird on film, but to be an artist about
it, to achieve good composition and proper balance of values, and, if possible, to catch a bit of the emotional quality that is essential to a good picture.

Index

Eagle, bald, 30, 85, 122-134, 137, 159, 206, 281
Eagle, golden, 130, 140, 159
Eagle, sea, 18, 134
Eastern Egg Rock, Me., 289
"Edge," 75
Edge, Mrs. C. N., 153
Egret, common, 73, 77, 194, 195, 206, 311
Egret, reddish, 199
Egret, snowy, 73, 77, 196, 200, 226
Eider, American, 31, 217
Eisenhower, Gen. Dwight D., 13
El Nino, 293
Elliott, John, 95
Emerson, Guy, 14, 16, 108, 116, 265
England, 10, 57, 75, 138, 140, 149 (*See* Great Britain)
Erosion, 78
Europe, 75, 134, 135, 138, 140, 173
Everglades, 197, 312
Extinct birds, 75

Falcon, 153, 159 (*See* Peregrine)
Falcon, prairie, 72, 142
Falconry, 135-151
Falconry Clubs, 140, 141, 147
Fast, Arthur, 46
Federal refuges, 77, 174, 203, 224, 225, 226
Field Guide to the Birds, 18, 39, 96, 230, 304
Field Guide to Western Birds, 230, 237, 265
Finch, Cassin's, 245
Finch, house, 93, 238, 257
Finch, purple, 46, 240
Finland, 173
Fish, William, 50
Fish and Wildlife Service, 59, 77, 93, 116, 173, 175, 203, 224-228
Fisher, Dr. A. K., 121
Fisher, James, 5, 59, 65, 259
Flame Birds, The, 199
Flamingo, 89, 111
Flicker, gilded, 255
Flicker, red-shafted, 79, 237

Flicker, yellow-shafted, 40, 54, 79, 107, 162, 281
Florida, 45, 59, 69, 77, 88, 117, 122, 127, 133, 172, 174, 181, 184, 186, 196, 197-199, 200, 204, 211, 218, 276, 281, 306, 312-328
Flycatcher, Acadian, 212
Flycatcher, Arizona crested, 255
Flycatcher, olivaceous, 251
Flycatcher, olive-sided, 240, 282
Flycatcher, sulphur-bellied, 251
Flycatcher, vermilion, 258
Forbush, E. H., 136
Ford, Henry, 92, 93
Fort Jefferson, Fla., 313
Fort Monmouth, N.J., 148
"Fossil" nests, 234
Fox, Jim, 139
Franklin, Benjamin, 132
Frederick II, 138, 140, 148
Friedmann, Dr. Herbert, 69
Fuertes, Louis Agassiz, 53
Fulmar, 259, 261

Gadwall, 48, 85, 218, 225, 226, 229
Gallinule, 13
Gallinule, purple, 107
Gannet, 59, 262, 312
Georgia, 7, 74, 227
Germany, 147
Gnatcatcher, blue-gray, 206, 212
Godwit, Hudsonian, 86, 309, 310
Godwit, marbled, 235
Golden-eye, 216, 218
Goldfinch, 6, 74, 239
Goldfinch, European, 95
Goldfinch, green-backed, 258
Goodman of Paris (Le Menagier de Paris), 149
Goodwin, Ben, 160
Goose, blue, 203, 227
Goose, Canada, 225
Goose, named, 108
Goose, Ross's, 226
Goose, snow, 203
Goring, Herman, 148
Goshawk, 153